THE SANG'S THE THING

This book is dedicated to the memory of the late Norman Buchan MP, one of the great pioneers of the Folk Revival for whom the title of this book would have been an appropriate motto.

THE SANG'S THE THING

VOICES FROM LOWLAND SCOTLAND

Compiled And Edited By Sheila Douglas

Polygon
EDINBURGH

First published by Polygon
22 George Square
Edinburgh

Set in 12/12½ pt Perpetua by Alden Multimedia Ltd, Northampton
printed and bound in Great Britain by
The Alden Press Ltd, Oxford

British Cataloguing in Publication Data is available

ISBN 0 7486 6119 0

The Publisher acknowledges subsidy from the
Scottish Arts Council towards the publication
of this volume.

CONTENTS

Introduction

This book celebrates the richness and variety of the Scottish Lowland song tradition as exemplified by a selection of singers from Liddesdale to the Laigh of Moray. The singers' life stories reveal the character of the times through which they have lived and the strong links that exist between their experiences and the songs they sing.

Song-collectors in the past, from Bishop Thomas Percy through to Gavin Greig, and including Robert Burns, believed they were helping to preserve a tradition that was dying and about to disappear. They have been mistaken. The carrying stream of song may change and may drop and pick up material as it flows along; it may even go underground, but it goes on. Initially, I wanted to call this collection *The Disappearing Generation*, until I realised that the focus of the title was wrong. People may come and go, but songs last. If proof were needed, I found it in the fact that the singers I recorded still sing versions of ballads and songs that have appeared in one or other of the song collections of the past, from Burns to Greig–Duncan. As one of the editorial team working with Dr Emily Lyle on the Greig–Duncan Collection, I found songs and fragments from the collection still on the lips of living singers, who learned them from a parent or grandparent or a friend at work, and not from the printed page. For example, Joe Rae of Beith learned 'Comin Owre The Craigs o' Kyle', and 'Rowin it in Her Apron', two songs to be found in Burns's collection, from his grandfather, a herd in Galloway, who also passed on to him a version of a Child ballad 'Annachie Gordon', learned from a soldier in the Gordon Highlanders in the Boer War. Traveller Willie MacPhee sings a version of 'Jamie Foyers', a ballad from the Napoleonic Wars which he learned so long ago that he has forgotten where; songs like 'The Banks of the Nile', from ploughman, Jock Lundie, now eighty-four, picked up from older singers in Perthshire bothies. Willie Mackenzie of

Elgin sings a song, learned from an old friend, that incorporates one of the bawdy fragments that will appear in Vol. 7 of the Greig–Duncan Collection, 'When Bella was Milking', which in turn appears to be a parody of an older song, 'Caa the Yowes tae the Knowes, Lovely Mally'. I've noticed that through the current Folk Revival, these singers have passed on songs to younger people, who continue to sing them in folk clubs and at festivals. On the eve of writing this, I heard 'Muckle Friday Fair' and 'The Fisherman's Wife' sung at Glenfarg Folk Club.

The Sang's the Thing as a title seems to me to suggest a more appropriate and optimistic way of looking at our song tradition and one which reflects the singers' attitudes to their songs. Of course, the singers themselves are important too and deserve to figure more prominently in collections. Learning what songs meant to them, how and when and why they learned them, and where and to whom they sang them can teach us a lot not only about the past but about the present too.

These singers do not use their songs; they love and enjoy them and want others to enjoy them too. 'If ye hiv a voice, ye should use it tae gie pleasure tae ither people' was the late Dick Cowan of Newcastleton's philosophy. 'Songs were a consolation' says Archie Frame of East Kilbride, thinking of homesick emigrants, toiling miners and the community in wartime. 'When I sing ballads, I remember the people I got them from', is how Elizabeth Stewart of Mintlaw sees it, recalling her aunt, Lucy Stewart, one of the great tradition-bearers of the North-East. Belle Stewart learned her father's version of 'The Twa Brithers' from her own twa brithers and cherishes it for that reason. Jack Beck of Dunfermline enjoys singing songs he can identify with as a Lowland Scot. Some, like Jim Brown of Cumbernauld, make songs about the things they know about in their work and in their own locality. There is nothing parochial about this: it is the way to learn a sense of identity that helps us to recognise and respect the traditions of others. Many of the singers like the late Sandy Watt of Glenfarg, whose genial singing style endeared him to people, hasten to make the disclaimer, 'I'm no a singer!' Others say, 'I've never done anything' or 'I'm just an ordinary person', then go on to relate extraordinary stories that demonstrate personal qualities of courage, kindness and cheerfulness in the face of poverty, social change and personal disaster. I came to the conclusion pretty quickly that there is no such thing as an *ordinary* person with an *ordinary* life.

With only one or two exceptions, all the singers in the book are people I have known, in many cases for years, and whom I have recorded over a period of time. We have sung together, ceilidhed together, taken part in concerts and festivals, visited one another, laughed and cried and talked endlessly. When I went to record their life stories, I was spending time with friends who were sufficiently at ease with me to tell their stories naturally. None of them seemed to be intimidated by the tape recorder or the video camera, and most of them enjoyed reliving the past.

These recording trips have been memorable for the wonderful hospitality we received. Like my husband Andrew, who has been a tremendous help, I feel very privileged to have done this work, and it has only served to increase our affection and admiration for our singing friends. Photographic trips with Ian Mackenzie of the School of Scottish Studies and Aåse Goldsmith have also been very enjoyable and my thanks are due to them for the use of the photographs. In the case of two singers who are no longer with us, Sandy Watt and Willie Barclay, I am indebted to Sandy's son, Peter, and Willie's daughter, Barbara, for giving me intimate accounts of their parents' lives. I am also greatly indebted to Willie Scott's son, Jimmy, for allowing me to use tape of him talking in company with his father. For only one singer, Tommy Bonthrone, was I unable to find someone to tell his story, although I recorded some of his songs. But his character and his story are so unusual that I felt I could not leave them out.

There emerges from the book a fairly detailed picture of life in rural and urban Scotland in the earlier part of the century where farming was flourishing and labour-intensive, the horse still pulled the plough, the Clyde was lined with shipyards whose busy hammers were the background music to the life around them, men worked down the mines amid dust and noise, and most people worked long hours for little pay and lived lives devoid of luxury and labour-saving devices; but there was plenty of social life and home-made entertainment, and that included singing. Nowadays, when there are fewer people needed in the workplace and modern technology provides everything from automated milking parlours to pop videos, young people particularly may wonder how their grandparents managed to live with so much work and so little of the type of entertainment they are used to. They will find a great deal to enlighten them in Tommy Blackhall of Falkirk's accounts of street parties, Jane Turriff of Mintlaw's description of the part music played in her home life or Frank Duthie of Findochty's explanation of the work of the fisher folk of the Banff and Moray coast. These people speak of good times, close-knit family relationships, loyal friends who helped one another out and a contented outlook born of the ability to make the best of things. Glimpses are caught of the old fairs and markets that used to brighten the working year for town and country, such as Copshawholm Fair in Newcastleton, Little Dunning in Perth and Muckle Friday in Aberdeen. The secret society of the Horseman's Word, a mixture of magic, free-masonry and practical management of stock, is seen alongside the trades unions' struggle to protect workers from exploitation. Other events like foal sales, ploughing-matches and cattle-shows, local galas, village-hall concerts, marquee dances, bothy nichts, herds' suppers, common ridings, berry-picking, tattie-lifting, harvest homes and maidens, Hogmanay and Hallowe'en capers, feet-washing, go-as-you-pleases, picking the mill-steens, fire-watching in wartime: all provided a pageant to enjoy.

Another satisfying feature of the book for me is the marvellous tapestry it presents of different kinds of Scots. Some singers speak the richest dialect of their area, others reflecting their schooling by using a more standard English while others use a mixture of Scots and English. What has been harder to capture, even with the most meticulous tape transcription, is the music of their language: the strongly Scottish accent and intonation that all of them have. The lilt of the Borders, the graphic succinctness of the Glasgow area, the rising inflections of Fife, the lengthened vowels of Ayrshire, the earthiness of Buchan, the sing-song of Moray and the clear, almost Highland tones of Perthshire are all a delight to the ear. How dull it would have made them if I had anglicised them all and left out vivid expressions like 'an ingaun ee' for a mineshaft in a hillside that you walk into, or 'Hae ye gotten winter?' to ask if the harvest has been gathered in. There's a treasury of such language in these life stories.

In spite of the riches of the collection, it contains only a fraction of the material and songs recorded and transcribed. Without the help of my musical son Colin, I would never have completed this marathon. There are also many other singers I would like to have included, for there is a multitude of singers all over Scotland who are carrying on the tradition in many different ways. Most of them are not star performers or big-name artistes, but the songs which they sing and make matter to them because they are part of our identity. There are all kinds of songs from the ancient, classic, storytelling ballads that go on being sung because they have never been surpassed, to broadsides, love songs, lullabies and laments, bothy ballads and music-hall songs, political songs and bawdy songs, songs of present-day concerns, all relevant to the life we live and the language we speak. Ask any of the singers in this book what songs and singing mean to them and they will mention words like pleasure, fun, enjoyment, consolation, good crack, happy memories and good times. Aye, the sang's the thing!

Acknowledgments

Grateful thanks are due to the following:

The Scottish Arts Council for research grant; The Authors' Foundation for research grant; The School of Scottish Studies for the use of tape of Willie Scott, Mabel Skelton and Tommy Bonthrone and permission to use photographs; Falkirk Museum for photograph; Ian Mackenzie, for photography; Aåse Goldsmith, for photography; Peter Cooke, for photograph; Andrew Douglas for help with recording; Colin Douglas for musical transcription; Jimmy Scott for information on Willie Scott; Barbara Findlay for information on Willie Barclay; Peter Watt for information on Sandy Watt and Reg Forsyth for information on Tommy Bonthrone.

Willie Scott
Photo: Ralph Morton

VOICES FROM THE BORDERS

If you take the narrow road that winds over the hills and moors from Hawick into Liddesdale, it is almost like going back in time. The landscape has an air of having been there since time immemorial. There's something in the air, an echo perhaps – it's almost impossible to quantify – but it's there all right: something older than the winding road with its hump-backed bridges. It's when you come to Hermitage Castle that you realise you are looking at something that encapsulates clearly all your nebulous impressions. Although the castle is a ruin now, it still presents a solid and forbidding appearance, a thirteenth-century Border keep with crenellated ramparts and arrow slits high up on its bare, massive walls. A place of defence and safety, it survived the struggles that raged back and forward across the Marches and Debateable Lands. The warlock Earl of Soulis who sold his soul to the Evil One might just be standing in the shadows. The Nine Stane Rigg on which he was boiled in oil for his sins is near at hand, a spot on which, according to retired shepherd and veteran singer Willie Scott, who once worked on the farm of the same name, nothing will grow even to this day.

Perhaps the most authentic echo of the past there is to be found in that 'uncouth and savage' ancient Border gathering song, as Sir Walter Scott described it, called 'The Fray of Suport', which was collected by Scott from an old singer nicknamed 'The Lang Quaker', but whose true name was Jonathan Graham, 'an itinerant cleaner of clocks and watches' and one of the last wandering balladeers. He was brought to sing the song to Sir Walter at the house of his friend Dr John Elliott of Newlands on one of his collecting trips to Liddesdale. The description of the tune as 'the uncoest howling', by Scott's companion Robert Shortreed, is all we have of it, but the words are in 'Minstrelsy of the Scottish Borders':

Sleep'ry Sim of the Lamb-hill
And snoring Jock of Suport-mill
Ye are baith right het and fou
But my wae wakens na you.
Last night I saw a sorry sight
Nought left me, o four and twenty guid owsen and ky
My weel ridden gelding and white quey,
But a toom byre and a wide,
And the twelve nogs on either side.

Chorus: Fy lads! Shout a'a'a'a'a',
             My gear's a' gane.

The call for the rough justice of the Hot Trod is in the ululation of the second-last line.

WILLIE SCOTT

The nearest thing to this echoing cry that I have heard from present-day Border singers is the huntsman's halloo uttered at the end of 'The Keilder Hunt' by Willie Scott, shepherd and singer from Liddesdale, who once described himself as 'an old Border reiver':

THE KEILDER HUNT

9 den;_____ There the shep - herds they were

11 gath' - ring up wi' mo - ny a guid yauld

13 grew,_____ wi'_____ wi - ry ter - rier

15 game and keen, an'_____ fox hunds fleet an'

CHORUS

17 true._____ Hark a - way!_____ hark a -

19 way!_____ Owre the bon - nie hills o'

21 Keil - der, hark a - way!_____

[Cried out in falsetto at the end]

23 Whoop, whoop, whoop!!!! _____

    2. There was Mowdie frae Emmethaugh, there was Royal frae Bakethinn,
      There were hunds frae Reed and Keilder Heid, an Ruby by the Linn;
      There were hunds of fame frae Irthingside, they try baith moss an crag,
      Hark, hark, that's Mowdie's loud clear note, he has bold Reynard's drag.

Chorus: Hark away! Hark away! . . . etc.

    3. Away an away, o'er the hill and dale, an up by yonder Stell,
      The music of the gallant pack resounds o'er muir and dell;
      See yon herd callant waves his plaid, list his loud tally-ho
      The fox is up and streaks away, o'er the edge o' Hawkhope Flow.

Chorus: Hark away! Hark away! . . . etc.

4.   Hark forward, hark ye gallant hunds, hark onward, hark away!
     He kens the holes on Tosson Hills, he kens the holes at Rae;
     There's no a den roon the Kale Stane but he kens weel I trow,
     An aa the holes on Lerriston he kens them throw and throw.

Chorus: Hark away! Hark away! . . . etc.

5.   There's Wanny's Crags an Sewing Shiels and Christenbury too,
     Or if he win to Hereshaw Linn, ye may bid him adieu;
     The Key Heugh an the Cloven-Crags, the cove an Darna Haa
     Chatlehope Spoots an the Wily holes, auld foxy kens them aa.

Chorus: Hark away! Hark away! . . . etc.

6.   Away an away o'er bank an brae, they drive the wily game,
     Where Mowdie, Ruby, Royal still uphaud their glorious fame;
     See yon leish yald shepherd lads, how Monkside heights they climb,
     They're the pride o' aa the Borders wide, for wind and wiry limb.

Chorus: Hark away! Hark away! . . . etc.

7.   Throw yon wild glen they view him now right for the Yearning Linn,
     By cairn an crag, o'er moss and hagg, sae glorious was the din;
     Weel dune, Harrah! They've run him doon, yon's Mowdie twirls him now,
     The hunt is done, his brush is won, I hear the death halloo.

Chorus: Hark away! Hark away! . . . etc.

8.   Then here's to Will o'Emmethaugh, for he's a sportsman true,
     Here's to Robie o'Bakethin an Rob o'Keilder too;
     At the Hopes Bewshaugh an Kersie Cleuch, Skaup Riggend an the Law,
     In Tyne an Reed and Irthing Heid, they're gallant sportsmen aa.

Chorus: Hark away! Hark away! . . . etc.

Oddly enough, Sir Walter Scott in his remarks on 'The Fray of Suport' in his 'Minstrelsy of the Scottish Borders' mentions that the Lang Quaker's cry was like a view halloo – and that is from actually hearing it. Because of the rough nature and steepness of the Border hills, the fox is hunted on foot with hounds, and Willie must have done this with other herds to protect his flock. Like his ancestors, Willie Scott knew every inch of Liddesdale by heart, as I learned once when we gave him a lift back to Hawick from Newcastleton after the annual traditional music festival. Hill and farm names came readily to his lips. He remembered everyone who had ever lived in the houses and cottages dotted here and there, even those that no longer existed. He had worked as a herd in several places that he pointed out to us, including the one where he met and married his wife Frances.

   Willie was born on 7th May 1897 in the parish of Canonbie into a family that had produced generations of shepherds and where a love of traditional music and song was shared by his parents and brothers and sisters. Like most country people who worked for others, the family moved about during Willie's childhood, crossing the Border into Cumberland where he first went to school at Brampton, and moving later back into Liddesdale. His first job was at Stobbs near Hawick when he was eleven, and at sixteen he moved to work along with his father in Teviotdale for two years, working a twelve-hour day for seven shillings a week. He married Frances Thomson, whose father was a Canonbie ploughman in 1917, and they had six children. Living and working in remote places as a shepherd with a wife and family meant that they had to be self-reliant.

Like all Borderers, Willie enjoyed the excitement of the annual Common Ridings, and he and his family gave colourful descriptions of the one at Hawick, which commemorates events following the Battle of Flodden in 1513, from which only one Hawick man returned alive with the town flag. A statue in the main street of Hawick depicts this local hero. In the following year when the Bishop of Hexham's men were marching on Hawick, the youth of the town, who were its only defenders since all the able-bodied grown men had fallen in the battle,

> Charged the foe wi native valour
> Rode to them and took their colour.

This happened at Hornshole, where the English were routed. At the Common Riding, the song is sung with a refrain of 'Teribus and Terioden', a slogan so ancient that its precise meaning has been lost sight of, but that does not deter the townsfolk from singing it with fervour. 'They get aa het up at this', as Willie's son, Jimmy, says. Jimmy also describes the start of the Common Riding:

'Well, it starts officially on the Thursday, wi the Colour Bussing and lasts Friday and Saturday. A holiday, sort o'thing. But it starts weeks beforehand really, every Saturday they ride the Marches all round, different places, forty horses. They always stop at a little inn somewhere and get dinner and a drink, and then home again, and the whole town comes out, cheering them back, ye ken. There's the Cornet, his right-hand and left-hand man, his acting father and all his followers. And there are no women allowed to ride in the thing – male equestrian supporters only. Actually there was a woman rode the moss one year and got away wi it, right until the minute before they presented the badges and she got found out. She went right round the whole way wi them. But before the presentation Charlie Whelan suspected her, questioned her then and foond oot. Apparently women did take part in earlier days, but a number of accidents caused the rule to be made that they should not take part with the men. The rout at Hornshole is commemorated by the Common Riding Chase, 'when the Cornet wi the flag leads the cavalcade harin up the hill'. But the day begins long before that, at six o'clock in the morning with the 'Snuffing'.

'There's an old traditional thing that they call the Snuffing. They keep the snuff in a big sheep's horn. This is kept along at the Town Hall. A man comes out wi that at six o'clock in the morning, marches round wi the fifes and drums and all the young men in Hawick is supposed to wrestle wi this man and take this horn o'snuff off him. An they wrestle for aboot half an hour. He's got a grip like a lion; he winna let go! Then when he calls a halt, he throws little bags o'snuff tae everybody. An they go into the hotel and they start it from a quarter past six. The official drink then is rum and milk. Then the riders all go up to have breakfast at a moorland farm of curds and cream with more rum and milk, and while they go off to ride the marches, everybody's in a pub wi their friends and they're aa singing these songs:

1. We'll hie to the muir a-riding
   Drumlanrig gave it for providing
   Our ancestors of martial order
   To drive the English off the Border.

2. At Flodden Field our fathers fought it
   And honour gained though dear they bought it
   By Teviotside they took this colour
   A dear memorial to their valour.

3. Though twice of old our town was burned
   Yet twice the foemen back we turned
   And ever should our rights be trod on
   We'll face the foe to Tirioden.

4. Up wi Hawick, it's right and Common!
   Up wi aa the Border bowmen!
   Tiribus and Tirioden
   We are up to guard the Common.'

When Willie died on 30th April 1989, the news spread across Scotland quickly. I heard the news in Glasgow en route for Germany, and I felt, like everyone else who knew Willie, that it was like the end of an era. One of the giants of the age had departed, leaving no one to fill his place. Apart from his knowledge of the countryside and his great physical strength and fitness, Willie was a man of great honesty and integrity, with high standards of personal conduct who prided himself on having served his masters faithfully and well. He spoke highly of the old farmer he first worked for when he left school.

*****

'That old man, when I left school, he was really a teacher of people about sheep. I had fower year wi him, and there was never a farmer that I ever served after that that ever said I was doing wrong or faulted anything I did. That was the best education I'd ha gotten anywhere. And ye had tae work! If everything wasnae his way, he told ye just on the spot. It did me a lot o'good; I'll never regret it. I often thought I was bein bullied, ye know, but I wasn't and it did me a lot o'good.

'It's a very interesting job, though, mind you. Tho' I canna say anybody interested me intil't, I'd no notion o'bein a shepherd, ye know, till that old man when I left school. At lambing, you often worked sixteen hours a day, and you often did things wi a lamp too. When I was at Hartwoodmyres, the sheep would start lambing February way and you had to get up at two o'clock in the morning and go wi a torch and look for them in the field. I had successful walking sticks, won everything far and near. I had aa the prizes at the Highland Show wi ma sheep, wherever I went. Now me coming into the singing doesnae fit everybody.

'Down in the Border country, there was no dances or any amusement. Everybody had to make their own amusement. There was a party in one house one night and a party in another house the next night. An they sort o'gathert together. There wasn't a hill cottage but there were a fiddle or two hangin in, ye know. There was always a song or a fiddle to play a tune and there was dancing, a sing-song, just a sort o'ceilidh, as they were called in the north o Scotland. We had some great nights. Ye can make your own entertainment:

THE SHEPHERD'S SONG

13 deed, but I wish the cauld east winds wad ne - ver

CHORUS

16 blaw._____ I can smear my sheep an'

19 dip, I can ud - der - lock an' clip, I can

22 lamb the yowes wi' o - ny o' them aa._____

25 I can par - rock, I can twin, aye, an'

28 cheat them wi' a skin, but I wish the cauld east

31 winds wad ne - ver blaw.

2. When the wintertime is here, for their lives I sometimes fear
   Tae some sheltered nook my flock I gently caa
   Or in the morning grey, I'll turn them tae the brae,
   Or seek them mang the tooring wreaths o'snaw.

CHORUS: I can smear ma sheep and dip, . . . etc.

3. In the lambing time I wot it was little sleep I got,
   But when the summer's sunny breezes blaw,
   On yon bonnie hill I'll lie and sleep my fill,
   When the lambs are rinnin roon aboot me braw.

CHORUS: I can smear ma sheep and dip, . . . etc.

4. I can cut an merk an spean, or drive them tae the train,
   Though their dams be rinnin bleatin in a raw,
   I can stand the mercat through and richt well I sell them too,
   And my maister's money safely bring it aa.

CHORUS: I can smear ma sheep and dip, . . . etc.

5.   I can work in time o'need, I can sow or hoe an weed,
     I can swing the scythe wi ony o'them aa,
     I can cut the corn and bin, and richt braw stooks leave behin,
     That will stand the autumn winds when hooses faa.

CHORUS: I can smear ma sheep and dip, . . . etc.

6.   And when I've done my wark though the nicht be ne'er sae dark,
     At a swaggering step I'll hie masel awa
     To the lassie dearest yin, she's the best aneath the sun,
     She'll name the day, we'll be nae langer twa.

CHORUS: I can smear ma sheep and dip, . . . etc.

7.   Noo my neebor herds beware when ye gang tae show or fair
     The fiery liquor never taste ava;
     Juist thole your drouth a wee, till your ain braw hills ye see,
     An the bonnie bubblin streams will quell it aa.

CHORUS: I can smear ma sheep and dip, . . . etc.

'We had to make everything. We got a loaf of bread once a fortnicht. Everything was to bake. Your messages was delivered over at the farm once a fortnicht and there was a loaf of bread. That was the only loaf we got. It got eaten but the girdle scones was always first. My wife used to bake every Friday. She'd heat the oven when ye went oot in the mornin and tried to get it by afore ye came back. She didnae like tae let folk see what she was daein. She won aa the competitions for baking and butter-making. We were aa chased awa tae bed whenever she started the nicht before. She won prizes at Newcastleton, baking utensils, different tins for putting cakes in. I also won prizes, four silver teapots playing carpet bools. A grand game.

'But if I'd my life to live over, I'd go back to shepherding, but I'd go north o'the Forth. They're a lot better off than we are down here. We had aa oor own hay tae cut wi a scythe and rake wi a hand-rake. The only thing we got a horse to do was to trail't home wi a sledge. When I retired I'd have been happier at Newcastleton or away aboot Stirling. I know far more o' the shepherds there than I know here. We only come to the Ram Sales here. I come hame here (Hawick) aboot half-past five and I very often never see a soul. I'm lonelier here than I was when I was on the hills.'

Willie Beattie
Photo: Ian F. MacKenzie

WILLIE BEATTIE

Another Border singer is Willie Beattie of Caulside, Canonbie. Willie is renowned for singing the ballad of 'Johnie Armstrang' at the festival at Newcastleton, which, like Gilnockie Tower, is only a few miles from his doorstep.

He is attached to his native Liddesdale in the way that people tend to love their own locality, with a warmth of sentiment that is more than sentimentality. He describes himself as 'a Common Riding enthusiast' and knows a lot of the history of the local event at Langholm, with which he identifies very closely. He has the strong sense of continuity of someone living where his roots are and is comfortable with the fact that the ritual of the Common Riding has hardly changed over the centuries.

He is familiar with the origins of the song 'Copshawholm Fair'. Copshawholm is the old name for the area on which the village of Newcastleton was built in 1793 by the Duke of Buccleuch, and its symmetrical outlines have changed little in the intervening two hundred years. The villagers continued to call it by the old name, Copshawholm, often shortened to the Holm; this provided the setting for the famous Fair.

*****

'I was born in Canonbie, 3rd January 1917. I am on borrowed ground now, but I hope there is plenty of it! I went to Canonbie School and left at fourteen and I have done every kind of work on the Buccleuch Estate: planting, pruning, felling timber, nursery work, fencing and draining. I worked most of the time by myself. I had a long walk up a wood road. Going up every morning, I composed 'The Innes Tweed', adding parts when having the bait. I composed some of my poems and tunes in this way.

'I married Mary Henry and I have one daughter, Elsie, and two grandchildren, Ian and Joy. Ian is at Newton Rigg College at present, learning to be an engineer. Joy is still at school, but works at the Crosskeys Hotel in Canonbie in her spare time, at weekends and holidays.

'The Langholm Common Riding began in 1759, that was the first Common Riding, and there was a Baldie Beattie, who must have been a relative away back. He carried the flag roon the Marches fifty years. They walked in those days. Now they go roon on horseback, led by the Cornet, but it wis walkin then. Fifty years he carried the flag roon the Marches. I walked it once or twice – I never was a horseman! I was faain off whenever I was on a horse! But I always wanted to do something in the Common Riding. I was lucky: I played button accordion in bands in the Common Riding dances, with Albie Tedham and others for many years. It was always something! I was on good terms wi aa the young people.

'They stuck to the tradition at Langholm, as much as any Common Riding, and I'm a traditionalist at heart – I always have been. I liked it for that. It went on uninterrupted right through the war years, 1914 and 1939. They used to meet the train, those that were coming were on, at nine o'clock. Of course the railway was done away with, but the band still goes to the station, comes back up and plays. They don't leave it out!

'Now women never rode the Common till 1918; it was always men. The first woman to ride the Common was Tibby Marshall from Canonbie in 1918. She lived just above the Cross Keys, in a big bungalow. It was burned doon in 1933. But she was the first woman and she insisted that other women followed after her. And oh, there's a lot now!

'They carry the Scots thistle, a barley bannock and a saut herrin – these are the emblems at Langholm. In the mornin the flute band perambulates the toon about five o'clock or half-past four, then they go up the hill for the Hunt Parade. Then they hand the flag in at nine o'clock at night. There are dances, and there are sports, like races and Cumberland wrestling.

'Hamish Henderson came doon here and he says, ''Willie, we're making a film o' the Common Riding. We'd like ye tae sing the ballad o' 'Johnnie Armstrang'. Will ye manage?'' ''Yes,'' I says, ''when is't?'' ''Next Wednesday. It's not giein ye much time.'' ''Oh,'' but I says, ''I'll be prepared.''

'He's got that friendly bit aboot him – ye take tae him! I says, ''Hamish, when I sing, I don't try tae be Kenneth Mackellar or somebody.'' ''That's just how I want ye. Jist be yourself.'' I says, ''I couldna be anybody else!''

'We sang at the castle – it was the only good day, or one o' the very few good days that summer. They had a picnic and they were aa spread oot tae hear me sing. I'd never had a drink or nowt.

'There was a fellow who had a stall at Copshawholm Fair, David Anderson. He spent the first seven years of his married life at Caulside and he went up to Newcastleton to work and he wrote 'Copshawholm Fair' in 1838. He had no money. Money would be scarce in them days, ye ken. All the books was sold by public subscription and they were printed in 1868 by Carruthers in Carlisle, only a certain number. I've been offered a lot o money for mine, but I wadna part wi it. I'd mine from Mary's father.

''The Brundenlaws' is a Border song. I think it refers to a farm in the Jedburgh area. I think sae, noo. It was a kind o' quiet night in the Liddesdale. I met this auld man called Davie Beattie who lived up Liddle Water. He got up an sing't twice an I got the tune off. I get the tunes off fairly quick. Then there was a fellow from the Holm, Willie Henry – he's custodian up at Hermitage Castle. He's a cousin o' Mary's here. His wife Margaret gien us the words for 'The Brundenlaws':

THE BRUNDENLAWS

1. It was ae night in sweet Ju - ly, the night was dark an' the wind was high when three young lads on mis - chief bent so off tae the Brun - den - laws they went,

CHORUS

Hid - dy did - dy hi - dum hi - dum hi - do, Hid - dy did - dy hi - dum hi - dum day.

2. For a ladder they did go
   And place it against the windae sole,
   Then Pate tae the tap o' the ladder did cling,
   Singin, 'Hey bonnie lassie, will ye no let us in?

CHORUS: Hiddy, diddy, . . . etc.

3. We chaffed them up till after two,
   Till daylight it was peepin through
   Then we said 'Fare-ye-weel, we're away'
   When we heard auld Tam comin up the stair.

CHORUS: Hiddy, diddy, . . . etc.

4. Down the ladder fast I ran,
   Sayin, 'Run, boys, run, for here comes Tam!'
   So away like hares we run
   An we hid in the fields where the hay was lang.

CHORUS: Hiddy, diddy, . . . etc.

5. We crept thegither tae form a plan,
   For back for the ladder we wad gang.
   Says I, 'I'll tell ye what we'll dae,
   We'll throw the bloomin aul thing away!'

CHORUS: Hiddy, diddy, . . . etc.

6. Nae sooner did I the plan propose
   Till yin tae each end o' the ladder goes,
   We carried it away right up tae the syke
   An flung the bloomin thing owre the dyke!

CHORUS: Hiddy, diddy, . . . etc.

7. Next mornin when aul Tam arose
   Straight to the broken ladder he goes,
   An when he saw it he did stare
   And cursed and swore and pulled his hair.

CHORUS: Hiddy, diddy, . . . etc.

8. Then straight to the cook wi aa his might
   Sayin, 'Jean, last night's been an affa night,
   So sit ye doon an tell me plain,
   An give me every yin o' their names!'

CHORUS: Hiddy, diddy, . . . etc.

9. Then tae Wilson he did steer
   Sayin, 'Gang an saddle up my meer.
   I'll hae tae gang tae Jeddart, faither,
   Tae get the lads in for breakin my ladder.'

CHORUS: Hiddy, diddy, . . . etc.

10. Next day a policeman he did come,
    Sayin, 'Faith, ma lad, what's this ye've done?
    Ye'll hae tae gae tae Jeddart tae plead your cause
    For breakin the ladder at the Brundenlaws!'

CHORUS: Hiddy, diddy, . . . etc.

11. 'For breakin the ladder, what's this ye say?
    Deil, I never heard o' it till this day!
    But if you think that I'm your man,
    Then you an Tam Charleton's gey faur wrang!'

CHORUS: Hiddy, diddy, . . . etc.

1 2.   So here's tae the lads and lasses dear,
        Ye havenae got onything mair tae hear.
        But if ever ye try tae speed up waas,
        Keep awa frae Tam frae the Brundenlaws.

CHORUS: Hiddy, diddy, . . . etc.

''Innes Tweed' was the first song I wrote. I never put the music down, I just memorised it. I made it up tae send tae this good friend o' mine Wilf Earsman, who was a gamekeeper up in Elgin. He sent us this kilt. I thought if I sent the money he'd be offended because he was well off, you know what I mean? If I send him this, he'll appreciate it. He showed it tae the laird, at the big house, an the laird was delighted. It was a private tweed and it was issued to the workers each year, the ghillies and the foresters. He says, ''I'll send ye an Innes tweed kilt if ye win at the festival.'' I says, ''I'll win at the festival.'' An that's how the kilt came about.

'The Elgin gamekeeper's brother lived down here. He was a gamekeeper an aa. It was a gamekeeperin family. He used to send his lassie owre wi a note to ging owre tae Bruntfauld, to another cousin. Bruntfauld is near Pentone, two-and-a-half miles to three miles from Caulside, in Cumberland, owre the Border. He was a worthy, Thomas; him an me got on! A real old Cumberland fellow. Aye, we used to spend some grand nights wi him. ''Do you not think, William, you've been wasting your time working in the woods?'' he used to say to me. ''You should be composing.''''

BRUNTFAULD

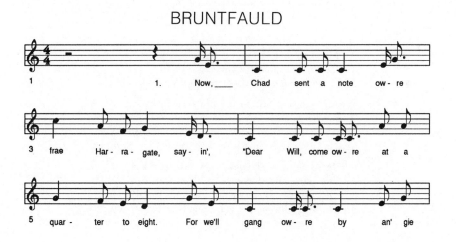

7 Tho - mas a call." And I kent that he meant we were

9 goin' tae Brunt - faul'.

2. So I quickly got ready and made owre the field
   And the lang road back oh I kent it sae weel,
   When Chad was now ready motorcycle and all
   Saying, 'Now, lad, what fettle? We'll gang tae Bruntfaul'.'

3. We very soon set off an did make no delay
   And doon the lang loaning we were on our way
   The east wind was howlin and oh! it was cauld
   But we ay bear the storm when we gan tae Bruntfaul'.

4. Some like television, they think it is grand
   And others like whist when they're gettin a good hand
   But we never care what's gaun on in the hall
   For there's nowt tae compare wi a night at Bruntfaul'.

5. Now we ay mak a halt when we get tae Pentone
   Just tae see Frank an Jean there before we gang on.
   Wi a few jars o'draught an the lager an aa
   And a wee nip or twa on the road tae Bruntfaul'.

6. Now there's some playin darts an they are of good cheer
   And Joe Telford's singin 'The Pub wi No Beer'
   But as time keeps gaun on an the stories grow tall
   We bid them fareweel an gang on tae Bruntfaul'.

7. Weel mounted again as we journey along
   Whiles croonin or singing some auld Scottish song
   For John Barleycorn has taen a bit haul
   As we turn up the loaning an intae Bruntfaul'.

8. Now a welcome frae Thomas that's warm an sincere
   An Margaret she says she is pleased when we're there.
   We receive hospitality, kindness and all,
   And a wee drappie o't when we gang tae Bruntfaul'.

9. We sit roon the fire wi the peats lowin bonnie
   An it's hard tae refuse a wee drap owre mony
   Till the grandfather clock lookin down frae the wall
   Says it's time we must leave an fareweel tae Bruntfaul'.

10. But Margaret and Thomas are wi us nae mair
    An the canty auld shielin is deserted and bare
    But the memory lingers and I oft times recall
    An can never forget the good nights at Bruntfaul'.

Dick Cowan

DICK COWAN

I first heard the late Dick Cowan from Liddesdale in 1970 at the first Newcastleton Festival. Dick was in his 77th year, a fact hard to believe when one heard his big voice. Dick was a true tradition-bearer. 'Well, you don't want them songs to die' was his reason for always being ready, as he sat in his customary chair in the Grapes, with his gill of Black Bottle before him, to give his friends or neighbours the songs they had all heard over and over again but never tired of hearing.

He was born on the day of the Copshawholm Fair in 1892. Dick's daughter, May Robson, told us that her father was born in Montague Street in Newcastleton and had an older brother and a younger brother and sister. Dick's father was a coal merchant and his mother came from just outside the village. Dick's first wife died in 1944, and Dick remarried but had no more children. After his second wife died, he lived with his daughter Jean for a few years, then lived with May until he died in 1981. He must have learned the song about Copshawholm Fair very early in life, for he knew it well enough to sing it at a family wedding as a boy.

Dick's working life began in the early 1900s as an apprentice to a tailor in Newcastleton. Clothes were still hand-made in those days, and tailors were busy people whose services were in constant demand. It seems remarkable that Dick, whose constitution did not allow him to do active service, was nevertheless able to thole almost half a century of shovelling coal at Riccarton Junction. Dick seems to have been glad that he left tailoring before its craftsmanship was replaced by mass production. Until the day he died, he wore suits of his own making, professionally cut and sewn, albeit in an old-fashioned style, and of good material, giving him a dapper and gentlemanly appearance.

During his working life, Dick learned songs from the people he worked with and was quick to memorise words and tunes. As a tailoring apprentice, he learned songs from his boss who sang as he worked. In the days when people had repetitive tasks and worked long hours, singing helped the work along and cheered the worker. It's very possible that the singing of the master tailor in Davidson's shop would have boosted the morale of the cutters and stitchers and created a happy working atmosphere.

*****

'People used to remark on what a strong voice I hid, tae be an auld man. It's like this to me. If they can put up wi us – and I ken I'm no a good singer – but if folk can put up wi us, and I'm asked to do a turn, I'll do it willingly. Because I think, if God gave ye a voice – use it, and give pleasure to ither people if ye can, forbye yourself. If it's a pleasure to you, it'll be a pleasure to them. That's the way I look at it.

'I was born on a Copshawholm Fair – 14th of April [1892]. It was a Friday. I can just mind on the Square – the carryvans used tae be on the Square. The far side of the Square they used tae be on, and on this side o' the Square. They were sellin gingerbreid and sweets and different things. I can remember, but I was a very small boy. And I remember, this girl took me – well, she would be a woman, I think – she took me on the hobby horses. I can mind o' that and I must hae been very little. There were hobby horses and roundabouts. It was a big fair that was here, and there was another at Carlisle. When I was young, there were a lot used to go to the fair at Carlisle. It used to be a big day there. This was when farmworkers used to fee for six months. The next yin would be November – what they called the term day. Then the farm workers were paid for the six month – I don't know how they got on – my Jove! When I got older, fairs was by. Don't think I ever went to Carlisle.

'The first time I sang 'Copshawholm Fair', I was about twelve years of age and I was at this wedding. It was an aunt that was gettin married. The weddins at that time, they were all in the house. You wed in the house and you had a dance and a sing-song. So this time, it was through the night an the man 'at was fiddlin – playin the fiddle for the dancin – he sang, and my Dad cam tae me an he says, ''Here, Dick, I'll gie ye sixpence if ye sing 'Copshawholm Fair''''. I was delighted. Sixpence was a lot o money then! An I sang't, and oh, they were delighted wi't, an I was pleased wi me sixpence!

'I remember the next time I sung was at a Burns do, and I'd never been at a Burns Supper before. I think I'd be twenty. It was in the Liddesdale, up the stair in yon big room. It was two rooms then and it was the far room we were in. So, when we congregated in the front room, before we went up to the dinner, this Bob Morrow, who had to do wi the thing, he comes up to me an says, "Will ye give us a song the night, Dick?" "Oh no," I says. "I'll no sing."

'So he went away and we went up an had the dinner and the singing started and the whisky started to go round. Just aboot midnight, he comes till us, an he says, "Will ye give us a song, Dick? We're short o' singers." "Yes," I said, "I'll gie ye a song!" He kent when tae come! I says, "I'll sing 'Mary Morison'." The man 'at was at the piano, he wis a barber and he had shifted fae Carlisle here, and he'd been here just aboot a twelvemonth. I don't know whether he knew the Scots songs or no, but he gets the thing and starts away and I starts to sing. Sticks! Bob Morrow came forrit. "Hold on, Dick, hold on! Try't again! Dinny gang away. Try't again!" I tried it again an I sticks again. "Och!" I says. "I'm gaun away. I've had enough o' this!"

"Hold on!" the man at the piano says. "Hold on, Dick! This'll no do!" he says. "I'm playing, 'To Mary in Heaven,'" "An I'm tryin tae sing 'Mary Morison'!" The barber told that over a few times! I was tryin tae sing 'Mary Morison'. I've never sung it since, and I don't think I've sung wi the piano since.

'I served me time as a tailor, and I was nineteen when I was oot o' me time. When the 1914 War started, I was working at Davidson's who had a tailoring business an the postmaster landit. He needed a postman, he was beat for a postman, an he knew I had failed for the army, an he said, "If ye go up to the doctor, Dick, an get a certificate," he says, "it'll be aaright." So I went up to the doctor an I got a certificate, an was on the post for six months. But I was finished at half-past one every day, an I went to the tailorin in the afternoon. Aye, I tailor't in the afternoon. So I was on six months an the man 'at went off [to the war] had been sent back oot o' the airmy an I lost the job. "Well," I said, "I'm no gaun back tae sit inside at aa. I'm gaun tae have a job ootside, I ken na what 'tis." I just went right intae hard work an I never took ony harm. I was forty-two year and a half on the railway. An I never rued leavin the tailorin one day. Like the man that did the cutting in Davidson's: in 1917, he was working on the coal bank at Riccarton – finished! The tailorin was gane way then, gane way tae machines.

'I canna tell ee who I got 'Copshawholm Fair' from. I was young when I learned that. I don't know, I can't remember who I heard singin it. But I had it off long before I was twelve, anyway, 'cause I could go through it an never stick:

COPSHAWHOLM FAIR

1. It fell on a Fri - day in the month o' Ap - rile, owre the hills cam the morn wi' a right sum- mer smile. The folk were aa throng - in' the roads ev' - ry - where, mak- in' haste tae be in at this Cop - shaw - holm Fair.

2. There was seen comin in fae baith mountain an glen
   Baith rosy-faced lasses an strappin young men,
   Aa jumpin wi joy an unburdened wi care
   Meetin auld freens at this Copshawholm Fair.

3. There was lads for the lasses, toys for the bairns,
   Blind ballad singers an folk wi nae airms.
   A fiddler is here an a thimbler is there
   Wi nut men an spice men at Copshawholm Fair.

4. There was pethers, there was potters, there was gingerbreid stands,
   There was peepshows, there was puff-dairts an great carryvans.
   An fruits fae aa nations exhibited there,
   An keel [kale] plants fae Hawick at this Copshawholm Fair.

5. It's a day when auld courtships are often renewed,
   When disputes are settled or more hotly pursued.
   When Barleycorn Johnnie sits fit dae declare,
   There's dancin an fightin at Copshawholm Fair.

6. Now next aboot hirin ye'll want tae hear tell;
    I'll tell it as weel as I ken it masel.
    What wages were gien it's sae hard tae declare,
    For sae muckle they vary at Copshawholm Fair.

7. There was yin I saw hired, a strappin young quean
    The fairmer speired whit her age was an where she had been,
    What work she'd been doin, hoo lang she'd been there,
    An what wage she was askin at Copshawholm Fair.

8. At first the bit lassie a wee while stood dumb;
    She stood an she scrapit her fit on the grun,
    Bit at last she took hert an did stootly declare,
    'I'll tak five pun an ten at this Copshawholm Fair.'

9. Says he, 'But ma lass, that's a verra big wage!'
    An turnin aboot as he'd been in a rage,
    'I'll gie ye five pun, an I'll gie ye nae mair,
    An I think ye maun tak it at Copshawholm Fair!'

10. He held oot the shillin tae arle the bit wench,
    In case it might enter her bit noddle tae flinch.
    She graspit it, mutterin, 'I shoulda had mair,
    But yet I will tak it at Copshawholm Fair!'

11. Now the hirin is owre, everything dune,
    It's off tae the ballroom tae join in the fun.
    I'm no goin to lie wi ma Mammy nae mair
    For the fiddle plays briskly at Copshawholm Fair!

12. Now, there's yin in the corner, afore him a gill,
    Another aside him is sippin his yill,
    Anither is strippit an sweerin richt sair,
    'Room will ye no gie me at Copshawholm Fair!'

13. Now some gan for whisky, some gan for sport,
    Some gan for a wee bittie lassie tae coort.
    But them that gans for whisky gets far the best share
    For they canna weel cairry it fae Copshawholm Fair.

14. So this is the fashion they aa pass the day.
    When nicht comes at last they aa lay away.
    But some are sae sick that they cannot dae mair,
    Wi dancin an fightin at Copshawholm Fair.

I've got a funny auld song caaed 'The Twistit Yin':

THE TWISTIT YIN

1. Now, gen-tle-men an' la-dies, just lis-ten for a while, and I will tell you some-thing that 'll cause you for to smile. For when I end I do be-gin an' when I start I'm done. So hats off men an' la-dies, till I get a breath of one.

2. Twas in one moonlight night in the wintertime in the middle of July
   The snow was fallin very fast, that's worse than any lie.
   I crept on board a tramcar to plough the ragin sea,
   An when I asked the ticket boy, the guard he punched my ear.

3. I fell in love with an Irish girl, she could sing a Gaelic dance,
   She was born in Tipperary, a few miles out of France.
   She was ugly, short and beautiful and her height was six feet three,
   Now don't be patient for a while and I'll tell you her pedigree.

4. Her sister was a polisman who never joined the force,
   She never was high-minded, she lived upstairs down a close.
   She was discharged one mornin because she coo'n't tell any lies,
   An now she's workin overtime in the brickworks catchin flies.

5. Her mother was a publican who lived in Donegal,
   She kept nightly lodgers through the day but they couldn't sleep at all,
   For she'd featherbeds of hedgehog hair and that I very soon found
   In a cellar above the garret, fifty yards below the ground.

6. Her brother was a dressmaker who worked with foot and hand,
   He served well his country but he ne'er wrocht on sea or land,
   He choked himself one mornin while chewin a bite of rum
   Poor married man he never was wed, his wife was deaf and dumb.

7. Her father was a tailor who sailed to a foreign shore
   He made patent wooden overcoats to last for evermore.
   He took toothache in the back and eye while crossing the raging sea
   And now he's back in Paddy's Land ten thousand miles away.

8. And her uncle was a dairymaid on board the Sunday boat,
   An he used to borrow lumps of coal for Barney Mulligan's goat.
   The goat they killed that very night which died six months before
   And now I think I'll finish for I don't know any more.

'When I served me time for a tailor, me boss used to sing that and I just learned it up. Every time he sat down at the board, he was singin away, singin away, all the time. What a man for music he was!

'I'm eighty-five noo, and I've seen affa changes. In my young days, there was no cars. It was horses and carts. And I mony a time look when I'm travellin – all the bridges are straight across. They're no jist straight across, and the width o' them. They've just been made for horses an carts. I mony a time look at that. There was no tarmacked roads, they were aa jist – the stones was pitten in, an blent, an a road roller over them. If you had a push-bike, you had to be very careful or you'd get a puncture. There canna be as many changes in the next eighty years, I dinna think. There was no aeroplanes, there was no cars, there was no wireless, no telly. I remember – well, I'd be in me teens – me Dad had a gramophone, you know, and the records, and we thought it was great! We thought it was great!'

Bobby Robb
Photo: Ian F. MacKenzie

VOICES FROM THE WEST

BOBBY ROBB

The Ayrshire coast is among the most beautiful in Scotland, dotted with holiday resorts and fishing villages. Thousands of working people at the Glasgow Fair went 'doon the watter', and the fishing industry was a flourishing one. My memories are full of the images of piers, cranes and ships, the smell of the sea, buckets of shells and fish teas. Bobby Robb of Girvan recalls working in the boatyard there and watching ships test-sailing down the Measured Mile. With his small beard and skip cap, Bobby looks like a sailor and does, in fact, sing about the sea, but his own work has been mainly in joinery and the building trade, probably because that was the best-paid work available to a man with seven children. He and his late wife Nancy were well-known figures around the folk clubs and festivals of Scotland, helping to support their local clubs and impelled to visit many others by their love of the music.

His background has two elements that are very common in the history of the people of the West of Scotland: a strong link with Ireland and with emigration. Bobby's father was from Ireland and had emigrated to Canada when he met Bobby's mother. They subsequently returned to Scotland when Bobby was very young.

*****

'I was born in Toronto, Canada. Ma father, who was from Derry, met ma mother, who was from Glasgow, there. I came to Girvan when I was about three year old. My oldest sister and I were born in Canada. I went to Doon School here, jist a wee school wi four classrooms and I think that's the first time I experienced folk music. It was in the music lessons at the school and any enthusiasm I had for it was swiftly knocked oot o' me. You know the type of songs, 'Spanish Ladies' and 'The Four Maries', stuff like this, and I didnae think much o' these at all. That's where my singin career began an ended in Primary Four, when the headmaster told me I was singin like an old crow and hit me owre the heid wi a ruler. That was the way in those days! How they cured bad handwritin was to leather your hand wi a belt. I was never much o' a singer up tae efter I left the school and started learning folk songs.

'My earliest memory was in Glasgow at my granny's hoose, just vague memories o' rinnin aboot the hoose. I don't remember much aboot bein ootside or anything. I went to school in Glasgow to Saracen School in Possilpark and I contracted diphtheria. Mind the epidemic? 1937 it was. When I come oot o' hospital, I was shunted back to Girvan, to the good country air. I was never back at school up there. I continued down here and then the war came, of course.

I left school at fourteen an I started wi a grocer as a message boy. My father warned me to sign on at the Broo when I left school. Ye had to sign on and say ye were gonnae start your workin career. "Don't go down a pit, whatever ye do, whatever job ye take," he says, "don't go down a pit." Most miners say that. That goes back to the days when their sons were *bound* to go down the pit. You know, miners' families were bound to go down the pit or else they got booted oot o' their job an their house. That's if ye lived in a company house.

'I can remember bein in Girvan, playin aboot the wee hoose in Kilpatrick Street. My father was a miner when he returned from Canada. He worked in the mines till the outbreak o' war, when they started building Turnberry Aerodrome. He managed to get a doctor's line and he managed to get a job wi Wimpey. Then he was in the building trade. During the War, he was in the Fire Brigade, first at Crosshill, near Girvan, and then he was transferred to Girvan. So through the war years, he was in the Fire Brigade in Girvan. But he was brought up in the country and his father was a ploughman, and he was a great man for walking aboot the hills and poachin rabbits and guddlin troot. That was some o' the earliest memories was goin up the burn, the wee Myoch Burn that rins doon at the foot o' the Byne Hill; or goin up the Byne Hill or up the Dow Hill, anywhere aboot the hills. He was a great man for walks. But a lot o' miners were, spendin their time underground. He wasnae of a mining community. He would be aboot ten years in the mines. Those were my earliest memories of going away wi him. Every Sunday, we'd go up the burn guddlin, richt up to Brochneil Farm, then we'd go up to the farm an get a can o' buttermilk – he loved buttermilk – then head for oor Sunday dinner.

'I remember when the Queen Mary was launched an standin on the shore an watchin it do its trials on the measured mile. An durin the War years, I saw quite a bit o' traffic goin up, convoys, destroyers. There used to be a practice range oot there. On one occasion, the shells overshot and landed on the shore at Turnberry. We were shelled by the Royal Navy! In the meantime, I got involved in the pipe band, Girvan Legion Pipe Band. Naturally, I was in the cadets, you know, the Air Cadets, the ATC and the Army Cadets. They aa had pipe bands, but they were all taught by one man, the harbourmaster, old Willie Carswell, who was a drummer tae trade! But he also taught the pipes and he was a stern taskmaster. This was during the War, and eventually the lads that he taught joined the army and most o' them joined pipe bands. So efter the War, they formed the British Legion Pipe Band, and I became a member o' it, because the ATC packed up just at the end o' the War. I was in the pipe band right up till 1963 and I started work out there at Grant's Distillery, building Grant's Distillery.

'That wasn't my first job. My first job was in the boat yard, actually, as a boat builder. I was three years in R. & T. Mackechnie's, a very old, established firm in Girvan, till I was seventeen. If I hadn't got intae a trade by the time I was seventeen, I would have had to go to the army. I wanted to go to the joinering but I just couldnae get an opening, so I managed to get a start in the boatyard, started my apprenticeship there. But I was seventeen at the time, which is rather late. I got a deferment for my time, an I was twenty-one or twenty-two when I went to the army and I was in the army for two years, eighteen months in Germany. I quite liked it but if I didnae have to, I wouldnae hae gone. But I had to go so I just accepted it. Quite enjoyed the life. Met a few blokes. I'd never really been South o the Border up till then. Well, once went on holiday to Sheffield wi a friend o mine I met in the boatyard. He was my best man eventually. Goin to the army broadens your outlook a bit. I was in the pipe band but I didnae particularly want to go to a Highland regiment, an infantry regiment – I'd hae gone intae the pipe band, bein a piper. So I went for my trade in an armoured regiment. I finished my time. I got married when I was in the army: I was twenty-two by then. I had been courtin my wife, Nancy McLean, who lived just roon the corner. Then I had to go to the army.

'I came home from the army to get married. I'd done three years in the boatyard and I left it. Och, the money wasnae good. I liked the job, but the money was terrible. So I went and finished my time wi Jimmy Lindsay at the joinering. And after that, it was just a matter of, you know, different jobs. You know what the building trade's like. And I eventually ended up at the building o' Grant's Distillery; in 1963 it started. It was all work and no play! Every hour that God sent, I was workin oot there so the band kin o' fell by the wayside. They were attending competitions at the time and I wasnae doin justice; I couldnae get practisin, I just didnae hae time tae practise. So I left the band temporarily, till the buildin work was done.

'When I come oot the army, I just commenced my career again, in the building trade. It was just a succession of different jobs. On one occasion, I had to list every job I'd had fae 1955, when I came oot o' the army. What a job it was! I'd been in so many. The building trade's like that. Unless ye stick wi a local firm, but there's nae money in that. Housing schemes, shuttering contracts, mainly in the area. I never travelled far, mainly Ayr or Girvan. There was plenty o' work goin at that time. The family was growin at regular intervals. Robert's the oldest, then Jean, then Melanie — there's two years between them, then David — he's a chemist, or he was a chemist; he's moved into management. Then there's Karen and Pamela. Pamela married an American. She doesn't live in America, she lives in Girvan. They bought a wee house and he's got a job here and they have a boy and a wee girl and she's expecting another baby. Beverley, the youngest, is unmarried.

'It was in 1964, I think, this folk music first appeared at Girvan, and you know it was in aa the pubs. I thought this was great — music, live music, that I liked, as opposed to pop groups and — the machines. One o' the fellows I worked wi, Tom Mitchell, an this John McGarrity, suggested we started a club in Girvan, which we did. We put an advert in the paper. Just about the same time, Ayr Folk Club started, so we got in touch wi them and an interchange o' singin nights took place. Then we decided to run a concert. Wir first concert was for charity of course, in the wee Legion Hall in Girvan. Oh, we had a massive audience! I always remember goin up on stage wi my big mate who played the guitar. I was too lazy tae learn the guitar! I done the singing an I startit away on 'Leezie Lindsay', an my mind just went blank after the first verse! An my mate's stannin there! I remember it. It was just nerves. It was the first time I'd ever really sung in public in a performing capacity and in front o' an audience. I learned the songs — you could say the oral tradition if ye like — on records, hearin other singers, radio programmes. Then we started goin tae the festivals. I think the first festival was the Blairgowrie Festival. That was even better, you know, that you could go about the country an we discovered they were getting more every year. Almost every week in the year, you could go to a festival somewhere in Britain. Then we discovered Irish music. We'd formed a wee group by this time. I played wi a group caa'd the Cottars. Two o my mates stayed up in the wee cottages up there, up in the back road next tae the Fire Station, so we decided we'd call the group the Cottars. We used to go about the pubs and the clubs an we got in tow wi a concert party fae one o' the villages, Barrhill, up the road. They toured roon aa the villages. That was good experience. You know, you had the Highland dancers, accordionists, different singers. A country concert party. That was very good. We eventually got bookings.

'The club in Girvan through the years was on an off. It died for lack of enthusiasm. People moved on. We've always been associated in Girvan with itinerants. For instance, we used to have Customs officers who'd come and do two or three years at the Distillery. They'd get involved in the club. We ran it in the Queen's Hotel, we ran it in the Hamilton Hotel at one time. This was after we moved out o' the wee Legion Hall. We were there for years. It was always a family sort o' thing in the Legion Hall because on a Sunday night, the licensing laws at that time, I think it was half nine or ten o'clock closing an it wasnae licensed in the Legion Hall, but we'd run oor night wi crisps and lemonade, so that Mammy and Daddy an the weans could come in. We charged sixpence a head, nothing for the weans, hopin they'd buy crisps. We had professional guests: Hamish Imlach, Matt McGinn, the usual boys that were on the scene at that time. I was just lookin at a book, the finances o' the club, and ye see the fees they appeared for. Fifteen shillings! It's unbelievable. But that was quite a sum in thae days. Then at one stage, the club moved up to the village o' Barr. He became a great friend o' ours, Bert Stewart. He'd been a cameraman for the BBC in Glasgow and he took over the Jolly Shepherds, so we went up one night. Eventually, we ran the club up there, we ran a bus up. An the Girvan people that wouldnae come doon tae the Queen's or the Hamilton, they wouldnae walk two or three steps doon the road, were clamourin tae get on this bus to go up tae Barr! It was mobbed every night.

'We went up to Marymass Fair [in Irvine, in August] one Saturday night. Och, we just couldnae get in anywhere an there were nae sessions gaun on then. So we just got back in the cars an came back doon tae the Queen's Hotel and were sitting having a pint. Harry says, "That's a hell of a way to run a festival, wi nae sessions. I think we'll run wir own." So with our respective wives, we formed a committee and started the Girvan Folk Festival. That would be 1975. We had phoned up Willie Scott and his son said, "Willie's in Australia, but," he says, "he'll be back on the Thursday before the festival." I didnae expect tae see him – no an auld fella like Willie. Mind you, he wasnae that auld then – just in his seventies. On the first night, I jumped in the car an went down to the festival shop. I was just comin back up when who should I see but this figure wi the shepherd's crook! I says, "Well, it cannae be bad if Willie's here. If he can make it, the rest'll make it!"

'Although I didn't start singin till the Folk Revival came along, I've a good ear and I remember how I've heard songs sung all my life. That's maybe why it's been said that I'm a singer in the old style. I love dialect. I like listening to different dialects. I just think I've an ear for it. I've always found it easy. Some younger singers pick up songs but they don't use the dialect or the old style. I remember hearing people sing in my earlier years and this is what attracted me. Most pop music is sung sort o' Mid-Atlantic, American style. Folk music is something o' aa different dialects.

'There is a book, an anthology o' Carrick, and there are quite a few local songs in there. 'Kirkdamdie Fair' is one o' them, for instance. It's after the fashion o' aa these songs aboot the fair, like 'Copshawholm Fair' and 'Muckle Friday Fair', aa the characters and aa the things that was happening at the fair. 'Kirkdamdie Fair' was an old fair up on the Barr road. Kirkdamdie Church — they held it in the churchyard. Burns tends to overshadow the folk scene in Ayrshire. We did find that. Maybe no a bad thing because an awfu lot o' Burns' work is folk music.

''The Toon o Dalry' is a song I heard Belle Stewart singing first, then I heard Angus Russell singing it. Then I had a record of a guy called Ian Manuel. He lives in Hull. I heard him singing it and that's the version I sing. It's slightly different from Belle's. Angus sings Belle's version. There were quite a lot o' good songs on that record. I quite like his style:

THE TOON O'DALRY

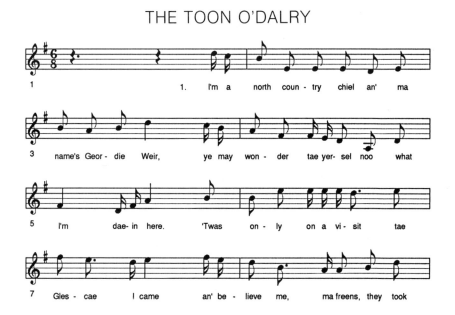

2. Noo when I landed there it's a mystery to me,
I hadn't as much as a crooked bawbee.
But I met an auld acquaintance and he didnae grudge
To pey for ma bed in a big model ludge.
Noo when I landed there twas a terrible night
I got under the clo'es an I got a richt fricht.
It was just like a battlefield under the claes,
O the troopers were fleein afore the Scots Greys.

CHORUS: Oh I wish I was back . . . etc.

3. As I walked doon the street I was feelin gey sair,
When a wee lass says, 'Jock, gie's a lock o' your hair!'
Ye no think tae yersel is there no a hairm did
When a dog comes an maks a lamp-post o' your leg?
As I walked doon the street I was feelin gey small
I went to a window to view a walked doll.
A wee lad said, 'Mister, your face dae ye slight.
If Mcleod sees your dial, he'll run ye inside.'

CHORUS: Oh I wish I was back . . . etc.

'There's a supernatural ballad that I sing. I've a feeling it's a fragment. I think there's a lot more to it:

THE BAY OF BISCAY O

2. One night as Mary lay a-sleeping
   A knock came to her bedroom door.
   Arise, arise, my dearest Mary
   For one glance o' your William O.

3. O William dear where are your blushes
   Those blushes I knew so long ago?
   O Mary dear the salt sea has them,
   For I'm just the ghost o' your William O.

4. O Mary dear the dawn is breaking,
   The time has come for me to go.
   And I must leave you quite broken-hearted
   For to cross the Bay of Biscay O.

5. If I had all the gold and silver
   And all the money in Mexico,
   I'd grant it all to the king of Erin
   For to bring me back my William O.

Joe Rae
Photo: Ian F. MacKenzie

JOE RAE

The country to the west is made up of little towns and villages, farmlands and hills with names many of which are derived from Gaelic. The area is well known to Joe Rae, who lives on a hill above Beith, and whose travels as a craftsman joiner throughout Scotland have furnished him with an impressive knowledge of history and tradition. For him, the past is real and ever-present, and he will point out from the driving-cabin of his van the road along which the poet Tannahill walked to visit his mother who was in service in a big house nearby. A small, quiet, humorous man, he has that sense of continuity possessed by a lot of his generation, and tells a story that happened twenty years after the death of Robert the Bruce as if it were yesterday.

Time-served as a joiner, he worked in an office for twenty years, as a result of which he missed what he calls 'the chipboard era', and since going back to his trade he has never used anything but natural wood. Working in an old, cluttered workshop in Kilmacolm, where he has had 'never had a slack day to gie it a guid redd oot' since he moved in fourteen years ago, he doesn't get rich, but he gets great satisfaction out of what he does.

*****

'I was born in December 1937 in Lanarkshire between Darvel and Strathaven, in Burnbank Cottage, where the road goes into the Bow Butts. My father was working at Rylandside Farm as a ploughman. My first memory is o' slidin doon the neck o' a big Clydesdale horse as it dipped its heid tae tak a drink oot the trough. An I mind them backing the cairts intae the burn tae wash them oot when they'd been spreading dung. Shortly thereafter, we moved intae Ayrshire to a place three miles south o' Galston called Sornhill. In these days it was horse work on farms, and they used tae mak the rucks in the hayfield an tak them intae the farm steading on a ruck lifter or a slipe, as we caaed it in Ayrshire. There was a ratchet and a pulley wheel at the front an ye took a rope roon either side o' the ruck and cleeked it in at the back an ye winched it up ontae the ruck lifter. I remember driving these rucks back. The first song I ever remember singin, was sittin up a tree at the walled garden at Cessnock Castle wi Davie Gibson, the gardener's boy, and it was:

> O the term time is comin
> And soon I'll get my brass,
> And if that farmer wants me back
> I'll tell him tae lick ma arse.

I've never ever heard it since and I don't know where we got it. It must be a bothy ballad.

'I was third-eldest in the family; I had a sister, then a brother, then masel, then four sisters and anither brother, eight o' us altogether. I started school at the Barr Primary School in Galston. Sornhill was jist fifty yards inside the three-mile limit, so we had to walk. I can always remember the old woman sittin at the school gate, smokin the cutty pipe wi the black shawl over her head. Next tae the school was the Barr castle, a tower house, just a square o' red sandstone and one wall. My father had two old uncles who would tell aboot hoo the folk o' Galston were world champions at handball and this was where they practised and played, against this wall. During the War, the government used the castle to store gas masks.

'We moved further oot to a place called Mairch Hoose, because it was the mairch o three parishes. I was aboot six when I went tae the country school, a one-teacher school with aboot twenty-five pupils up to twelve-year-olds. When I was a wee fella at the Mairch Hoose, my grandfather was at a place called Blackside just above Thorn. He was a herd and he was paid only once a year. That's my mother's father, his name was Rogerson, and after my granny died he was living on his own. I spent a lot o time with him. He was a herd fae the real oot-bye places. He started his working life at the age o' ten at the Glenheid o' Glentrool – John Macmillan was the fairmer there – yin o these Galloway sheep fairms that was mair stane than grass, an it was that big they didna measure it in acres but in square miles. But for aa its size, they could only keep yae coo, because they could only grow enough fodder tae see yae coo through the winter! When he started there in 1894, the great friend o' these Macmillans was Sam Crockatt, S.R. Crockatt – an my grandfather heard a lot o' the stories o' the area fae him. There was 'Tam MacKissock and the Mermaid', 'The White Worm o' the Clachan', 'The Dole o' the Thirteen Herrin', 'The Laird o' Ettrick Shaws' and 'How the Soutars o' Selkirk got a Reputation for Honesty'. Did ye ever hear the saying, 'We're aa Jock Tamson's Bairns'? In Galloway, oot-bye men used tae drink tae Jock Tamson's health. It cam aboot in the time o' Bruce that his brother Edward, the Earl o' Carrick, collected aa the Galloway men, aboot twa thoosand, and went over tae Ireland tae fecht wi the English there. He was jined by a few o' the native Irish, but when they met up wi the English, they were ootnumbered fifteen thoosand to two. The Irish decided discretion wis the better part o' valour, but Bruce was a bit o' a rummle, as we say in the country, and decided he wid have a go wi his ain Galloway men and charged wi them. Bruce and his lieutenants were aa slain and his men were left wi naebody leadin them. Then forward stepped this Jock Tamson and he took charge and fought a rearguard action and got them back oot o' it, and got them tae Carrickfergus and shipped them aa hame. That was how Jock Tamson was aye toasted in Galloway, wi 'We're aa Jock Tamson's bairns', because it was literally true.

'In 1895, there was *the* hard winter o' centuries, and at the May term, my grandfather's family took the herdin o' the Back Hill o' the Bush, the farthest-oot hoose, nine miles fae the nearest road: everything went in on the back o' a powny. The first three years his mother never saw another woman. Then they got new neighbours and a young woman in her mid-twenties cam owre in July tae visit his mother for the day an he had the job o' escortin her home. It cam on a big thunderstorm an they were shelterin in a cave in ablow these rocks as big as hooses, an he was fifteen. He said, "This young woman tried everything – but I didna ken what she was needin." Can ye imagine that today? Anyhow, she showed him what tae dae an it cam as such a shock tae his system that he went away and enlisted in the army an it was the Boer War that was on. He jined the Gordon Highlanders and was a year or sae away in South Africa, an cam back tae the Back Hill o the Bush in 1901. When he came back, one o' the songs he sung – an it's yin o' the ballads – wis 'Annachie Gordon'. That was his favourite, and he reckoned he got it when he was in the Gordons in the Boer War. Another one he sang wis:

NITHSDALE BALLAD

1. Oh__ oor young____ la - dy's a -
hun - tin'_____ gane, Hawk or
hound she____ has - nae tane.
She's borne her young son or she's____ come____
hame an' she's rowed him in her
a pron.

2. Her apron was o' the Holland sma
   Rowed aroon wi laces aa,
   She was feart her babe wad faa
   So she rowed him in her apron.

3. Her apron was o' the Holland fine,
   Rowed aroon wi laces nine,
   She was feart her babe wad tine,
   So she rowed him in her apron.

4. Her faither says within the haa,
   Amang the lords an nobles aa,
   I thocht I heard a young babe caa
   In oor young lady's chamber.

5. O faither dear, it is a bairn,
   I trust that ye'll dae it nae hairm,
   For the laddie I loe he loed me again,
   For the rowin it in my apron.

6. O is he a lord or is he a loon,
    This man wha brocht thy fair body doon?
    I wadna hae't for aa in this toon,
    The rowin it in your apron.

7. O young Terregles is nae loon,
    He is the toss [toast] o' Edinburgh toon,
    Aye and he'll buy me a braw new goun
    For rowin it in my apron.

8. It's oot an spak Lord Maxwell then,
    He was the chief o' aa his kin,
    'Wi my son Terregles ye shall be wad,
    For rowin it in thy apron.'

9. For it's I hae castles and I hae tooers,
    I hae barns and I hae booers,
    And aa that's mine it shall be thine
    For rowin it in thy apron.

He used tae sing that yin: I've never seen it in print. It sounds kind o' Nithsdale – the Maxwells were aa that airt.

'My grandfather was back in the First World War wi the Gordon Highlanders and he was at the Battle o' the Somme. Aa his medals are at my mother's hoose yet. He didnae talk much aboot the war at all. The only story he told was when he was taken prisoner along wi his captain, Captain Brook o'Glentanar up in Deeside. They were in a mansion beside a lake and they made up their mind tae escape. Now, my grandfather was descended fae the same Murrays as Alexander Murray that became Professor of Languages at Edinburgh University in the eighteenth century, and he had seven languages. I don't know how he'd learned them in the oot-bye places he'd bided in! Captain Brook couldnae speak any foreign languages but he could swim and my grandfather couldnae swim. So the way they escaped was, Captain Brook swam across the lake wi my grandfather on his back, and my grandfather spoke their way oot. He arrived home a week after a telegram from the King saying he was missing, presumed dead! The owner o'Glentanar, the father o' this captain, offered him any farm of his choice on the Glentanar estate tae rent, but he was a kin o' independent man and he didna take that. He continued his herdin in Galloway.

'In the wee one-teacher school I went to when I was at the Mairch Hoose, there was only once I was ever belted. We had what ye caaed the whipper-in, who came once a fortnight to check the register: this man arrived in his car an he seemed someone to be feared. I must have forgotten it was the whipper-in's day, an the Eglinton Hunt came by an we spied the hunt afore dinnertime an we followed it. We didn't get back till half-past three and the whipper-in was there. So old Mrs Scott had tae belt us!

'Aa the place-names aroon there, like Auchencloich — the field o the stones — aa the ferms we could see fae that school had a Gaelic name — Barbeich, Barnaich, Killoch — so don't tell me Gaelic wasnae the indigenous language o' the haill o' Scotland! We were snowed in for six weeks in the hard winter o' 1947. The Mairch Hoose had a well a hundred yards fae the hoose an we had tae dig a way tae the well. There were great big drifts an ye could go over hedges an drystanc dykes and no ken they were there!

'In 1949, we moved tae Mauchline because the family was gettin bigger. I was aboot six month at Mauchline Primary School and then I went to the Academy at Cumnock. I left the school at fifteen and became an apprentice joiner in a country joiner shop aboot three mile oot o' Mauchline. They were still makin cairts for horses in 1953 but by the time my time was oot, ye were jist gettin them tae repair. I could still mak a cairt wheel yet; I can aye mind the sizes. If ye look at a Scots cairt wheel, it's a beautiful piece o' work. All the wood's trimmed away tae relieve the weight and it's bevelled away an it's decorative. Ane o' the jobs I was introduced to as a green apprentice in the early Spring was the making of bras, an if ye wonder whit kin o' bra ye wad make in a country jiner shop, it wis a widden yin! These bras were for members o' the bovine species who were appearing at cattle shows! Widden brassieres for cattle tae shape the udder tae the right shape. It wis a flat board wi a curved part at the back, wi a ratchet ye could adjust tae bring the udder up tae the right shape. It was highly illegal, of course!

'In the jiner's shop, Jimmy Gibson was aye singin tae the tune o' 'La Russe':

> O ye'll gang gey often tae the pawn
> Wi yer wee bit bundle in yer haun,
> Ye'll gang gey often tae the pawn
> The day ye mairry a jiner chiel!

I served maist o' my time in the shop, but I mind goin oot tae the ferm at Adamhill that had belonged tae John Rankin, Burns's friend, and there were two young bricklayers that were goin tae dip me in the horse-trough tae initiate me. I took off doon the field and come owre the breist o' this brae wi them rinnin efter me, an comin towards us was this great big Ayrshire bull. Ayrshire bulls are kin o' unchancy brutes. So we shot off at right angles and these two young bricklayers, jist yin on each side o' me, grabbed me an threw me owre this great high thorn dyke an they had tae scramble through it. They were covered in thorns.

'I was there for six years in the country jiner's shop. In thae days, I attended night school to take my National Certificate and I left the practical side o' it to go into a builder's office in Glasgow. When I got married, I lived in a wee place called Sorn, three miles east o' Mauchline on the banks o' the Ayr. Not long after we moved in, my wife and I were sitting one Saturday night and a knock came to the door. It wis a local character called Hardy Bobby and he says, "Here, Joe, I hear ye collect old songs. Get this yin doon." It was a song caaed 'The Auld Ferm Hoose', and he said his mither used tae sing it tae them when they were wee.

'We lived at Sorn for four years and then the Coonty Cooncil wanted tae build a bowling green for the village where oor hoose wis, so we moved up tae Cauldhame near Beith, twenty-three years ago. The first mention in the title deeds is 1802, when it was sold off by the Crummock Estate. It might have been 1740 when it was built. They were all wee crofts wi twenty-odd acre. Ours had twenty-four acre up till 1904, when the ground was put in wi the neighbouring farm.

'My family are: David, the eldest, Billy, Robert and Morag who's just comin twenty and she just got married. The ithers are showin no signs o' gettin married. For as their mother's connection wi Burns, there's no one o' them can even whistle! Her mother was a Greig o' Pitrinny Mill up near Auchenblae. They were there for four or five hundred years till her uncle died in the mid '60s. Greig o' Pitrinny Mill was a cousin o' Burns's father. My wife's father's mother was a connection o' Soutar Johnny Davidson from Kirkoswald, and Soutar Johnny was a cousin o' Burns's mother. So she's connected wi both sides o' the family.

'When my boys were comin on and none o' them were showin much inclination for staying on at school, this workshop in Kilmacolm was for sale and I bocht it fourteen years ago and went back tae the practical side o' the joinering. I like makin things – in fact, I maybe like it that much that I don't make nae money at it! I tend to be a perfectionist. I missed the chipboard days, being twenty year away fae it. I've never worked wi chipboard in ma life. We make old-fashioned things like doors and windows. Folk are going back to the solid wood. The plastic age is past. That suits me. The laddies having got something at their fingertips, which they wouldnae have had in this last recession, which I saw comin. There's schoolmates o' theirs have never worked. I'd hae been better off financially continuing to work in Glasgow, but money's no everything. I like what I'm doin an ye can pick an choose wi the kind o stuff I'm doin. I don't need to do the mundane stuff. Folk workin oot the back o' a van can dae that. I get asked to make some quite unusual things. I've just finished a four-poster bed. We had a nice job in a Greek Thompson house in Glasgow, an A-listed interior. We made a mezzanine floor, designed in the Greek Thompson style, and a square spiral staircase.

'Ye used tae hear auld sangs at these herd's fairs and suppers my grandfather used tae go to. There's only one herd's supper left in

Ayrshire noo, an that's New Cumnock, which has been goin since the time o' Burns, since aboot 1780 or 1770. But ye canna get a ticket for't for love nor money. Ye've tae be born intae it. This is anither auld sang ye micht hear:

FARE YE WEEL, MA AULD WIFE

1. It's fare ye weel ma auld wife. Sing bum bee ber-ry bum It's fare ye weel, ma auld wife, the stee - rer up o' stirt and strife. The maut a-bune the meal the nicht wi' some, some, some.

2. Fare ye weel ma auld meer,
   Sing bum bee berry bum,
   Fare ye weel ma auld meer,
   A fit for me ye wadna steer,
   The maut's abune the meal the nicht
   Wi some, some, some.

3. Fare ye weel the auld toon,
   Sing bum bee berry bum,
   Fare ye weel the auld toon,
   It's where she aft-times played the loon,
   The maut's abune the meal the nicht
   Wi some, some, some.

Sheila Douglas
Photo: Aåse Goldsmith

SHEILA DOUGLAS

The West of Scotland is also the part where I grew up, living in Renfrew, but with strong family links with Ayrshire. My father worked on the River Clyde, and its busy traffic of big ships, pleasure steamers, tugs, scows and fishing boats and the oily, metallic smell of a ship's engine-room figure large in my childhood recollections. The streets of Glasgow were, in my imagination, places where wonders were to be seen, where danger seemed to stalk and where the whole world seemed to jostle and throng. Music always played a big part in my life, and singing came as naturally to me as breathing. I can't imagine what my life would have been without songs and, as with Bobby Robb and many others, the Folk Music Revival that began in the Sixties was one of the greatest life-enhancing experiences I have had.

*****

'I was born on 19th June 1932 in Sowerby Bridge in West Yorkshire where my mother came from, in a tall, thin house with three floors and a cellar with a copper boiler and a clanking mangle, and an outside lavatory. My mother had grown up in Ayrshire, where her father had worked as a blanket weaver. She met my father there in his native Dalry. He'd gone to sea as a marine engineer and, when I was born, he was on the Indian Ocean and the China Seas, from which he brought back beautiful ornaments and china. I didn't see him until I was three, when he came home on leave and never went back. He spent the next two years trying to get a decent job ashore in engineering. In the end, his father's cousin got him a job on the Clyde as a chief engineer on one of the Clyde Trust's hopper barges. He worked there until he retired.

'In Sowerby Bridge, the house was always full of people singing – everything from Handel's 'Messiah' to 'Keep the Home Fires Burning'. There was an old-fashioned pedal organ which my mother could play, and she sang too. When I tried it, of course, it would only groan and wheeze – a great disappointment to me. I could sing, however, and did, I'm told, night and day. We were staying in my Grandma's house, my grandfather having died before my parents married. Grandma sang old music-hall songs like 'Two Little Girls in Blue' and 'The Man Who Broke the Bank at Monte Carlo', and she told me a long-running, never-ending serial story about a fairy who lived at the top of a tree. My mother's Uncle Wilfred sang 'Why Do the Nations so Furiously Rage Together?' and 'The Bold Gendarmes' along with her cousin, Ernest Ainsley. Outside in the street, I learned 'The Big Ship Sails on the Eeli-alli-O'. I've also a vivid memory of boys singing in the street what I later recognised as a First World War parody of 'Little Redwing', an American pop song of the time:

> Oh the sun shines bright on Charlie Chaplin
> His boots are cracking for want of blacking,
> And his little baggy trousers they'll need mending
> Before we send him to the Dardanelles.

'We moved to Renfrew when I was nearly five and my brother was only five months old, and it was like moving to another planet. Our house was newly built in 1930s style, a semi-detached in a scheme that was not completed when the Second World War broke out. The ground was flat and although we were between Babcock and Wilcox engineering works and the Rolls-Royce factory at Hillington, nevertheless there were green fields nearby. It couldn't have been more different from hilly Sowerby Bridge, although even there, from where we lived, we could see the moors, where I loved to go for a picnic and to run among heather and gorse.

'I went to school at Moorpark Public School and, because I'd been to a nursery school in Sowerby Bridge and could read, write and count, I was put into a class with children older than myself. Someone made fun of my Yorkshire accent and I bit her, which, needless to say, didn't make me popular! However, I did my own thing and tried not to let the opposition worry me.

'When the War broke out in 1939, I was seven years old and didn't really understand what was happening, except that it was exciting. I remember the day it was announced on the radio: I could see that my parents were upset and, when I asked what was happening, was told that the War had begun. I danced about the house crying, ''The War's on! The War's on!'' as if it were some kind of gala and was somewhat puzzled when my father skelped me! During the War, my pals and I had put on back-garden concerts to raise money for Salute the Soldier or Wings for Victory and we sang all the Vera Lynn, Bing Crosby and Carmen Miranda hits. At school, I loved the French and German songs we learned in the language class. I had a curious experience with the French song 'Ma Normandie'. When we learned it, I knew it already! I've never been able to explain that. I became interested in the music of other countries as well, partly through playing 'The National Anthems of the Allies' like they did on the radio quite often. When I got the chance, I would sit at the piano and sing songs from my mother's Morven Collection of Scots songs, Kennedy-Fraser Hebridean songs (I knew no better), French songs, Schubert songs, pop songs, hymns – anything that could be sung – and, of course, I made my own songs. Soldiers were billeted in our school, so the school had to move into local church halls. You didn't move from Primary Three to Primary Four, you moved from St Margaret's to Trinity.

'One night, my father came in from visiting a workmate nearby and remarked on there being a full moon. ''What a night for a raid!'' he said. He'd hardly spoken when the sirens sounded. That was the start of the Clydeside blitz. For two nights, my mother, my brother and I sheltered under an iron bedstead against the ground-floor back wall of my Grandma's bedroom and listened to the ominous vroom, vroom of German bombers overhead, heard the crump of bombs falling and the roar and rattle of the anti-aircraft guns that were concentrated in the Glasgow area after the first night. My father took me out on the front porch, where he kept watch all night, to see the searchlights and the tracer bullets making their patterns in the sky. After the second night, my father evacuated us to Ayrshire.

'The Clydeside blitz interrupted my schooling in Renfrew, but my few months at Dalry School, when we stayed with my aunt and uncle, seemed to stimulate me to do even better. I was dux of the primary school and, later on, dux of Renfrew High School, from where I went on to the famous – or infamous – Paisley Grammar School on a bursary. Most of my friends went on to Camphill Secondary and I experienced the effects of both snobbery and inverted snobbery. One lot of people started speaking to me and another lot stopped. I felt they were both equally silly. For me, social class didn't figure in my scheme of things. It still doesn't. Like Burns's 'man of independent mind', I look and laugh at aa that.

'At Paisley Grammar, I pursued a heavily academic course of five Highers, none of which were my two favourite subjects, Art and Music. These were fripperies for those who weren't able for the real world, according to the educational outlook of the time. I continued to sing, play the piano and compose songs and tunes out of school. Maybe it's just as well that I didn't take music as a school subject, since the school music course was all about classical music, which I loved although I knew there were other kinds just as interesting and valuable.

'With the help of grants and a lot of sacrifice on the part of my parents, I went from Paisley Grammar to Glasgow University in 1950-1, the Fifth Centenary Year, and the year during which the Stone of Destiny was recovered from Westminster Abbey. To say it was an exciting time is an understatement. I joined the International Club and met all kinds of people from many countries, including my husband Andrew. We marched together in the torchlight procession from Glasgow Cross to Gilmorehill and attended the famous Rectorial Installation of Nationalist John McCormick during which the ermine robes of the Glasgow Council got covered in eggs, flour and tomatoes from the battling factions in the hall. 'What a disgraceful sight for the overseas visitors at the ceremony!' wailed the papers. Like hell! The overseas visitors were returning the missiles and enjoying it hugely! There was some expectation that the Stone would turn up at the Rectorial, and indeed, burly CID men ineffectively disguised as students had infiltrated the hall, and at one point we all thought it was happening. But when something like the Stone made its appearance, it was carried in by two characters in ballet skirts and bowler hats, who opened it up and distributed Coca-Cola from it amid gales of laughter.

'At the International Club, I became responsible for organising the Saturday evening entertainment, which usually took the form of coaxing, brow-beating or bullying the students of any one nationality into putting on a programme of music, dance or whatever from their own native tradition. The easiest night was the African Night: as long as I could get the African students to come along, we were assured of great entertainment. No rehearsal, no special instruments, no reluctance for them. They were natural performers, able to create irresistible drum rhythms from table-tops and bits of wood, graceful and exuberant in the dance, amazing in vocal harmony, drawing everybody into their joyful celebration of life and living, in which I felt then as I still feel now, the heartbeat of the human race. I enjoyed other music too, the calypsos of the West Indians, the subtle ragas of the Bengalis, haunting Jewish music, beautiful songs from the Greek Islands, American country music, Scandinavian hopsas, passionate Arab laments and love songs, Nigerian High Life, French ballads and songs from Poland, Hungary and Italy. It seemed to me that there was hope for world peace if only people would let music show them how to enjoy life. Naïve perhaps, but I was young then.

'After I had left University and tholed my year at Jordanhill, I taught in Glasgow for four years before getting married and moving to Perth in

1959. I've never stopped feeling how lucky I am to live in such a bonnie part of the country. During that time, I was aware of the skiffle craze that was to be one of the triggers of the Folksong Revival, the songs of Lonnie Donnegan, which my brother liked, and those of Burl Ives. But it was only after the birth of my elder son that I became involved with the Folk Club that had just started locally. Most people were singing Bob Dylan songs or Tom Paxton songs: protest was in the air, the Joan Baez songbook was on sale, the guitar was *de rigueur*. The Corries appeared on the scene and I liked their spirited renderings of Scottish songs. Then I heard a singer with a sensitive voice and a charismatic style, called Archie Fisher. The Folk Club night became the highlight of the week, with new discoveries coming thick and fast: Ewan McColl unforgettably singing 'The Cruel Mother' and opening up the world of ballads to me, Matt McGinn showing me the possibilities of songwriting and, most important of all, the Stewarts of Blair with their uninhibited unaccompanied singing that showed me that I didn't need a guitar. I began singing at the club and at other clubs too, in Dundee, Stirling, Leuchars, St Andrews, Edinburgh, Forfar, Irvine, Elgin and Buckhaven. It was during this period that fire destroyed the Michael Colliery in which many of the members of the Buckhaven Club worked, and I wrote a song about it:

MICHAEL COLLIERY

11 Col - lie - ry!   Black   smoke   un -   der -

13 ground!   Six   men   dead   in   a

15 pit   of   hell,   and   three   who   were   not ____

17 found.

2. Though many reached the daylight
And drew in sweet fresh air,
Eleven men were trapped below
And some were past all care.

CHORUS: Fire at Michael Colliery! . . . etc.

3. A mile below the pithead,
Jock McArthur and his mate
Were struggling through the darkness
Though they feared it was too late

CHORUS: Fire at Michael Colliery! . . . etc.

4. Jock knew the roads a lifetime,
Found a place where air was clear,
They banged upon the rock
And heard a rescue party near.

CHORUS: Fire at Michael Colliery! . . . etc.

5. Down in the burning coalroads,
Husbands and fathers died.
The firemen could not master
The raging flames inside.

CHORUS: Fire at Michael Colliery! . . . etc.

6. Dark was the billowing smoke-cloud
Hanging o'er shaft Number Two.
But darker, the miner's future
If there's no more work to do.

CHORUS: Fire at Michael Colliery! . . . etc.

'At a New Year reunion at Buckhaven Folk Club after the disaster, I had to sing that song. It was an experience I'll never forget. It convinced me forever that song tradition is not just a source of entertainment but an expression of humanity. Norman Buchan and Peter Hall didn't put my song into the Scottish Folksinger because they said it was too pessimistic. But I had several songs published, in Chapbook, the folk magazine, and in Ewan MacColl and Peggy Seeger's New City Songster.

'In the 1960s, Perth Folk Club met in the County Hotel to begin with, but later moved to York House Hotel, then to the Plough Inn, where it stayed and flourished for six years. Luckily, there were few real disasters and an awful lot of great nights. Every Tuesday night, I compered the evening and enjoyed hearing all the guest artistes who were classified at that time as 'traditional' or 'contemporary'. Both of these terms were somewhat vague. 'Traditional' could mean anything from an unaccompanied ballad to a group of people with instruments harmonising on 'Johnny Cope'. 'Contemporary' sometimes meant a good, recently written song, but more often an introspective wallow in juvenile emotions, described by Ian Campbell as 'the wet-dream school of song-writing'. There were many people using the Folk Revival as a stepping-stone into the world of show business, like Billy Connolly, Barbara Dickson and even the Corries, who soon deserted the clubs for the more commercial (and lucrative) solo concert circuit. Unaccompanied singers were looked at somewhat askance, until Hamish Henderson and the Traditional Music and Song Association gave a platform to people like Jeannie Robertson, Willie Scott, the Stewarts and Jimmy McBeath, the source singers whose influence was to revolutionise the Revival in Scotland. During this time, I also guested at other clubs and at festivals, won singing and songwriting competitions, ran concerts, published the Scone Ceilidh Songbook and a small magazine called Folk News, started the Scottish Folk Directory, which I was to edit for twenty years, and organised three festivals in Perth as part of Perth Festival of the Arts. After I gave up running the Folk Club, I became active in the TMSA, running ceilidhs and helping to run festivals, eventually serving five years as Chairman.

'My song bag was full of all kinds of songs, as it had always been, and I've written a wide variety of songs too. I loved to sing the old storytelling ballads like 'Johnny o' Braidislie' and 'Eppie Morrie', and learned songs from Belle Stewart, whom I first met in the Sixties, and with whom I'm still good friends. 'The Queen among the Heather', 'The Twa Brithers', 'The Berryfields o' Blair' and 'Betsy Bell' were the favourites. From Belle and her family, I also learned stories and a lot of the wisdom of the travelling people, whom I came to admire and appreciate very much. They're people who've adapted to change for hundreds of years with tremendous courage and who value the non-material things in life. I liked comic and bawdy songs, like 'The Cuckoo's Nest' and 'John Anderson my Jo' (old version), as well as songs about work and working life, love, death and war. I wrote all kinds of songs, both tragic and comic, about Aberfan (translated into Welsh and sung by Siwsann George), about the breathalyser, about the oil boom in the North, about a bull and an electric fence, about Vietnam, about night-visiting, about the sexual symbolism of musical instruments, about politicians, about anything that is a talking-point:

THE MEN O' THE NORTH

CHORUS

Oh the men o' the north are aa gane gyte, aa gane gyte the-gi-ther O! As the der-ricks rise tae the nor-thern skies, the ___ past is gane for e-ver O.

    1.   As I cam in by Peterheid
             I saw it changing sairly O
             For the tankers grey stand in the bay
             And the oil is flowing rarely O.

CHORUS: The men o' the north . . . etc.

    2.   The lads frae the Broch hae left the fairm
             Aff tae the rigs they're rushing O
             For ye get mair pay for an oil-man's day
             So they heedna the plough or the fishin O.

CHORUS: The men o' the north . . . etc.

    3.   I met wi a man fae Aiberdeen
             That city aye sae bonnie O,
             He said there's a spree by the dark North Sea
             And an affa smell o' money O.

CHORUS: The men o' the north . . . etc.

    4.   What wad ye gie for the gowden sand
             The whaup's cry in the morning O
             The rowan fair an the caller air
             An the tide as it's gently turnin O.

CHORUS: The men o' the north . . . etc.

Tommy Blackhall
Photo: Ian F. MacKenzie

VOICES FROM THE SHIPYARDS, MINES AND FACTORIES

When the Forth and the Clyde were lined with shipyards and surrounded by the foundries and engineering works required to support their work, the men who toiled among the deafening hammers and towering cranes, blazing furnaces and dust-filled coalroads were a particularly tough and resilient breed with passionate hearts. Most would have been raised in poverty and hardship from which there was little relief. Small wonder that so many of them became involved in the struggle for better conditions and pay as active trades' unionists.

In talking to men like Tommy Blackhall from Falkirk, Jim Brown from Maryhill and Archie Frame from Newton, I came to realise that their political views and outlook on life were forged in the heat of the passion they felt for the injustices suffered by their families and communities in twentieth-century industrial life. The stories they tell of their childhoods and working lives reveal the heroism of parents and grandparents who laboured through the relentless, heavy, drudgery of lives devoid of luxury of any kind. Yet in spite of hardships, these people sang, played music and entertained themselves in the family circle or the street or pub. As children, they didn't feel deprived, never having known anything better, and improvised all kinds of fun and games.

Overcrowded living conditions was one of the reasons for the boom in walking, climbing and youth-hostelling among city-dwellers. Both Jim Brown and Tommy Blackhall developed a love of the outdoors, the hills and the sports connected with them. Archie Frame's thirst was for education and, as a mature student, he made a new career for himself when the mining industry declined.

Anyone who has been to any of the folk festivals that have taken place all over Scotland in the last twenty years will have seen and heard Tommy Blackhall at the heart of any informal session. Whether wholeheartedly singing or energetically playing a set of tunes on the melodeon, or accompanying other musicians on the bones, he is the very embodiment of musical enjoyment.

TOMMY BLACKHALL

'I was born on the 28th of May, 1929 in the Kerse Lane, in the old part of Falkirk a week afore ma faither and mother got mairrit and I was baptised in the nearest church, which happened to be the Episcopalian church, the English Church. I've had a lot o' free transfers since then! I became an atheist eventually. When I was about five year old, I got knocked doon by a bus and I got my skull fractured. It was only agitation by people after two or three accidents that they widened that road.

'My Dad – he never worked because he had a bad leg. We were brought up on Parish assistance; everybody at that time didnae have very much money: you're talkin aboot the early 1930s away up till the War started. My earliest recollection was o' my auld granny giein me a penny. I must hae been aboot three or four year old. There was one o' the auld street singers that used tae come roon an she says, "Gie the man a big penny an get him tae sing your granny's two favourite songs." An it was 'Annie's Tryst' and 'The Auld Rugged Cross'. On a Sunday night, we aa congregated in ma granny's hoose. My Auntie Lizzie was blind an she used tae tell stories, a great storyteller; she used tae tell aa types o' stories. She used tae sing a wee bit as well, but my faither and them used tae get rowed up wi the melodeon, the tin whistle, a wee bit o' singin, but it was mainly instrumental. My grandfather and my uncles an ma faither aa played the auld-fashioned melodeon, the old International. I was absolutely crazy as a wee lad on the melodeon. My faither always had the melodeon and my uncle Jock played the whistle wi his nose in the Roxy Theatre Go-as-you-pleases.

'Sometimes, I went tae my Auntie Lizzie's hoose, because she was blind and I can aye mind that. The women were sittin breist-feedin the weans. There were the big hook owre the fire an the pot o' soup was hung on it for the next day. Yin o' ma aunties used tae sit wi twa bottles wi the milk fae the coo, an she used tae set yin under each fit and rin it back an furrit, knittin, feedin the wean an makin butter in the bottles. It was just like Charlie Chaplin in his film 'Modern Times'.

'We flitted fae there tae a place caaed Bruce Street in Falkirk, an that would be the 1935 cooncil hooses. I come right through the war years in that area. I went to Victoria School and because I'd had an accident, I went intae a B class and then I came intae an A class and I passed the Qualy and control exams – and I got a bursary. But because we were that poor an ye had tae buy claes if ye won a bursary tae go tae the High School, I went tae the Technical School and completed my secondary education there. In the school I was aye pretty good at the sports and the running and I always liked the singing. An early impression in the Junior School: we were getting the Middle Ages, serfs and people wi collars roon their necks, an even at that early age I used tae think, "How the hell was there sae many o' them at that time suffering?" Another thing was there was a big blank map an oor teacher told us, "That's the USSR." An there was only aboot four or five toons on it: Moscow an Archangel an Kiev, on a big broon map, a mass o' land. An aa she said, I can mind, was there was a Workers' Revolution there and we dinnae ken what happens there – an that was the history o' the Soviet Union an the geography o' Russia! That kin o' rins in my mind.

'Durin the War, I got ma first bike. This boy was gaun awa tae the Merchant Navy and I met him in the chip shop an he said: "I'll gie ye my bike for whatever money ye've got. I'm gaun awa tae the convoys tae Archangel." He didnae come back. It was a BSA wi a Sturmey-Archer back gear. I turned the hannle bars upside doon and I managed tae get anither back wheel, twenty-six by one-and-a-quarter inches, an I put twa fixed wheels on it, one for rinnin aboot wi an one for racin wi. An I ended up daein that in later years. I started away on that bike in Denny Road Club when I was only fifteen. I was a founder member. I was bike-racin mad.

'I ended up gettin a job. My uncle Robert Peel was a foreman in the Grangemouth boatyaird an he spoke for me an I got in as an apprentice blacksmith. Ye worked under the steam hammers in the shipyaird an the conditions in there were really bad. Ye're workin under the steam hammers, an every time the hammer hit the metal, ile and muck, thick ile an watter an steam aa condensed an came fleein aff it, an every time ye hit it, your face got aa spattered like a Dalmatian by the end o the day. Yin o' my mates, when the steam hammer was up one day, he wis flickin stuff wi his finger, when the hammer came doon an took his finger aff. This made a big impression on me an through the years, I've always been very strong as far as safety and health was concerned, fightin for rights and conditions for people.

'The War was aboot owre – it was about 1945 – I was seventeen and a half anyway, and I got my books, because I was continually agitating wi trade union stuff. The men were in the union but they didnae bloody fight. Some o' the country blacksmiths were in there and aa the people were that greedy for money and for piece-work, they couldnae get enough money and they broke the prices o' jobs. So efter the War was feenished, the companies were revertin back to the old system an were takin the War bonuses off. When they did this, their wages werenae worth tuppence. The men got some o' their problems sorted oot, but I got my books. I continued wi my apprenticeship at Sunnyside Foondry.

'It was all belt-driven machinery in there – like walkin away back intae Dickens' times – wi a biler wi a master shaft in it and everything worked aff it wi an old belt. I was only in there a wee while, when wan day we were aa sittin roon the combustion stove – an they were aa lookin at their pey lines an hidin them. I was walkin roon lookin at aa their pey lines. Naebody noticed me because I was a laddie, the apprentice, jist walkin roon. Then I turned roon tae yin boy an I says, "He got 8/6 a week an you only got 7/6. Ye should be showin each ither your pey lines, no hidin them," I says, "because twa-three'll be gettin that money, the rest'll be gettin none, an ye should aa get that money." That was the case. I forced a Union meeting an it happens tae be in the same office I'm in noo as a full-time Union Organiser. They all agreed everybody should be gettin 8/6 as an engineer, an blacksmiths should get 7/6 extra, if they did twa hours' maintenance work every day, which they did. I got up at the meeting and asked, "What aboot the apprentice? What does he get?" They said, "Ye get nothin till your time's oot."

'Aa through my life, it was always melodeons or the tin whistle an I played the mooth organ for a spell, but I was aye singin and aye singin aa types o' sangs. At thirteen, I went tae Willie Hannah, the Scottish Country dancing. At first, what attracted me wisnae sae much the dancing as Willie Hannah wha was one o' the auld melodeon players. I had an auld label sayin, 'Hear Willie Hannah 2/6' an they had them at 1/9, some o' the records o' Willie Hannah an then there was some aulder ones than his: Peter Wyper an Danny Wyper, old 78s. My faither and uncles played aa that. When the blackoot was on, they had tae play in the hooses, but on the simmer nichts they played ootside in the streets an there were great street activity in thae days. The lassies played at beds an jumpin ropes. Ye used tae play fitba wi your bare feet in the street, or cricket up against the lamp-post. The people comin oot o' the tenements or comin oot o' the cooncil scheme still had this friendliness o' helpin each ither.

'I can mind there were only two wirelesses in the street. My Auntie Lizzie was blind and had a charity crystal set. My Uncle Tom had a job

– he was an engine-driver – so they were well-off. Every Friday, I used tae go an get the Red Star Weekly and the Secrets, the women's magazines, an because she was blind, I used tae read tae her. I was an affa bugger for readin! I'd read anything, ye ken. I used tae read short stories an serials an sometimes, I read books tae her. I was readin them at the same time an sometimes I'd read them an I had tae read them owre again, which I widnae mind daein. She used tae be guid crack.

'At that time, they had nae fridges and under the steeple at Falkirk, the butcher, efter a certain time on a Saturday night, he sold threepenny and sixpenny parcels, wi sausages or chops or a bit o' steak. An ye'd see aa the drunk men, some o' them wi sausages hingin oot their pockets, an dugs pinchin them as they staggered doon the road. Ma faither used tae busk in nearly aa the pubs an he'd get twa or three bob an aa his drink. He had a guid serge suit, which he got aff the Parish, a navy blue suit an it lasted him for years. He only wore it at weekends, on Friday and Saturday nichts, then he wad pit it in the pawn. He got something like thirty bob on his suit on the Monday and my mither had tae pull it oot on the Friday when he got the Parish money. Then when he got it, he wad go an busk in the pubs again.

'When the War feenished, I was away roon the Youth Hostels – it was a May holiday an as we were comin doon intae Callander, it was Victory in Europe Day. At Strathyre, it cam owre the wireless that the War had feenished. In Callander, there wis a wee bit mair activity an we came tae the toon, then intae Stirling an there was mair excitement, an we were anxious tae get hame then. When I got hame, the wid was piled high wi everything, furniture an bits o' wid, everything they could pit their hands on. It was aa oot in the middle o the street an they started the bonfire, the chairs were oot an the booze was gaun an ma faither was oot there wi his melodeon an everybody was haein a go. It went on aa night, tae aboot eight o'clock in the mornin. We went tae bed an we woke up in the efternoon an there was a big pile o' ash and a great big hole in the road, where the tar had melted the stanes, aa smoulderin aa night while the celebrations went on.

'When I was in the army, the best o' bein in Germany was ye were able tae get the Hohner mooth organs. I got a melodeon tae, but it was the D-G type and the C-F, no like the Scottish type wi the B-C and C-C#, only semitones apart. I aye wanted a G-D melodeon, tae play wi fiddlers and concertina players. Old Scottish International melodeons were C-C# and D-Cs and I've got an old Scottish International melodeon an it's in C#-D. I can aye mind o' ma faither when I used tae sit in wi him an I was playin an auld battered thing. I didnae read music an they used tae sing wee bits o' vulgar songs along wi the tunes tae remember them. I can aye mind we used tae sing when we were doin an eightsome reel:

[To the tune 'Turkey In The Straw']

O ye ken Mary Ann, she doesnae gie a damn
When she lifts up her petticoat an pisses like a man,
She's a belly like a drum, a big fat bum,
An a hole below her belly for ma toodle-oodle-um.

[Then diddled until the end of the tune.]

'I was a founder member o' the ICI Folk Club, at the same time as I was involved wi the Falkirk Folk Club. At that time, they were tryin tae start a Folk Federation led by Arthur Argo, who had the Chapbook in Aiberdeen at that time, in the early Sixties. They started off in the Cycling Club at Falkirk and then they moved oot o' there into the Temperance Cafe and fae there tae the Metropole Hotel. There was one wee period that we started Saturday night sessions in the Star Inn in Falkirk and it was absolutely brilliant. It was an old-fashioned bar up the stair that hadnae been open for years. It had a wee bar in the centre o the place and you could serve drink and keep the session goin. It only lasted twa-three weeks 'cause the polis came in an closed it. There were too many people up the stair and there werenae enough fire escapes and the flair kin o' hollowed a wee bit inside it. But och, for tradition, for songs, for atmosphere it must have been one o the best ever!

'In the ICI Club, we started awa wi Matt McGinn and Hamish Imlach and that got us a good turn-oot, and they were baith good an they only took a tenner – they could hae got mair. Eventually, we put it up to fifteen. Matt McGinn gave me 'Three Nights and a Sunday Double Time'. I learnt it aff him when I was steamin an he was steamin!

THREE NIGHTS AND A SUNDAY

1. There's a fel - la doon the road that I a-void. He's one o' them we caa the un-em-ployed. Says he, it's be-cause o' blokes like me, he

10 can- ny get a job 'cause I've got three, for I've three nights an' a

CHORUS

13 Sun - day dou - ble time. For I've three nights an' a

16 Sun - day dou- ble time. I work aa day an' I

19 work aa night; tae hell wi' you Jack, I'm aa - right. I've

22 three nights an' a Sun - day dou - ble time.

    2. At the work they've introduced a new machine
       There's ten men where there once was seventeen,
       The machine does the work o' seven ye see,
       I dae the work o' the ither three,
       For I've three nights and a Sunday double time.

CHORUS: Three nights . . . etc.

    3. My wife came to the works the ither day
       Tae say we've anither wee yin on the way.
       Says I, Nae wonder ye can laugh,
       I've never been hame for a year and a half
       Three nights and a Sunday double time.

CHORUS: Three nights . . . etc.

    4. I never miss the pub on a Friday night
       It's there ye always find me gay and bright,
       I'm never oot of the Auld Bay Horse,
       I'm a weekend waiter there, of course,
       Three nights and a Sunday double time.

CHORUS: Three nights . . . etc.

    5. I've a big Post Office bank book, it is true,
       An in it I've a fiver mair than you,
       For I've saved by eatin potted heid,
       It'll pey for the hearse when I drap deid,
       Three nights and a Sunday double time.

CHORUS: Three nights . . . etc.

6. I won't go to Heaven when I die
   To find a Dunlopillo in the sky,
   I'll be gaun tae the ither place,
   An idle time I couldnae face,
   Three nights and a Sunday double time.

CHORUS: Three nights . . . etc.

'I got the fifth verse years later from Matt, the night I took him hame fae the ICI Club — the same time as he was given the artist's copy of his 45 record, 'Dundee Ghost' and 'Pining For The Pill'. He printed it in verse four in his handwritten notes. Years later, I gave this original to someone collecting songs for a socialist song book. It was later printed in the Big Red Book 1949. I think I may have been the first to get the song because of his written notes.

'When I was workin as a blacksmith and welder up in the hydro-electric schemes, the Irish boys used tae come up for the start and opened their insurance cairds and it was £2 for the start and it was £3 for a job at the face, where the bigger bonus wis. If ye didnae gie that: "Sorry, nae job." When ye worked up the tunnels, it was really tough goin because there was nae Union or anything like that up there. But I liked the tunnels. I'd have the melodeon up on the job, waitin on the bus comin up the hill, at the smiddy fire. I had a big, half-inch thick plate roon the top o' this fire, then I had the coal bit in the centre, so that ye could get a couple o' chairs on each side o' it in the winter time and a blazin fire and a can o' tea. When the shift was finished, ye could get the melodeon oot and hae a bit sing-song.

'I stood nine times as a Communist candidate in the Falkirk local elections and for the last four years I stood, the election agent was John Mitchell. Noo, John Mitchell wis the first secretary o the John Maclean Party. He later cam intae the Communist Party. He had a sister Betty and a son caaed Jack. I became friendly wi the haill faimily o the Mitchells. Years later, I met up wi Molly at the first folk night in Molly's place. I dunno if it was aa organised that Molly wis the maist eligible spinster and me the maist eligible bachelor, and I ended up gettin mairrit tae Molly a year later. Now. Molly wis feart tae tell her family that I wis a Communist, so I waited till I visited Molly's mither and Myles, her faither that night and Molly says, "Eh, Tommy's in the Communist Party." "Oh!" she says, "I nearly joined the Young Communists masel. I went tae the meetins wi ma pal, Betty Mitchell, John Mitchell's sister. It was fae Jack Mitchell that I got the tune of 'The Auchengeich Disaster' '':

THE AUCHENGEICH DISASTER

1. In Au-chen-geich, there stauns a pit, the wheel a-bove it is-nae tur-nin'. For on that grey Sep-tem-ber morn, the flames o' Hell be-low are bur-nin'.

2. Tho' in below the coal lay rich,
   It's richer noo for aa the burnin.
   For forty-seiven brave men are deid
   The wives hae sweethairts nae returnin.

3. The seams are thick at Auchengeich
   The coal below is black and glistenin.
   But oh, this cost us far owre dear
   For human life, there is nae reckonin.

4. Oh coal is black and coal is red
   Ah coal is rich beyond aa treasure.
   It's black wi work and red wi bluid
   It's richness noo in lives we measure.

5. It's better though we'd never wrought
   A thoosand years o' work and grievin.
   The coal is black like the mournin shroud,
   The wimmen leave behind their weavin.

6. In Auchengeich, there stauns a pit,
   The wheel above it isnae turnin.
   For on that grey September morn,
   The flames o' Hell below were burnin.

Jim Brown
Photo: Ian F. MacKenzie

JIM BROWN

Jim Brown is a shipyard worker, a wiry, hard-working man, with an ironic sense of humour that masks his romantic and sensitive nature: a man who makes a joke of the things he cares most about. But the underlying warmth and deep feelings he has radiate through the protective cover, and this is nowhere more apparent than in his songs: never sentimental, down to earth, yet full of the dreams and follies of ordinary people. The songs Jim weaves out of the modern industrial scene reflect the life about him and the kind of man he is.

*****

'I'm like Sean Connery and Clint Eastwood, I'm coming up for the big Six-O. I was born in Glasgow in 1930, of that I'm pretty sure, within earshot – or roar – of Partick Thistle's football ground at Firhill. Life was quite primitive, really. Ma father had the misfortune of having a leg shot off in World War One. He was struggling as a war pensioner to support ma mother and maself. Unfortunately, in those days, they didn't prepare them much for civilian life other than giving sorts of rough training in something they could earn their living by. In my father's case, they trained him in Cathcart to repair clocks and watches. This more or less was it. My Dad would repair the neighbour's watches for them at half a crown a time. He chased ma mother and me out to the cinema to get out his road, while he worked on the shoogly card table, trying to keep the wee screws from falling onto the carpet. One terrible day, I got the thrashing of my life. He'd gone out and I played wi some o' his watches wi a magnet!

'I think I got lot o' ma imagination from the cinema. I spent a hell of a lot of time in the cinema, wi ma mother, just tae get out of the way. We lived in a single end and life was cramped. There had been a brother before me, but he died of a mastoid. His name was Charles Edward. There must have been a streak o' the Jacobite in calling my brother Charles Edward Hedeville Brown. My father lost his leg at Hedeville, somewhere in France. His name was James Baptiste De Molder Brown. His father had been a Corporation cooncillor and he had a friend who was a French sea-captain and his name was Baptiste De Molder, so my Dad got the handle Baptiste De Molder! When it come my turn, all I got was James Brown. In a way, I was annoyed wi that. Having red hair was bad enough; ye got teased. It's no red noo! But if anyone asked your name, a policeman or anybody, an ye said "James Brown," no-one ever believed ye! Strangely enough, as the years have gone by, I got to accepting it was not such a bad name after all. I work in the shipyards and guys like tae shout, "Hey Jimmy Broon!" It's a kind o' itch – they jist like tae hear themselves say it. If one will shout it, in the course o' the day, half a dozen will. "Hey Jimmy Broon!" It's a kind o' Glasgow cry. It seems to give them some kind o' reassurance. In the square mile, there are probably more Broons in Glasgow than anywhere else on earth. Funnily enough, when I started writing songs, I decided to say, "Jim Broon". I felt it sounded a wee bit more sort o educated. Anyway, as far as the yards go, I'm Jimmy.

'I was raised in Maryhill and it was quite a happy enough childhood really. Not like many others who felt deprived, I had lots o' fun in the games that kids play. I got the first taste o' song culture from watching the buskers comin round the back yards o' the tenements. There used tae be an auld guy came roon aboot once a month, I don't know if it was a Sunday, but he always chose religious songs. He always sang 'The Old Rugged Cross', shaking as he sang and lookin as if he needed a good meal. But the real star attraction was a bloke who won everybody's hearts and he was known as Old Joe. He wore a greasy raincoat and what we called a paddy hat, an old battered soft hat, and he had this banjo and his plectrum was a bit o' broken beer bottle. This guy was a wow, for when he came into our back yard, immediately every kid in the district, including maself, would rush to where he was and we'd hang onto his coat, and then we'd all hang onto each other, until there was a human crocodile o' kids in the yard. He always played – and I think it was the only song he knew – 'She'll be Comin round the Mountain when She Comes'. That delighted the mothers and the pennies were gettin flung oot the windows galore, and this old guy was doin really well. He'd go fae back yard tae back yard right along the whole street and down another street. I would follow him everywhere, wi this chum o' mine, and I really adored him. I suppose there were musical tendencies in masel. I remember one time he done our street, and I followed him everywhere until he'd finished his stint, and I even followed him doon towards Maryhill Road, doon tae Queen's Cross, as a matter of fact, me an this chum o' mine. I've got to describe the guy: he'd a huge big white beard, like Father Christmas and big blue eyes. When we got tae Queen's Cross, we wondered where he'd go next and got ready to hang onto his coat tails again. To our absolute horror, we saw him go into a public hoose, wi big heavy swing doors. He shoved the door, to go in, and we tried to follow him an he turned round an he bent down an he said, wi his big blue eyes lookin at us, he said, ''Hey, sonny – get tae fuck!'' What a shattering experience for a young boy. That lovely man! Maybe that toughened me up a wee bit. Everything's not as it appears to be.

'I had a good diet o' Hollywood movies and I began to get this idea of wanting to travel the world. When it came time to earn a living, I opted to be an served my time as a marine engineer. I'd this idea I wanted to travel the world, and I would be hangin over the ship's side while the Hawaiian islanders came out to the ship – I could see it all in my mind's eye. I served five years hard on Clydeside doon near thon Finnieston Crane, in Elliot Street, Davie Rowan's Marine Engineers and Boiler-makers. They built the engines and the boilers. The big Finnieston crane would lower them in. I remember being down the stoke hold when they were lowering in a boiler. At that time, they made the stoke holds small and crammed in everything they could get into them. This big crane, when it brought the boiler down, it just blotted oot the daylight. Your job was to land it on its stool, bolt it down, and everything was done by hand signals, no walkie-talkies then! One mistake and you were goin tae be intae an Oxo cube.

'When my time was out, I did go to sea. Some o' my mates had gone to British Columbia. They kept writing letters to me saying, ''Why don't you chuck the sea and come and join us?'' They were out in the Rockies by this time, and I got this idea, because I had done a lot o' hiking and rock-climbing and skiing, when I was serving ma time in the yards. Every weekend, summer or winter, I was away under canvas – never could stay at home because o the cramped conditions. I spent all my spare time roamin the Highlands and pickin up songs and stuff that I absorbed *before* the Folk Revival. I played the pipes. I learned the pipes in the Boys Brigade and then graduated into the Clan Fraser Pipe Band. That's a first-grade band. I'm quite good at the pipes. I only wish I could play the guitar the way I can play the pipes. I can play the pipes, drunk or sober! But two or three pints, wi the guitar, an I feel as if I've got gloves on.

'I went all round Africa when I was at sea, doon the West Coast and up the East Coast, and over to the States on oil tankers. But I'd still this burning desire to go to Canada, where some o' my mates were workin on ski tows. I got booked up for a workin passage on a deep-sea trawler to go to Canada for a delivery job. I can still remember the name o' the company – Abrahams in Hope Street. They signed me on and all I had to do was wait till the boat was completed and away we'd go. I began to get nervous because National Service was comin, so I shot aff to the Forestry Commission.

'I thought I could handle it because I thought I knew what hard work was. But I didn't know what hard work was till I joined the Forestry Commission. Hard work, poor food and low wages! The first day in the woods wi an axe in my hand, I was attacking the trees square-on – wallop! – and jarrin every bone and muscle in my body. I was back to the bunkhouse at night in a severe state o' paralysis, unable to move. It went on like this for days, till somebody told me to strike at an angle and make sure the axe is bloody sharp and honed up, and sinks into the wood instead o' batterin off it. That was lesson one. Other jobs were diggin ditches – that was pretty hard goin – I'm talkin about the days before it was aa mechanised. We dug ditches wi shovels and cut doon trees wi axes. An the double-handed saw – that was the nightmare o' nightmares. Sometimes, ye got coupled up for the day wi some big country yokel, that was out to earn bonus. Ye'd tae try an keep up wi these guys an ye were down on your knees an your very intestines were nearly falling out, trying tae saw in time wi the guy's frantic pace. Ye tried tae keep the fixed grin an "I can take it!" But it was absolute agony! I reckon we were undernourished because the cook in the cookhouse was an old ex-Glasgow modeller and the guy only knew two feeds – greasy stew and mince and totties; breid an jam for takin on the hill.

'I was in Strathyre and in the Loch Katrine area and I used to go climbin there, up aboot Ben Aan and I thought it would be wonderful workin there. Again, it's bein duped by Hollywood movies o' Canadian lumberjacks wi MacKenzie River shirts, whackin down big redwoods among the snow-capped mountains. The reality in Scotland was you're in among trees that looked like pit-props, an that's aa they're fit for, the rain's comin down an the midgies are biting. Sometimes they'll send ye in to do a bit o' brashin, cuttin off the lower small branches, and ye'd sit there and hae a smoke wi your mate, then – crack! – a twig would break, an ye'd look round and see the old foreman behind the trees, creepin up on ye. Ye'd say, "Christ Almighty, I'm doin aa this for £7 a week!" and they'd take your board off that.

'My enjoyment some nights was to go doon to Callander on someone's push-bike. I'd been quickly snapped up by the Callander Pipe Band, along wi another guy who played. We used tae be sittin in the public bar o' the Dreadnought Hotel on a Saturday morning having a quiet pint, when the pipe major would rush in, "Hey Jimmy, Bobby, get a set o pipes!

Come oot here – we're short-handed!'' Somebody'd throw ye a set o' bagpipes and ye'd suddenly join the band and march away along the main street to the adulation o' the tourists. Some nights, we went to a place aboot Comrie tae hear Jimmy Shand.

'But I learned one very, very valuable lesson. I'd spent ma teenage years as a weekender. There were two Glasgow working-class climbing clubs; the Lomond Mountaineering Club and the Craigdhu Mountaineering Club an there was great rivalry between them. I grew up associating the open air as being the fun place, the beautiful place. See when ye have tae work in it? It's a different story altogether!

'I'd thought if I got away into the undergrowth, the authorities wad never find me for my National Service, but they got on ma trail. So I buggered off to Southern Ireland wi a mate o' mine. We had a month over there, drinking Guinness stout and gettin penniless. I came back; ma mother was in tears, and I'd only a ha'penny left and she said, ''They're callin ye up, son.''

'I'd that cock-eyed optimism – I suppose it must have been my age – and I said, ''Och, they'll send me tae Austria skiing every day.'' They sent me tae North Africa. I'd two bloody years out there and the only thing that relieved the monotony was they put me in the Scots Greys pipe band. I got away on a Mediterranean cruise wi them. Ma piping really improved, because I had nothing else to do but play that chanter every day. The army certainly helped me musically. When I got home, I tried to go to Canada again. I was booked up an my father took ill and I cancelled it and I got booked again an he took ill again, cancelled it again. Then I met Joan. Finally, my ideas changed entirely. Funnily enough, my daughter's now married and she's aff with her young husband – to Canada!

'I met Joan in the Highlander's Institute of all places. She said I won her over, because we were dancing away and there were stags' heads all round the room and I said, ''I bet all their eyes light up when they play the eightsome reel!'' She says that was the moment when she fell in love with me!

'The Folk Revival started and Drew Moyes had his Folk Centre. I started going up an I was quite content tae listen. It was like opening a big treasure chest. I'd no idea the millions o' good songs in Scotland, an absolute wealth o' jewels in there; it was a complete revelation and I had tae tell everybody, ''Hey, ye don't know what you've got! Scotland's rich in songs and music! It's wonderful, wonderful!'' Of course, it was an education seeing all those who were performing, doing their stuff up there. I was quite content tae play the pipes, but when I heard Bert Jansch playing the guitar, I had to run out and buy one, thinking, ''The guy's a genius on the pipes. He'll pick up the guitar no trouble at all.'' Wasn't to be the case at all. Joan was expecting Gavin and you couldn't have the pipes in the house. By the time Gavin was born, I could play three chords. By the time Alison was born, I began to imagine I could write songs. The first song I wrote was about Alison. Ewan MacColl and Peggy Seeger were visiting Cumbernauld and somebody told them I had written this song about a little girl. So I was commanded to come to their workshop on Saturday morning in the Cottage Theatre. I sung this song and they liked it so much they published it, and started corresponding with me and encouraging me to write more. They gave me the confidence to keep on writin.

'I was invited down to London to meet Ewan and Peggy at home. I got a good bit of advice from Ewan MacColl. "Look," he said, "if you're goin to write songs, write about what you know best. Don't try to write about things you don't know anything about." So I thought, "What do I know about?" I realised that all I really did know about was workin life on Clydeside, so I thought I'll concentrate on that. Here's a kin o' daft sort o' song. It's really a play on place-names, an it's also a song about a young fella who cam from Moscow. No, no the big Moscow in the Soviet Union; oor wee Moscow doon in Ayrshire. This lad had ambitions to be a professional footballer, but things turned oot rather differently, because he was what they call, in football, 'ball-shy' — feart o' gettin walloped in the face by the ball, and that's very bad, isn't it[!]:

THE BALL-SHY BOY FROM MOSCOW

— 72 —

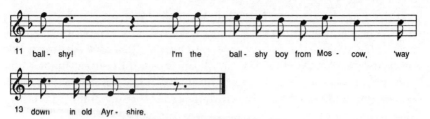

11 ball - shy!   I'm the   ball - shy boy from Mos - cow,   'way

13 down   in old Ayr - shire.

2. An ma faither came frac north of here
   From a wee place known as Stepps,
   Wi a population mixture
   From miners tae company reps.
   An he was good at fitba
   But I'm no in the race,
   For I'm feart I'll get a wallop
   Frae a fitba in the face.

CHORUS: Because I'm ball-shy! . . . etc.

3. An ma mither was a Moscow girl,
   Moscow born an bred.
   She was the local hockey star,
   An of balls she had no dread,
   For she was the goalie
   An very brave, ye see.
   But I sometimes think she might have been
   A bit ashamed of me.

CHORUS: Because I'm ball-shy! . . . etc.

4. An when I played at fitba,
   The crowd wad always roar,
   'Ye're a flippin ballet dancer!'
   'Cause I never seemed to score.
   But ma fitwork, it was special
   An someone else watched me.
   'Twas a talent scout frae overseas
   From a ballet company.

CHORUS: Because I'm ball-shy! . . . etc.

5. So now ye'll see me dancin
   All o'er the world sae wide,
   Twirlin lassies roon ma heid
   As on the stage I glide.
   An in a way, I'm happy.
   The crowd they were so rude!
   Oh ye see, it's just anither case
   Of 'LOCAL BOY MAKES GOOD!'

CHORUS: Noo, I dance wi Bolshoi!
   An I prance wi Bolshoi!
   I'm the Bolshoi boy from Moscow,
   An ma folks are proud of me!

— 73 —

'I also was anxious to try an sing in the dialect and not necessarily funny songs, because for too long the music-hall, funny, Glasgow song was accepted as twentieth-century Scottish culture. I thought I'll try to sing *passionately* in the dialect, because there's not a lot o' that aboot. I got onto writin this song which, again, Ewan and Peggy published. It's about the Glasgow I knew when I was working under that big crane, something entirely in the past:

OLD GLASGOW TOWN

2. Some children wore the Parish clothes
    Women stood wi weans in shawls,
    And a hundred pubs saw a hundred brawls,
    In Garscube Road, in Garscube Road.

3. An the shipyard hooter's morning sound,
    Was always heard for miles around.
    And a thousand hammers would start to pound,
    On ice-cold steel and red-hot steel.

4. An the tramcars rattled through the fog,
    And the carters made their horses jog,
    While men and boys would homeward slog
    On cobbled streets and gaslit streets.

5. Well, the rough old days pass with the years,
    But the tough new days are ever here,
    And children's voices sound so clear
    From the concrete towers above the town.

6. So good luck kids in all you do,
    Old Glasgow now belongs to you,
    I'm just a friend who's passing through
    And remembers yesterday.

7. Old Glasgow town, I knew you well,
    I knew your colour, I knew your smell,
    When a tenement was heaven or hell
    So long ago, so long ago.

'It's changing rapidly, I don't know if it's changing for the better or no. In some ways it is, but the soul's kin o' gone out of it. But there again, who am I to say what way it has to go? It'll go its way whatever we think aboot it. Anyway, folk music's healthy and alive in the city an that's a good thing. I sang in the yard social club during the miners' strike. That was a bit o' a revelation for them! Big Mick Broderick was there wi the Whistlebinkies. He was working in the yard as well. I think the lads quite like the idea of having a resident songwriter. I suppose Matt McGinn kin o' paved the road for that. It's Yarrow's where I work. Aye, making frigates. I don't take any great pride in that, by the way. Ye can disagree wi what I say, once ye stop payin your income tax. We're aa guilty. I'd rather we were makin combine harvesters or cargo ships or anything but what we're buildin. But then, ye can argue that in this troubled world every country needs a navy. Anyway it's just a job that pays the rent. I worked in Falkirk in the Carron Iron Works, an I was made redundant, and I worked here in Cumbernauld, but the job wouldnae pay the rent. I ended up havin to go back to the Clydeside. I never thought I could face it. I'd been away quite a long time from it; I'd been in refrigeration. I hadn't been in the yards since boyhood, and it was very, very hard to go back, I can tell you: the noise and the conditions were frightening. But it's like goin doon the mines – ye get adjusted and ye don't notice it after a bit. But I must confess, I'd be quite happy to be retired tomorrow: ye get stiff in the joints – it's a young man's game. Like the mines, it's no a sedentary job.'

Archie Frame
Photo: Ian F. MacKenzie

ARCHIE FRAME

I first met Archie Frame when he came to Glenfarg Folk Club with a party from Glassford Folk Club. He sang in a style I had come to recognise as the hallmark of the traditional singer of the older generation – whole-hearted and committed to the song. When I learned more about the extraordinary life he had led – emigrating to Australia and coming back again, working in the mines for years, leaving them and embarking upon a new and different way of life – my respect and admiration grew. Many people may see him as a stocky wee man with a genial smile who likes a song and a pint, but behind that unpretentious appearance, there is great strength of character, determination and a real generosity of spirit.

*****

'I was born in Newton into a mining community in the last year of the First War, 1918. This particular community lived in five barrack-like streets, every house just looking into the other. You had a situation where nobody could keep secrets. One thing was certain: that people were open-heart-ed and wouldn't allow a neighbour to be in distress without giving a hand. The big thing about village life, particularly when most of the men worked in local pits, was we had this feeling that we were all together. Injured men, for example, requiring some relief from the boredom of lying in bed with a broken back, would be trundled out into the streets and we'd have a wee concert or a ceilidh round about their beds to cheer them up in some way.

'But in any case, during my formative years, I went to school early in that village. I think I was quite unusual in going there when only four years of age, and I seemed to be a wee bit precocious. I was readin the

Times and readin murder stories, so much so, that my parents were warned after I'd had a number of nightmares, to keep me off readin too much. One of the penalties of bein a good reader was that I was promoted quickly at school and found myself bein moved up classes. I was sort o' dominated by larger people than myself and I had to make my presence felt in other ways.

'It was during my early school days that the General Strike of 1926 came along. I was just eight at that time and I took my chance wi the rest, linin up for my soup in the village at the wash-houses. Now, I'm not goin to say we were in dire straits, because we had one or two connections and ye had to use them. My mother's sister was married to a man who was manager of a grocery shop in Glasgow, and at least she could go in there and get stale buns and stale cakes very cheap, whereas the normal thing during that long strike was that folk depended on parcels bein handed in. One of the aftermaths of the strike was that many miners felt that the best thing to do was to emigrate. Because my mother had an uncle out in Australia who was supposed to have a farm and a fairly good position, the family moved off in 1927 and we arrived in a place called Williamstown.

'Of course, my schooldays had to be continued under different circumstances. I may say, probably even less favourable, because bein the son of a Pommie — even although ye were a Scots Pommie, which wasnae regarded in such a bad light as English Pommies — ye still had to defend your position an say that your Dad hadn't come over to take an Australian's job; he was just escaping from bad conditions at home.

'One of the things that buoyed me up in Australia, as it had done at home, was that we had this fund of Scots culture and we attended the Caledonian Society and other groups that were set up. We used to go and listen to Scots music and Scots songs and during the five years we were there, we learned more, probably, became more conscious than if we'd stayed at home. My old man, during the five years we were there, I think he counted up to twenty temporary jobs. My mother was the main person who contributed to the family finances. She went out washing morning and afternoon, and in the heat of Australia without modern washing-machines or any tackle like that, it was a hard day's work. Ye could live rather cheap in terms o' the cost o' livin, so we could live and save and actually, after this four-and-a-half years, we came back home on this boat.

'I'm not saying the future was rosy. I had seven months to go at the school, when I reached this magical age of fourteen. I went to a local school down there at Gateside, Cambuslang. It was one o' these places like something out o' Dickens. It was a holding operation. I didn't learn anything at that school and I left it. I wasnae quite fourteen. I'd tae sign a paper that I would do two years at night school, an my grandfather, who was a contractor in the pit, gave me as a birthday present a line for a lamp. Whether he'd done me a service or not, I don't know.

'It wis intae the pits I went, as a pan engine boy and my wage wasnae too bad, because my grandfather was the contractor, a sort o' middleman between the owner and the men and he took a contract to take out so much coal at so much per ton, or drive roads at so much a yard. It was a bad system – I learnt that later on. I started my life as a miner and this pit was really my University, because in it there were people, knowledgeable men of all kinds. I mean, apart from working hard and learning the craft of being a miner, you had to go up through the stages of being a haulage boy, until you worked towards the coal face and you became a face man, with a higher wage of course.

'But all through this period, there was many things happening in the world. From my experience of seeing how working people had to live on a pittance, and the savage laws against them, I began to take on a kind of socialist attitude, a Communist attitude in some cases. The big watershed for me was the Spanish Civil War in 1936. Because a number of people from our area went to fight there, some miners from the pit I was in went and got themselves killed. So all during this period, we would listen to the broadcasts from Spain and naturally we took sides with the Republicans. All these ideas were creating a ferment among the working population, so that eventually I became active in the Union and a member of the Branch Committee and began to see myself in some kind of political role, trying to help to change the world. An of course, here again was where music also played a big part.

'In the coal mines, there were always songs like 'The Blantyre Explosion' which were sung and were part of the tradition of the mining area and, of course, we were just a hop, step and a jump from Blantyre. The song would be sung very frequently at parties we attended:

THE BLANTYRE EXPLOSION

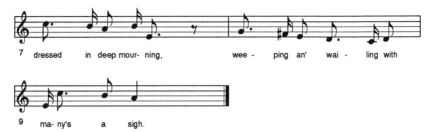

7 dressed in deep mour- ning, wee - ping an' wai - ling with

9 ma- ny's a sigh.

2. I stepped up beside her and thus I addressed her
   'Pray tell me fair maid o' your trouble and pain.'
   Sobbing and sighing at last she did answer,
   'John Murphy, kind sir, was my true lover's name.'

3. 'Twenty-one years of age, full of youth and good-looking,
   To work down the mine from High Blantyre he came.
   The wedding was fixed and the guests were assembled
   Yon calm summer evening when young Johnny was slain.'

4. 'When the explosion was heard, the women and children
   With pale anxious faces they ran to the mine.
   When the truth was made known, the hills rang with their mourning:
   Two hundred and twenty young miners were slain.'

'Going on in my mining life, the war came along, of course, and I was one of those individuals who missed being a militiaman by a few months. They set up a team for guarding the pits from incendiary bombs, fire-watchers, in other words. I was conscripted into this, being an active member of the Union. I remember turning up the first night it was instituted and the pit delegate, a man called Willie Innes. They'd laid doon army-type beds in the manager's office. Willie and I arrived up after four or five pints in the pub and went into the beds in the manager's office. The day shift started at seven in the morning, an the manager came in at eight, and we were still lying doggo in these beds! He read the riot act! A manager had considerable powers and needless to say the bed system was abandoned from them on.

'I won't say that all through this period o' the War it was aa gloom and doom. In the villages and towns, we had organisations set up to provide comforts for the soldiers, and the comforts funds were set up. I'd learned to play a sax in a very indifferent fashion, I'd a two- or three-piece band and I remember at the beginning it was really awful. My repertoire was so poor – in fact, the whole band were learners more or less. We'd learned about a dozen tunes and when ye're having a late night, when ye have to go through the whole mill of eightsome reels, foxtrots, quicksteps, we found that we had to repeat these same tunes many, many times. One o' the things that used to happen was they gave out a bag o' buns about half-time, and the latter part o' the night would be not as much a test o' musicianship as a test of dodging buns! We did have fun!

'My fondness for folk music began to develop about the same time. I learned a few tunes, and there's one called 'My Jo Janet':

MY JO JANET

1. Sweet sir for your cour - te - sy, when you come by the bass then, for the love you bear tae me, buy me a kee- kin glass then. Keek in to the draw well, Ja - net, Ja -__ net. An' there ye'll see yer bon- nie sel, my Jo Ja-__ net.

2. Keekin in the draw-well clear
   What if I faa in then?
   Syne aa my kin will say an sweer
   I drooned masel for sin then.
   Haud the better tae the brae
   Janet, Janet,
   Haud the better tae the brae,
   My Jo Janet.

3. Guid sir for your courtesy
   Comin through Aberdeen then,
   For the love ye bear tae me
   Buy me a pair o' sheen then.
   Clout the old, the new are dear,
   Janet, Janet,
   A pair may gain ye half a year,
   My Jo Janet.

4. But what if dancing on the green
   An skippin like a maukin
   They should see my clooted sheen,
   O me they will be talking.
   Dance aye laigh an late at een,
   Janet, Janet,
   Syne aa their fauts will nae be seen,
   My Jo Janet.

5. Kind sir for your courtesy,
   When ye gae tae the Cross then,
   For the love ye bear tae me,
   Buy me a pacing horse then.
   Pace upon your spinnin wheel,
   Janet, Janet,
   Pace upon your spinnin wheel,
   My Jo Janet.

6. My spinnin wheel is old and stiff,
   The rock o't winna stand sir,
   Tae keep the temper pin in tiff,
   It flies richt aff my hand sir.
   Mak the best o't that ye can,
   Janet, Janet,
   But like it never wale a man,
   My Jo Janet!

'Just after the war, 1946 actually, I spent the next two years at Ruskin College, Oxford, living the life more or less o' a gentleman. Well, after the arduous work o' the pits, it seemed to me like a gentleman's life. I got a diploma in economics and political science. But it really wasnae worth a great deal, 'cause I'd pledged masel to go back to the pits. I'd this mistaken belief that I had some kind o' mission in life tae lead miners.

'Anyhow, I slogged on in the same pit up till 1953 and, of course, just about that time I got married and in order to get a house, I had to move. I took a job in a pit up near Clackmannan, called the Zetland mine. It was one o' these ingaun eens. Ye jist walked into the hillside and ye worked away. I had transferred from one pit to another but the work didn't get any lighter, much heavier, in fact. It was still a very dangerous job. Ye just couldn't hear your ears for the grinding o' the machinery. Ye couldn't even tell whether there were goin to be some fall o' roof nearby. If a man was injured, you didn't know because you could hardly see for the dust that was swirling through the section, especially if ye were on the topside of this machine. As I say, I soldiered on for five years, then the children began to come, three before I left the mining industry.

'Songs were a consolation, though ye didnae get much chance tae sing in the pit, because o' the roar o' the scraper and power loader. Maybe there wasnae much tae sing aboot in the pit. Socially, when we were living in Tullibody, at that period, it was a sort o' meltin-pot o' miners, people entering the mining industry comin out the Forces. Tullibody was the sort o' place that attracted folk because ye could get housed very quickly. The village was originally built roond a new pit called the Glenochil, a very modern, up-to-date pit. They spent twenty million pounds on the infrastructure, but unknown to the Coal Board, the pit was worthless, because all the coal had already been taken out by the Alloa Coal Company and that money went down the drain. Now, of course, the premises are used as a Young Offenders' Institution.

'By 1959, I'd done twelve years since Ruskin. My wife, at this stage, had entered into a mature students' scheme. I thought, I've done my share of heavy work and I've nothing to lose by applying, maself. So, I did this and in 1959, I got a year's grant to allow me to go and study for Highers and get into University. In order to do this, I enrolled in a place called the British Educational Institute in Bath Street [Glasgow]. I travelled every day from Tullibody, quite a distance, an hour and a half's journey each way. I worked fairly hard; my stumbling block was, of course, ye had to have an Attestation of Fitness in the normal University entrance.

'I made a decision to come back to the West here, nearer to Glasgow and nearer to places where I could attend night school. I managed after working as a porter in the railway station at East Kilbride. I got a house, fortunately, near the station. Strathclyde, one o the new Universities, opened in 1963 and by this time I'd managed to get at least an O Grade French and one or two Highers and I believe they welcomed me into Strathclyde with open arms, because I was a mature student – in fact, I was a very mature student! Some people used to mistake me for staff and direct me into the staff rooms and the staff bar, which I didn't mind at all! The only problem for me at University was finding the level of work to undertake. With nothing but a big shovel behind me, I mean, I wasn't there to waste my time I can assure ye. I struggled on and I got through.

'Only snag was, when it came to my last year, I had the chance of doing an Honours year but the authorities thought I should be in the front line, teaching. It meant I had to go in front of a full board at Jordanhill to justify my application for another year. Of course, my main reason for taking another year was that there was £6 a week more if ye were an Honours graduate and that was the big incentive for me.

'Then the question became, where would I work? Now, I could have gone into the school system, but it meant another year at Jordanhill. I was fifty by this time and I thought it a more promising thing if I could work in a further education college. The situation at the College of Building was that they were expanding so rapidly they were willing to have me as it was with my in-service training later and it suited me very well, so I went and worked in this college for fifteen years. I taught Economics, which is a dismal science. Later on, I became a chief examiner in the world for the Institute of Quantity Surveyors and I set the examination papers. Needless to say, I had a very high pass rate!

'As for the young apprentices, building slaters, roofers and plasterers – they hated every minute we tried tae teach them Communications. They wanted to be up and about and sometimes ye did relent and take them out tae places like the People's Palace or the Acropolis. You could do a very good sort of lesson in a graveyard. In that particular graveyard, it was mainly the wealthy in Glasgow and from the point of view of sociology, you could talk about the merchant class in Glasgow and the importance they had in the city's development. In the People's Palace there used to be parrots in the big greenhouse and some o the lads used to try and teach these parrots language that was hardly parliamentary, in other words, foul.

'One day a week we had Modules. I did, among many things, one on Poverty – that was the title. I claimed to be an expert on it. I was also roped in to give lectures to young offenders in Barlinnie, and the only thing that disturbed me about the lectures was that ye were supposed to go over there and talk about thrift and how to bank money and insure for your old age and all eventualities. They called it Civics, and none of these lads were interested in Civics at all. What they wanted to hear about and talk about was women and drink. As often as ye could bring in these kind o' topics, ye could see their eyes lightin up.

'I also had to entertain them and usually tried to pick out a film that would last as long as possible on the subject I was dealing with. I was supposed to have a preview, first. I remember going up and taking a film on spec. It had to do with insurance, as I thought. I took it over to Barlinnie. It had to do with insurance certainly – but it was showing ye, ninety-nine-and-a-half per cent o' the film was showing ye how to break into a warehouse, and about two minutes was showing you how the guys got caught. Talk about a school for crime!

'I had the option of maybe working at the prison full-time, but the College of Building was much more preferable to the atmosphere of Barlinnie.

'I soldiered on in the teaching business until, of course, by Act of Parliament, I had to leave. I was sorry to go, because I maintained, as long as I could totter up that brae towards the College, I would carry on. But I took my golden handshake and retired gracefully like a man, and I've been trying tae sing like a lintie ever since. Here's a song which I've been associated with and have loved; it's called 'Jeanie's Black Ee':

JEANIE'S BLACK EE

1. The sun shone sae ro - sy, the grey hills a - dor - ning, light sprang the lav'- rock and moun - ted sae hie. When true tae the tryst o' blythe May's de- wy mor - ning Jea- nie cam lin - kin oot ow- re the green lea. To mark her im - pa - tience I crept 'mang the bra - ckens, aft, aft tae the kent gate she turned her black ee. Then ly- ing doon do- wi - lie, sighed by a wil- low tree, "I am a- sleep, din- na wau- ken me."

2. Saft thro' the green birks I stole to my jewel,
    Streek'd on sprin's carpet aneath the saugh tree;
    'Think na dear lassie that Willie's been cruel.'
    'I am asleep, do not waken me.'
    'Wi love's warm sensations I've marked your impatience,
    Lang hid 'midst the breckans, I watched your black ee;
    You're no sleepin, pawkie Jean, open that lovely ee.'
    'I am asleep, do not waken me.'

3. Bright is the whin's bloom, ilk green knowe adorning,
    Sweet is the primrose, despangled wi dew;
    Yonder comes Peggy to welcome May morning,
    Dark wave her hafflet locks o'er her white brow.
    O light, light, she's dancing keen on the gowany green,
    Barefoot and kilted half up to the knee;
    While Jeanie is sleeping still, I'll rin and sport my fill,
    'I was asleep and ye've wakened me.'

4. I'll rin and whirl her around, Jeanie is sleeping sound.
    Kiss her frae lug to lug, no-one can see;
    Sweet, sweet's her hinny mou' – well, I'm no sleeping noo.
    I was asleep but ye've wakened me.
    Laughing till like to drap, swith to my Jean I lap,
    Kissed her ripe roses, and blest her black ee.
    And aye since when e'er we meet, sing for the sound is sweet,
    'I was asleep and ye've wakened me.'

Jim Wallace
Photo: Aåse Goldsmith

VOICES FROM THE EAST COAST

JIM WALLACE

Jim Wallace was born into a Fife farming community, and his recollections create a vivid picture of country life when horses were still in use and harvest homes or 'Maidens' were still held. His grandfather's notebook of horsemanship, with its solemn oaths and religious tone, brings a strong whiff of the stable from the days when 'a shak o' Auld Hornie' was obligatory for every budding ploughman. Most of the notebook consists of a long series of practical instructions for the management and care of horses, based on the precept that the only way to control an animal is through kindness, which contrasts bizarrely with the terrible fates invoked on whoever broke the Horseman's Oath. Jim found farm life without the horse unattractive, so, through his love of dogs, he became a shepherd and worked in Fife, Kinross and further north into the Highlands and Islands, which was where he met his wife, Dolly, a Gaelic speaker and storyteller from Harris.

*****

'I was born at Haresteens Farm in 1928, between Woodend and Kinglassie in Fife, youngest of a family of six. My father took a bad heart and we moved to Redford at Thornton. I left the schuil there, of course, and we were just two year there. I left the schuil there and I started to work wi Sandy Clarke at Strathore at Thornton. That's a brother o' Tommy up here at the Muirton. Then in 1943, we moved up to Milnathort and we were nine year up there upon two or three o the fairms roon aboot there. I worked maistly wi horses at that time. The Horseman's Word was still on the go.

'I still have my grandfather's notebook of horsemanship with the Horseman's Oath in it and several lessons in horsemanship. At one time, it wouldnae done tae let ye see it, but it doesnae maitter noo:

THE HORSEMAN'S OATH – ANSWERS AND INSTRUCTIONS

Q. Who is there?
A. A brother and a blind man.

Q. What do you want here with a blind man?
A. To be made a horseman the same as myself.

Q. How do you know you are a horseman?
A. Because I have been tried and retried and ready to be tried by you.

Q. What way come you here?
A. Through crooks and straits as the road led.

Q. What brought you here?
A. To find the secret.

Q. Did anyone send you here?
A. No.

[The man to be initiated was brought to the ceremony by a sponsor]

The oath is a very solom [sic] one which we make of you is to hold up your right hand and place yourself in a position, neither walking nor swinging, siting [sic], lying, standing clothed nor unclothed, boots on, nor boots off.

I do most solomly [sic] take upon me the vows and secrets of horseman-ship before God and these witnesses and may God help [sic] me to keep my vows and secrets of which I will have to give account on the last day that I will always conceal and never reveal to father nor mother, sister nor brother, wife nor winch [sic] nor to the babe that siteth [sic] on my knee nor to anyone, he or she, nor show any of the signs of horsemanship. I vow and swear that I will not give it nor see it given under the sum of £1 sterling and a bottle of whisky paid down as I did myself.

I further vow and swear that I will not give it, nor see it given under the numbers 3, 5, 7, 9 nor 11 swearn brethren being present to be the same as myself.

I further vow and swear that I will not see it given to a drunkard, nor to a swearer, nor to a liar, nor to a revealer of secrets, nor to anyone I think will abuse horses, nor see them abused without telling them they are doing so. I will attend all brothers' signs or summons within the distance of five miles except in five cases: my master's time, my wife in childbed, going for a doctor, in sickness in my family or a house on fire.

I further vow and swear that I will not give it, nor see it given to any one under eighteen, nor above forty-five years, nor to a tradesman except to a blacksmith, and very few of them, and not to a woman at all.

I further vow and swear that I will not cut it nor carve it, write it nor engrave it upon parchments, paper, snow or stone, or anything movable nor unmovable under the canopy of heaven, nor do as much as wave a single letter to cause it to be known.

PRAYER

O help me my God to keep my secrets and perform my vows as a horseman and if I break any of them, I wish no better to come over me that my heart to be torn from my left breast by a wild horse and my body quartered in four and hung up to the four winds of heaven and taken down and buried in the sands of the sea shore where the tide ebbs and flows twice in the twenty-four hours to show that I have been a deceiver of the faith. [Amen]

Always be kind to a horse and he will have confidence in you. Kindness has a power over animals.

'In 1942, that was the first year I left the schuil, I got a trip to the Glasgow Stallion Show at Scotstoun. It was aa Clydesdales at that time, hunders o' Clydesdales, and it lasted fower days. We left Thornton at half-past six in the mornin wi fower stallions and a man wi a horse and cairt wi the kist on it, wi the show stuff, the harness for the horses and oor rations. Aa things were rationed at the time; ye couldna get nothin. We gaed doon tae the station, we loaded them on the train at Thornton an we gaed doon tae Glescae an got shoved in a sidin at Cowlairs. We had tae wait on a trainload comin in, tae take oot tae Scotstoun. They jist gien ye an engine when there was maybe twenty or thirty – ye had tae hing aboot there. We sat there for aboot fower oors an then the engine came an took us tae Scotstoun.

'We got the horse off an there was a big boy, Dave Wilson – Dave was an auld bobby in Glescae, but by this time, he was a coal merchant in Thornton. I was just a laddie. I was there tae haud them for the ither yins tae dress them up for the show. So they were oot every day exercisin them roond this track. We got tae Scotstoun an big Dave, bein cook, the first thing was intae the kist tae see whit wis for eatin, twa or three dozen eggs an ma mother made a big dumplin, a fine handy thing – nae cookin required. Dave gets in there an I can aye mind yet, as he opens the lid, "What a smell in here!" he says, an diggin, diggin richt doon tae the bottom, did she no pit in a lump o fish! It was maybe packed on Thursday an it was near a week efter! But big Dave said, if it got some air it was maybe richt enough. It was jist kin o' strong in there. He got a lump o' newspaper jist ootside the door. There was a lot o' railway sleepers lyin. So he's goin along layin oot the newspaper an the fish one at a time along this railway sleeper. He laid them oot an he'd jist come in onywey. There wis this boy, Davie Taylor, cam rinnin in tae Dave Wilson an he shouts, ''Dave! Dave! There's a cat at your fish!'' So Dave gaed oot an here's this big black tom, paradin up an doon at this fish. So he got a stick an he did the sentry duty up an doon at the front o' the fish, till he thocht they were cooled aff enough tae eat. He gaithered them up an brocht them back an we ate the lot. They were richt enough. Well, we're aye livin!

'I've done a bit o' singin. I was quite young when I picked up songs. People used tae sing quite a lot. In thae days, they didn't need much excuse tae sing. Even the old man – there wasn't a note o' music in him – but he was aye gaun aboot hummin away tae hissel. An when he got one owre mony, it was him that done 'The Cottage in Old Donegal':

THE COTTAGE IN OLD DONEGAL

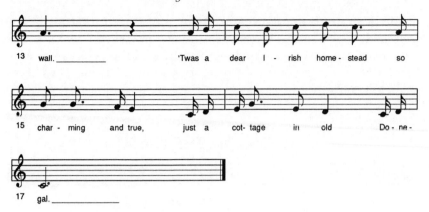

13 wall._____ 'Twas a dear I - rish home - stead so

15 char - ming and true, just a cot- tage in old Do - ne -

17 gal._____

2. It brought back the joy of a bright Irish day,
The memory is still in my mind
When a barefooted boy dragged the long hours away
In peace and contentment to find.
But in search of a living then I had to stray,
An emigrant boy got his call.
So I left my dear homeland and sailed far away
From the cottage in old Donegal.

3. And now in life's Autumn, my race almost run,
Too plainly the story is told;
The long years have passed and the mother is gone
And left me forgotten and old.
Oh the primrose will bloom in the cool leafy lane,
The cuckoo in Spring time will call
Where kindly green moss hides the hallowed remains
Of that cottage in old Donegal.

4. I fled from the bar room, the smoke and the haze,
My feelings I could not disguise
From a barman who looked with a questioning gaze,
'Is that the tears streaming down from my eyes?'
In a church on the corner, I knelt down to pray,
My voice sounding humble and small.
'God bless you, my homeland and guard you each day,
Every cottage in old Donegal.'

'He was the only one I ever heard singin that. I've never heard it since. But he was in Canada when he was young an he picked it up in the big logging camps in Canada.

'There was aa kinds o' things. There was Maidens — efter the harvest, the big thing, ye ken, the hairvest hame — but we cried them Maidens. That een at Cardenbarns, where my Uncle Tam was — God almichty! It was kent faur an near; it wis looked furrit to for months, the Maiden at Cardenbarns! It was a big nicht. They killed the pig an there was plenty o' biled ham an roast pork. He was a kin o' professional at the pig-killing. Everybody took a turn at the Maidens, daein something. There was a fair bit o' talent roon aboot. Aa kinds o' songs, ye ken, things that ye've never heard since, or ever heard before. Here's ane o' them which has a guid-goin chorus:

KISSING IN THE DARK

1. Oh for lang I coor-ted Jea-nie and I
focht wi' micht an' main tae get a pu-ckle sil-ler an' a
big-gin o' ma ain. Il-ka nicht when gaun tae see her, be it
late or be it lark, I tak her in ma airms, aye, an'

CHORUS
kiss her in the dark. Oh the dark, the dark, the
dark, the dark, the dark. I tak her in ma airms an' I
kiss her in the dark.

2. Noo, ae nicht when gaun tae see her, oh ma Jeanie, bein frae hame,
I step't up tae the windie an I rattled on the pane.
When oot cam Jeanie's mither an the nicht, it bein sae lark,
I tuik her in ma airms an I kissed her in the dark.

CHORUS: Oh the dark, the dark, the dark, the dark, the dark,
I tuik her in ma airms an I kissed her in the dark.

3.   Oh she ruggit an she tuggit an she tried tae rin awa,
But I held her aye the closer an I gien her anither twa.
When oot she burst a-laughin, she says, 'This is affa wark
Tae toosle an auld biddy, aye, and kiss her in the dark!'

CHORUS: Oh the dark, the dark, the dark, the dark, the dark,
Tae toosle an auld biddy an kiss her in the dark.

4.   Oh syne I made for rinnin, but she held me sure an fast.
She says, 'Ye needna hurry, lad, the secret's oot at last.
Yer Jeanie's doon at Auntie's an she'll get an affa start
When I tell her hoo ye toosled me an kissed me in the dark!'

CHORUS: Oh the dark, the dark, the dark, the dark, the dark
When I tell her hoo ye toosled me an kissed me in the dark.

5.   So I waited wi her mither till ma Jeanie she cam hame,
She tellt her aa the story which I thocht an affa shame.
But noo I've got ma Jeanie efter aa the coortin wark,
There's few that land sae lucky wi the kissin in the dark.

CHORUS: Oh the dark, the dark, the dark, the dark, the dark
There's few that land sae lucky wi the kissin in the dark.

6.   Oh we hadna lang been mairrit when her mither she tuik ill.
She sent for the lawyer, for she had tae mak her will.
She left me aa her siller, aye, an mony a kin remark,
I think the auld wife likit it, the kissin in the dark!

CHORUS: Oh the dark, the dark, the dark, the dark, the dark
I think the auld wife likit it, the kissin in the dark.

'The horses I worked wi, they aa had weys o' their ain. Even the big Clydesdale horses, they aa had tricks in them. It wis jist a maitter o' kennin the tricks. Ye kent what tae expect. I've seen me tae when I was at the sheep – dogs are the same. I've seen dogs, whenever ye let the chain off in the mornin, ye kent whit kin o' a day ye were gaun tae hae, dependin whit kin o' greetin ye got fae them. Horse were the same. That's the great thing aboot stock. A lot o' folk think it's like drivin a tractor, whaur when ye pit the steerin wheel wan way, it'll gang wan way. Stock's no like that. They've got a mind o' their ain tae. Ye've got tae kin o' humour them tae get the best oot o them. It's no sae easy wi them as it is wi mechanical means. But there's a lot mair enjoyment in it, at the end o' the day, if ye can put a thing tae dae what ye want it tae dae, a lot mair interest in it.

'My Uncle Tam at Cardenbarns was a great horseman. He wis the ringleader if there was any bluidy cairry-on gaun on at aa; Tam was gey often in the middle o't. He wis a character! He'd been oot in the Falkland Islands when he was young; he'd been a butcher there. He killed pigs, he killed aa thing. During the War, he made a blooming fortune on the black market. He was caught once wi a pig hingin up, an old boar. It was hangin up at Cardenbarns an the police went up an caught him. He was fined – at that time it was a lot o' money, £25 or something. Anyway, his excuse was that the pig had choked and he didnae see nae sense in lettin it dee, so he jist cut its throat. An he jist aboot got away wi it. After it was all over, Tam said, "My God, it was a good job they didnae come last nicht! I had twenty-seiven sheep hangin up there!"

'But, him that was so good wi the horses, he eventually got killed by a pony. This pony had been rubbin on an ice-cream cart or somethin, an the boy was wantin tae sell it. Tam bocht the pony that wis rinnin in the field an they couldnae even get a haud o' it. Well, we hunted that beast for a whole day and, eventually, we caught it in the open reed at Easter Balgedie. Tam put it in the lorry that day an took it hame. Within a fortnicht, he had one o' his wee grandsons on its back, gaun owre wee jumps in the stackyaird. He had it just where he wanted it, an he had it lyin doon an standin on barrels. This Setterday nicht, Bob Taylor fae Ballingry had been doon at Tam's and the twa o them had landed on the bottle. Onywey, nothin but he wad take Bob tae see the powny. It was in a wee shed made o railway sleepers at the end o' the steadin at Cardenbarns. He opened the door an walked in an it was black dark, because there was no electric. He jist says, "Giddup!", ye ken, an pit his hand oot like that an it turned roond an both its hind feet intae his stomach. Tam rin aboot for two or three days an oh, he wis jist dyin! Eventually, they got the doctor an took him intae Kirkcaldy Hospital. That was the end o Tam. Everybody had thocht it wad be a gun job tae get rid o him! One o' thae worthies, ye ken.

'Oh, I aye liked the horses! I ploughed an aa thing, but I didnae gae tae ploughin matches. I think I was twice at one. It taks up a lot o time, for ye have days an days before it, gettin ready for it. It's a thing that taks up a lot o time. But nooadays, I've been tae twa or three, but it's no the same kin o thing at all. I mind o' the field below the Lomond Hotel at Kinnesswood. I mind o' forty-echt pair o' horses in there at a plooin match. That's since the War, aboot 1946 or 47. Noo, ye'll go the whole length o' Kinross and ye'll no see one.

'If the horses had still been there, I wad never hae been at the sheep. It was the dogs that were the attraction. Efter the horses disappeared, I got a dog and I got interested in that, I started at the shepherding; I went to the sheep. I didn't like the ferm work withoot the horse. So I started oot wi a sheepdog an I spent thirty or forty year among them. Wandered all the road fae Milnathort tae Inverness and the Isle o' Skye and I finally landed in Perth. We've been here for twa year. I met Dolly in 1971 – this wis anither disaster! We met at Inverness on the Black Isle and we were married at Braeroy at Roy Bridge, and his nibs [Colin] turned up one autumn day, 2nd October 1973.

'The Braeroy lambs gaed tae Stirling, when we were up at Roy Bridge. They gaed awa the day before an we gaed doon in the mornin an we aye left aboot half past five in the mornin. Then doon tae Stirling. We used tae gang this way – well, no intae Perth. When we were goin tae Stirling, we used tae come doon an richt up Loch Laggan, through Dalwhinnie and doon the A9 to Dunkeld, then in thro Amulree and Muthill an oot at Greenloaning and doon through Dunblane. We aye cam that wey in the mornin, then we gaed hame by Glencoe in the efternune. An I think there was aboot ten minutes o' a difference in the twa roads. We travelled doon by car, then back up at night again. It was a long day! I've seen it half past five in the mornin and aa oors at nicht afore ye got hame, dependin on the sale. The sheep's aa awa, ye ken. Nearly aa plantit wi trees, noo. But it was aye a big day, the sales.'

Tam Webster
Photo: Aåse Goldsmith

TAM WEBSTER

Bothy Nichts concert parties are very popular in some country areas, and it is in this context that Tam Webster has become one of the best-known names in the East of Scotland and beyond. Tam became involved in entertainment at an early age, and has performed all over Scotland as a whistler, singer and comedian. Founder of the Lomond Cornkisters, he has appeared on television, and combines his work as a postman in Kinross with a punishing schedule of ceilidhs and concerts.

*****

'I was born in a little farm cottage called Southfield, on a farm called Cuthil Towers, just outside Milnathort on the auld Glenfarg road. And ma mother always told me that I was born in a cabbage and efter that, all ma brothers and sisters used tae go huntin the cabbages tae see if there was any more brothers and sisters. I remember I was told that I was lying in ma cot and a rat bit ma finger, and ye can see that mark tae this day. We came intae Milnathort and we got the first council house because there was eight of a family and there was too many for the house we stayed in on the farm.

'Well, I grew up and went tae Milnathort Primary and from there, I went tae Kinross High. I left the school tae be a grocer, then after six months, I didna like servin the public – too many complaints! So I decided tae serve ma time as a gardener, and I've never regretted it. I've always loved gardening and then I went tae the army. But before I went tae the army, I joined the Boys Brigade. I found out that I could whistle and yodel, and every one of ma brothers and sisters were all good singers, and ma brothers could yodel and I think they taught me what tae do. And over the years, I began tae sing, yodel and whistle and I started off in the Boys Brigade shows and joined the Young Farmers and did their concerts. Then I went intae the army shows and done all the army shows when I was in the forces down in Wiltshire and Reading and places like that. Then when I came out, I entered lots of go-as-you-please competitions, and won through to the Final of Butlin's Ayr and won a free holiday. I also joined the Bill Wilkie Show in Perth. I always remember Bill said he was looking for a ''siffleur'' and I always thought he said ''a chauffeur''. Of course, a siffleur was a whistler, and I said tae ma mother, ''Bill Wilkie was on the phone wantin tae see if I'd come as a chauffeur tae his concert party. I don't know why he's wantin me as a chauffeur!'' So I went up tae see Mr Wilkie and he said, ''No, no, a siffleur is a whistler!''

'So I got the job as a whistler in his show and we went all over Scotland, wi nights in Inverness and he used tae bring me home in his big car because I didna have a car then, as I'd just come out of the army and gone back tae gardening. He used tae bring me back and forward from Forfar and Inverness, and there were so many good lads in the show then: lads like Jimmy Blue, Mickey Ainsworth, Ian Powrie, Jimmy Lyndsay, all the well-known button-key players and fiddlers and that were all in the Bill Wilkie Show when I first started. And it's just recently they had a big surprise forty years party for Bill Wilkie in the Station Hotel in Perth and I was invited up with all these lads; all the entertainers from the bygone years.

'Then I went from the Bill Wilkie Show intae the Andy Morris Show. He was a chap from Cowdenbeath who had a show and I went round most of the hotels and clubs in different areas of Scotland. Ye had tae come home and go tae yer work the next day, ye know, when ye were absolutely shattered, and start yer work all over again, and then away out tae another concert or something the next night.

'Then in maybe 1968, Mrs Sutherland of The Fife Yokels asked me if I would come on her Bothy Nicht evening. Well, I'd never done bothy songs up until then; it was always whistling and sort of folk songs and country music and things like that. But I'd enjoyed the bothy ballads, so I got all rigged out and in the first two years on Grampian Television's 'Bothy Nichts', I won the Male Entertainer Of The Year twice. Then I left The Fife Yokels and founded The Lomond Cornkisters in 1970, and in the first year, we won the Brose Caup. So we became famous then and I was asked tae go and record with Grampian Records in Wick. So we did a Bothy Nicht record and then I brought out another two records and cassettes with them. Then I was offered to go with Ross Records of Turriff and I've since brought out four cassettes and LPs with them.

'Well, I've gone all round the countryside and I've judged at the Kinross Festival for some years. We enjoyed having the folk festival here in Kinross and we were quite sad when it left Kinross, because it brought so many talented people from all over the land, it was very enjoyable, it helped all the shops and hotels and we really missed it in Kinross, I can assure ye. Even yet, lots of people say it's a pity we don't have the folk festival because it was something to look forward to and those really tremendous characters like Davy Glen and the auld boy fae the Borders, Willie Scott, the shepherd, Jimmy Reid of the Foundry Bar Band, Alex Green, the penny whistler, Aly Bain, the fiddler, and his teacher, Tom Anderson. I don't really know why it stopped because we had all the facilities to cope with it here and we miss seeing all these people. Sometimes I bump intae one or two of them like Jimmy Reid and I've been up tae see Willie Fraser and lads like that, just passin through.

'Since then, I've entertained all over the land, twice been tae Germany, and I'm goin tae Austria next year with a Scottish show, and I've been tae most places in England and I've enjoyed it thoroughly. I do a lot locally, a lot of charity jobs to raise quite a bit of money over the years, like most of us entertainers do. I don't think I would've turned professional, although I've been offered it when I came out of the army. I felt I'm happier when I'm doin what I do. I love gardening and I still spend a lot of time doing it, although I'm a postman now.

'I've been a postman for twenty years and I'm known as the singin, yodellin, whistlin postman because I do it when I'm on ma round. I was on the wireless about a month ago and they took me out on the postie-bus and I was singin a song that Sam Gibson, a friend o mine, wrote called 'Bonnie Loch Leven', which takes ye round the loch and mountains, all the villages and important places.

'One of the bothy ballads I did was 'The Ploughboy' and it became so famous in the north that they asked me to do a record called 'Amang The Neeps And The Barley', and on it was Sandy Dawson, Tam and Geordie. Now, Sandy – he was the farmer who's paralysed now through a terrible accident on his farm – his wife Christine and Jean and I are great friends of Jimmy and Anne Shand. Jimmy wrote two lovely tunes for Christine and Sandy and often comes up to Sandy's farm and play a few tunes and stay for supper. Geordie was the well-known Geordie Hepburn, who has since died. Then I made another one quite famous, which I called 'The Waddin' and it's since been recorded by a couple of folksingers, because I heard it on the wireless on MacGregor's Gathering, and it's a good one too. It's all about the work on the farm:

THE WADDIN

1. Noo, I ne-ver thocht when I was young that I wad tak a wife. They tell me when ye mair-ry ye are ne-ver free fae strife. But noo I've taen the plunge an' the morn I'll mair-ried be, for I've gone an' asked a bon-nie wee lass wha said she'll mair-ry me.

CHORUS

Noo, I'm gaun tae hae a bon-nie wee hoose that I can caa ma ain I'm gaun tae hae a bon-nie wee wife that nae-bo-dy else can claim. A bon-nie wee gair-den full o' flooers, a kit - chen plot an' aa, wi' car-rots an' neeps, ing-ins an' leeks, sproots, ce-le-ry, beans an' beets, cab-ba-ges, broc-c'li, let-tu-ces aa grown in a bon-nie wee raa. Oh aa-bo-dy loves a wad - din,

21 aa- bo- dy loves a do, where gran- ny does the eight - some reel an'

23 grand - pa he gets fu. Aa - bo- dy kens a wad - din was

25 on - ly meant for two an' the next time ye see the cou- ple they've

27 ad - ded on ___ a crew.

2. Noo, I laid aside ma tackety buits, likewise ma nicky tams.
Ye'll no see me oot here the morn in the fields atween the trams,
For I'll pit on ma nairry breeks, ma collar an ma bow.
An when the minister ties that knot, ye'll hear me shoutin oh.

CHORUS: Noo I'm gaun tae hae a bonnie wee hoose . . . etc.

3. Noo, I'll tak her for a day tae Perth an then we'll settle doon.
I'll hand her aa ma wages an ye'll never hear me froon,
For in this house wi ma bonnie wee wife, as suir as a pig's a ham,
It'll no be long afore ye'll see me hurlin a bonnie wee pram.

CHORUS: For I'm gaun tae hae a bonnie wee hoose . . . etc.

Well, that one, I think, is on the 'Amang The Neeps And The Barley'
tape. Then there was 'The Ploughman', which became quite famous:

THE PLOOMAN

1 1. Noo, I mind o' the time I got

3 tired o' the ferm, an' I made up ma mind I wad

5 leave at the term. I'd go tae the ci - ty, a

2. Noo, I gaed tae the jute works in bonnie Dundee,
An I mairried a lassie wha cam fae Lochee.
But she spent aa ma siller an left me ma lane,
Langin tae be in the country again.

CHORUS: Amang the neeps an the barley, . . . etc.

3. Noo, I'm back on the ferm whaur I'll bide aa ma days,
Whaur I'm suir o' ma meat an enough tae buy claes,
Wi ma milk an ma tatties, in the bothy I'll bide,
Never again leave ma ain countryside.

CHORUS: Amang the neeps an the barley, . . . etc.

'That's an awfy good song. Both these songs were written by Mrs Sutherland of the Fife Yokels. 'The Orraman's Lament' was another good one. I never recorded it, but Sam did and so did Sandy. I can't remember all the words tae it masel. I've recorded a lot o' the bothy ballads like 'Mormon Braes' and 'The Braes o Benald' – that's a good one – 'The Auld Meal Mill', a lot o' John Mearns' on cassettes like 'The Slippery Stane', 'Dufftown Fair', 'A Lassic Lives By Yonder Burn', 'The Corncrake Amang The Whinney Knowes', 'Hame and Guid Nicht' and 'Bonnie Bessie Logan'.

'I met John Mearns a lot o' times and I've got three or four scrapbooks with all the stuff in them, and when I was on the Bothy Nichts tae begin with, John Mearns was there all the time. And then there's Myra Thow and all these well-known bothy ballad fowk from the north, and then Jimmy Spankie took over when John retired. I went up tae do a night at the Auld Meal Mill, which I just did again this year with Ross Records, and they bring all the Scots that are on Ross Records records and tapes all together for different years and different ones for a night at the Auld Meal Mill, and it's got the auld water wheel and everything. John Mearns used tae sing 'The Auld Meal Mill', but he wasn't on this year because I think he's too auld now – he's eighty odds.

'When I was a gardener, I worked at Ladeside Nurseries in Milnathort, and tae finish ma time, I got exemption off ma National Service for six months – instead of going in July, I went in January to finish ma three-year apprenticeship as a gardener. And when I came out, I started gardening again and I was Head Gardener at Glenlomond Hospital, and I finished up working at Windlestrae under an auld fella called Donald MacDonald. He was one of the auld school and I'll never forget him. I've landscaped dozens of gardens in Kinross-shire – Crook o' Devon and all these villages – and I'm landscaping a big one now, with a burn running through it and I'm bringing a bridge owre it. I was taught by the right auld fella and he used tae say tae me when we built stone dykes, 'Tom, never lift a stone an put it back again. If ye lift it, it should fit tae where it's goin.' And this is how this man worked; he lifted the stone and it fitted the dyke and the next one fitted in the next place, and he *never* put it back again. It *always* fitted in when he looked for just what he was needing. Now, ye just dinna get these boys nooadays; they're sort of a dying breed and it's very fortunate I learned fae a lot o' good men.

'I left Windlestrae because the lady of the house wasnae well at all, and Sir Alan Smith, the owner and owns the wool mill in Kinross and all over Scotland – Todd & Duncan, Pringle and all these knitting companies which come under Dawson International – was keener on his wool than on his garden, so I thought, well, time for a change. So I got the chance of being a postman. I still do gardens as well.

'Going back to 1960, I met and fell in love with a wee Collessie, Fife, lass called Jean Jarvis and we married in 1961 – that's thirty years ago this year – and have four children. Collessie was also the home of our famous 'Collessie Kate', a great character and friend. We also have three grandsons, and a granddaughter, so here's hoping one of them will be an entertainer.

'I've surely got a few humorous stories about when I travelled the length and breadth of the country like yersels, and I've enjoyed many a great laugh. One time, we were going tae do a show at a village outside Kirriemuir and we had dancers with us. There was a lovely girl singer and another beautiful girl who started off on the Bothy Nichts with me – Helen Campbell her name was and she finished up as a professional dancer all over the world. She was about eighteen years auld then and there was another two girls, Sam and I and the rest of the group. We were heading for a wee village outside Kirriemuir for this Bothy Nicht and when we came to this hall, we got all our stuff out at the front door and then we saw these other lads taking their stuff in the back door. I says, "What are they doin? They must be at the wrong place." So we went round the corner and we bumped intae Jimmy Blue, and I says tae him, "Where are ye playin the night, Jimmy?" He says, "In here." I says, "But we're playin in here!" He says, "Where are ye goin?" and I told him an he says, "Ah, Tam, ye've another five miles tae go. But when I sees what ye've got wi ye [all the lovely girls], I think I'll just go wi you boys!" So he got in the van and he was ready tae go another five miles wi all the lassies. That was a good laugh.

'Another time, I was goin tae do a Bothy Nicht at the wee village of California, near Falkirk, and the woman says, "Have ye got a piano?" "Aye," I says, "we have, but I canny bring it down." Well she says, "The only thing I havenae got is a piano and there's no much chance o gettin one." So I says, 'Well, never venture, never win" and we got a trailer from Sandy and we took the piano on the back of the trailer fae Milnathort, and the police stopped us. It had moved on the trailer and was lying in a dangerous position, so the police pulled us in and he says, "Where are ye goin?" and I says, "Tae California!" And he says, "Are ye trying tae be funny?" "No," I says, "we really *are* going tae California." "CALIFORNIA in America?" he says, "No, California near Falkirk." "Oh," he says, "I thought ye were tryin tae be funny."

'That was just one of the hundreds of laughs ye get on the road. I always think I must be crackers doing this because I come home in the small hours and I've still tae go tae ma work as a postman at five o'clock in the morning. But when ye get a call, ye make a crack at getting there and I've met a lot of nice people in ma travels and I think it's been only the odd one that's been a prima donna, you know. I always feel that if ye're humble, and enjoy it and make other people enjoy it as well, ye got on far better. Always remember that when ye go out on stage, there's maybe a lot of people sitting out there that's far better than you, even though *you're* on stage, so ye needna think ye're the greatest. I never profess tae be a singer; I'm maybe more of an entertainer. Music is a great thing and we all do it because we get a lot of pleasure from it over the years. Everyone will tell you that.'

Kate Halliday (Tam Webster is to the left of the picture.)

KATE HALLIDAY

Looking through Tam Webster's scrapbooks of the Bothy Nichts concert parties, you'll see the cheerful, smiling face of Kate Halliday, who, with Tam, won trophies in the competitions held for such groups. She was well-known in Fife by the nickname of Collessie Kate, after the locality of the farm she worked on. Born in the West of Scotland, she spent her working life in Fife on a farm noted for the breeding of good horses. Her singing and entertaining developed naturally out of her background and life.

*****

'I was born at Rosneath, down the River Clyde, just round fae Gareloch Head an ma father worked on a farm there, called The Clachan. He was there for quite a number o' years an he was always on the land an making up poems an so forth, an he was a great Burns man. Well, I can always remember I was only four, an this was at Rosneath where I was born, an it's just like yesterday. I was walking along the top o' this gate; ma aunt was stayin there at the time, an she was in charge, an I fell an landit on the top o' this big sharp stone an I broke ma arm. Ma cousin was there at the time, an we went over on the ferry from Rosneath into Craigendoran and away up tae this wee hospital – the Victoria. It wasnae long before I was back and it had tae get reset. I was quite a wild careless girl, ye know. I've had a few accidents in my life, when the coo kicket oot.

'We left there in the Twenties an went down to West Kilbride an we stayed quite a time there. We moved from there down to Kirkmichael near Maybole an roon that area in the Burns country. I had a young brother born there an ma father thought on callin him Kyle because, as

I said, he loved his Burns. We moved on from there back to Cardross, just down fae Dumbarton into the Thirties, when the Clyde was busy wi the boat-buildin an that. In fact, ma cousin an I went down there the other day to see the QE2 at the Tail o' the Bank fae Ardmore Point, just as a picnic, an it was nice tae be back where ma father had been ploughin roon about the fields in that area in days past. We came up the road past the other farm where he'd worked – Milestone Farm. Then we spent quite a lot o' time in this little cottage that's now a ruin, thinkin about the days gone by an the times we'd enjoyed wirselves wi ma brothers an parents.

'Durin that time we were in Cardross, we went to school there, an then we went to the Hermitage in Helensburgh, an durin the time we were there, times were hard. Ma two brothers an I were on this milk cairt an we used tae sit an sing there on the side o' the lorry, an we were always late for school. I always liked to sing an I enjoyed the poetry too. Durin the time we were there, about 1935, we used to ging tae wee school concerts an that, singin, an ma brothers were good singers too. One o' them is a great piper, well, he likes the pipes an that, an he stays owre in St Andrews now.

'Just before the War started, we decided tae move again because the house was too sma an there was the auld pump round the corner where we got our water from a well. We were still happy there because we looked straight owre at Greenock an Gourock, an we moved on tae Uddingston. Ma father was still workin on the land then, but I went ma way to a place in Dumbarton an I was there for two years an then ma father moved on wi the family to the Lothians an I moved through to Fife in 1940 an ma aulder brother, he went to war. I went to Newton of Collessie, near Ladybank, but before that, I had one or two wee jobs, but they just didn't suit me. When I went to Fife, I was to stay there just for a wee while because I missed ma brother's company an ma mother an father an that, an it was kin o' lonely to begin wi. I would go up to the village at night an meet up wi the different Watts an the Young family an the Jarvises an that, ye know. The War was at its height then an roon about these fields the army dug thir big trenches. The local lads in the village joined the Home Guard.

'It was a big dairy farm I was on an I was there for over twenty years an durin that time, we went out tae different concerts an charity things for the soldiers an so forth. An we always went to the dancin in Giffordtown Hall, every Saturday night. We had two dancin classes durin the week an we were just mad on dancin, ye know. Durin that time, it was the blackout an I used to go on the bike with all ma pals. In those days, no one was afraid in the dark. Everyone was happy and contented, no TV and few holidays. Two or three o' us used to cycle so far into

Ladybank, an we met wi Jim Crawford an his wife an company, who had a band who played in Giffordtown Hall. Of course, they'd only a sma torch on the front o' this wee trolly thing an she had sandwiches, lemonade an so forth, an it was good fun, ye know. There was the dancin, an maybe somebody would get up an sing. I always went up an ma favourite was always 'The Soor Milk Cairt' because I'd originated fae the West, an they always wanted me to sing that:

THE SOOR MILK CAIRT

2. O the ither mornin early
    As the Boreland I did pass,
    Twas there that I forgithered
    Wi a winsome country lass.
    Say's I, "Ma boannie lassie,
    If ye are goin ma airt,
    I will drive ye intae Glesca
    In ma soor milk cairt."

CHORUS: Wi her cheeks as red as roses
         An her een sae boannie blue,
         Entrancin and glancing
         She pierced me through an through.
         Oh she fairly won ma fancy
         An she stole awa ma hairt
         When we're drivin intae Glesca
         In the soor milk cairt.

3. O she jumpit up aside me
   An we soon got on the crack.
   Wi a blush she tellt me
   Her name was Maggie Watt.
   Passing by the water fit
   Whaur the Cairt rins lood and clear,
   I slipt ma airm aroon her waist
   An spoke love in her ear.

4. I've heard o' lords an ladies
   Makin love in shady bowers.
   Hoo they wooed an won amongst
   The roses an the flowers
   I'll ne'er forget this mornin
   When Cupid threw his dairt
   An it made me pop the question
   In the soor milk cairt.

CHORUS: Wi her cheeks as red as roses . . . etc.

5. Oh the lass she has consented
   Sae gin term time comes aroon,
   I mean tae buy the harness plaid
   An a braw new silken goun.
   We're earnin tae get mairried
   Just aboot next August Fair
   An we're hopin oor auld acquaintances
   Will manage tae be there.

6. For she never had a hurl
   In a cairriage aa her days
   When I proposed tae get a coach
   An a pair o' greys
   'Naw naw,' she says, 'oor siller's scarce
   Lord, we canna spare it
   When we're drivin intae Glesca
   In the soor milk cairt.'

CHORUS: Wi her cheeks as red as roses . . . etc.

'It went on for quite a number o' years and then the war was comin to an end, but then there was always those harvest homes an different things roon about at Kingskettle an I can remember aa those different bands that took their turn in the district. Old-Tyme dancing would keep you fit! They were great years!

'It didnae seem long, the time I was on the farm an that either, because I was up in the mornin wi the cows an the milk run, an there was one or two people who worked on the farm. I went through there when the coupled got mairried an I was there still when all their family got mairried. There were two girls an two boys at Newton of Collessie. I was a jack of all trades there. They would go away to shows an so forth an the bairns were better at home, ye know, an they had a caravan an travelled in the summertime to the Highland Show an there was always one o' the boys left for the ponies an that; they had to be fed an just couldnae be left alone an another lady cycled up fae Ladybank twice a week to help out, an ma cousin, Jean, occasionally stayed wi me durin the holidays an there were good times. Ma friend, Tam Webster, used tae visit the village, but in the dark nights, I seen him but he didnae see me an there were different pranks I'd play on him. I gathered later that he liked wee Jean Jarvis.

'In the village, there was just the auld pub an that an I joined the church at Collessie an the minister was Mr Taylor at that time. Durin ma time there, I used tae do the milkin at Collessie an we used tae sit singin an the cows really enjoyed the music. But now, it's more modern an that in the milkin parlours and it's no just the same. Some o' them just prefer bringin their cows in, standin an tyin them up an milkin them an that's it. But on a winter's morn, it's nice tae get intae the byre an this lovely smell o' the cows an they're aa that warm an Jack Frost's outside an I'm no. Sometimes, if ye were late goin tae yer bed, it wasnae easy gettin up in the mornin an that. I also enjoyed ma life workin wi the ponies an the kids when they were younger, an we used tae have a wee trap an we'd go out for wee runs in it. Then they grew aulder, of course, an they'd to go to work themselves.

'There were a lot o' sing-songs at the harvest homes an that, which were held at Kingskettle, Ladybank and Pitlessie an places roon about, an one or two o' the ferms roon about gave the barn dances an that, but they were mostly along the Wormit way, ye know, an Letham, an I can remember the new Letham Hall was a great night, but we used to go to the auld Letham Hall which was up the back o the village.

'Tam Webster, he was singin around at the time an we joined up together an he was wi the Fife Yokels, an I was wi another lot called the Howe Bothy Boys. They were good too an they had their different ideas an we used to have oor arguments about things, but some o' them hadnae seen as much in life as what I'd seen, travelling around wi ma family an I was able to speak up. But when I did meet Tam, however, he'd to go up to Aberdeen for the Lomond Cornkisters, an the adjudicator up there, she liked the way I was dressed as a dairy maid. I loved wearin yon big boots an I felt I was lucky wi them an many's a time I kicked Tam and I *did* enjoy it. I went up wi the Howe Bothy Boys and won the Middleton Trophy an then I left them because some o' them left to get mairried and so forth, an later I joined Tam an company wi the Lomond Cornkisters. So Tam an I were lucky the first time we went up there; we got the individual prize each – this was the Bothy Nichts prize for the smart lady an the smart boy – an Tam an I won it two years in succession an we were presented wi the trophies by John Mearns again in 1969. I was back myself on a Grampian TV programme called *Fermtoun Folk* in June 1979, which was shown in *Sounds of Britain*.

'I was known as 'Collessie Kate' when I travelled around wi the Cornkisters an it was fun wi a crowd o' ye doin a play, with yer own individual part, an the country folk seemed to like it. I used to enjoy playin the mouth organ. I still have them up there in the loft an ma auld gramophone, but there's many auld songs which ye don't hear now like 'The Auld Quarry Knowe' — Jean sings that an it's a nice old song.

'I've done many recordings on television shows. The first time we went up to compete — I was in the Howe Bothy Boys then — we did quite a good show that day. We were actually fourth out of maybe twelve entries but, as I said, Tam an I got picked out o' the twa different teams. We were up again, but the time the next year came, there was something happened and the Bothy Nichts just disappeared. Sadly, it was stopped by the professionals. It was to do with traditional and ordinary amateur people, or semi-professional people that were entertainin aa up an doon the country in formed groups and it went on for twenty-odd years, but once the professionals felt that it was doin them out of work, they said, if there was going to be a Bothy Nichts, it would have to be done by professionals because it was their livelihood, which was a contradiction in terms. So Grampian said they would have nothing to do with it and they brought in the unions and stopped it and they couldn't do it any more.

'It was a real shame because there was over a million viewers watchin it every week in the north; the fermers dropped their ploughs an their harrows an everybody went in to watch the Bothy Nichts. Everybody watched Bothy Nichts then because it was for the people from the country. It was only kept to a certain area because they wouldnae hae understood it further south.

'They brought me in as a 'cousin from Kilmarnock' in the story. It was aa done on scripts an we aa had oor own stories an it was aa a joint cooperative effort. When you were on TV, ye had tae keep goin. In the Howe Bothy Boys, we had a good dog, an I went around, an I had stewed steak underneath ma apron an this was to keep the dog sittin there while the camera was on ye; it knew that I had steak in ma pocket, an they tried to make it sing an that, an that was quite interestin. Ye took yer own stuff wi ye. I've still got ma grandfather's wooden luggie; I always took it wi me for luck, an ye had yer auld-fashioned irons and the kist which I liked dancin on an, as I said, Tam was mostly the shepherd aa the time and he'd try oot aa the pranks, an we had a lot o' fun.

'The main thing was it had to be traditional and it had to be entertaining, so that people wouldnae turn it off. There was a whole variety o' things, – the songs, the stories, the fitba – an it was aa traditional, an there was this Brose Caup that they aa competed for, an the two trophies for the best individual man and woman. The Lomond Cornkisters won the Brose Caup once in 1970.

'I'm through in Kirkintilloch now, but I still go around ma friends that I met an when we go up to Skye, this auld couple – MacFarlane is their name – they always wanted me to sing 'MacFarlane O The Sprots O Birnie Boozie' an the band starts playin this an he shouts, "I'm MacFarlane – it's me, it's me!" an it's quite laughable when ye see him an that. Up there too, in Skye, it's mostly Gaelic an they like to hear a different kin o song, the likes o 'The Soor Milk Cairt' an 'The Kilmarnock Bunnet' an that, an the band can accompany ye an they obviously want more. They obviously understand it an the more ye go there, the more friendly they get. So when I retired, I've always managed to do something for the auld folks an that, an ma cousin, Jean, she sings too. Tam Webster has really been a good friend to us an there's also Sandy Dawson who I also visit. He was wi the Cornkisters an I enjoyed his company when he was there.

'I've many happy memories to look back on. I can mind happy times when ma mother an father an the family aa stayed down at Bo'ness at a place called the Fisheries, which looked across the Forth. Ma brother was in the pipe band then an ma mother was proud of him. In the '30s, ma father addressed the haggis an did 'Tam O'Shanter' an did 'The Twa Dogs' together wi a man fae up the road called Geordie Meikle an I've still got the ticket fae 1932 in Cardross near Dumbarton.'

Jack Beck
Photo: Aåse Goldsmith

JACK BECK

One of the finest singers to come out of the Folk Revival in Fife is Jack Beck, who came into folk music through jazz and is a good example of the revivalist who has rediscovered his roots and a true direction in singing Scots songs. He has had a non-musical professional career, in which he is still deeply involved and has been reluctant to give it up, in spite of his success as a singer.

*****

'I was born in 1942 in Dunfermline and my earliest memory is of going on holiday to Weston super Mare at the end of the War. My Dad had been an airframe-fitter in the RAF and he'd been in Egypt for a good part of the War, but was then stationed in Weston super Mare awaiting demob. I found the train journey terrible and was sick most of the way. It was my first experience of an enormous beach and big waves. Another thing I have memories of is cod-liver oil and orange juice. I can remember the flat bottles it came in, like medicine bottles, with the Ministry of Food label. My Mum had this mistaken idea that the way to get you to drink the cod-liver oil was to mix it with the orange juice. Of course, they don't mix. To this very day, when I get the first sniff of a glass of orange, it can make me quite nauseous. My Dad managed to send, or bring back from Egypt, a banana. By the time it got back home, it was black, but, as a great treat, I was to get it! I remember being cajoled to eat this terrible, rotten banana, and to this day, I can't eat bananas.

'We lived in a street off a hill called Townhill Road in Dunfermline and if ye continued up the hill, ye came to a camp set up during the war for sailors. I remember troops marching up Townhill Road, maybe at the end of the war, to do with VE Day or VJ Day. I remember the winter of 1947 with the tremendous snow, looking out our window in Shamrock Street and seeing a channel cut through the snow from our door, like the Cresta Run, with walls of snow on either side, to the Cooperative shop at the corner, where ye got your rolls in the morning. Various channels met up wi one coming down the middle of the street, like World War One trenches. I had the measles at the time, and was confined to the house. All the other kids had a ball, playing in the snow!

'I remember being in the Cubs and taking part in the Gang Show in the Carnegie Hall – the Dunfermline one. I was a toy soldier and I remember the home-made uniform and being made up with pink spots on the cheek. There was a marching routine on stage, and I was the one that turned the wrong way! By the age o' twelve, I'd become a bit bolshy and did a side-step from joining organisations, so I never made the Scouts.

'I left school with no qualifications at all. My secondary school career was meteoric – downwards! I went into Dunfermline High School in 1B, which was as high as ye could go in, and I ended up in 4H, which was about as low as ye could get. I wasn't a very motivated pupil. I'm an advert for the FE system, because once I'd left school, I got trade qualifications to as high a level as ye can through night classes and I also sat Higher English and thoroughly enjoyed doing it.

'When I left school, I served my apprenticeship as a painter and decorator in my Dad's firm. He served his time before the War as a sign-writer and grainer. Nowadays, ye wouldn't serve a whole apprenticeship in that, but in the 1920s it wasn't unusual. He served his time in a painting and decorating firm and went on to become very highly regarded in that firm. In some ways, his experiences were similar to the hero of a book called 'The Ragged Trousered Philanthropist', who was also a sign-writer and grainer. My Dad wasn't a radical, but the descriptions in the book of going home and drawing up things at night to use for decorative features of a room the next day was very much the kind of training he had. When he came out of the RAF, he went on to start his own firm in partnership with another chap. I've memories of him making his own water-soluble crayons for graining. I remember him sitting and making a dough with Spanish whiting, size and umber tints, with egg-white to bind them and laying them in lines on the shelves by the black-leaded fire. The year before I left school, I remember going and helping him up at Kinross House, beside Loch Leven, where he did all the work for Sir David Montgomery. Working in places like that, ye saw tremendous quality of work. That was the kind of environment that I left school and went into.

'My first interest in music began on a family holiday to Morecambe, before I left school. We went to the shows and the music of the time was the Everly Brothers, my first experience of pop music. My other memory is of my grandfather, who was a widower and stayed with us. I got to know him particularly well. He had an allotment and he used to come back from it with his pocket full of peas and kids used to meet him at the corner of the street and he'd be doling out peas to the kids: he was known as the Pea Man. He used to sit in his favourite wooden-sided chair and drum on it and sing 'The Muckin o Geordie's Byre'. It saddens me greatly now that, right up until he died, I never appreciated what I was hearing. It was just Grandad's daft old songs. They meant *nothing* to me. It wasn't till long after he died that I thought what I could have learned from him, if only I had been a bit older and more clear-sighted. At that age, yir heid's fu o' mince. He must have had a great repertoire of songs.

'The music I then encountered, which totally swept me away, was jazz. At the age of about seventeen, I started to hear skiffle and people like Lonnie Donegan, who once played banjo in Ken Colyer's and Chris Barber's bands. I became interested in traditional jazz and I got a banjo. I was very pleased to find the banjo was one instrument you could play at least one chord on without having to learn any chords. I got by for a long time, kidding people on for years: in fact, some people might say I still do! I was soon playing in a group, based in Edinburgh, called the East Claremont Street Stompers, which sounds like New Orleans but it was where the student digs were. Then I got a guitar and I felt when I'd learned three chords, I'd really cracked it!

'At that time, it was normal, when ye finished your apprenticeship, to leave the firm and go somewhere else, to broaden your experience. Some people did much bigger things like going round the world – so two friends and I decided that's what we would do. We decided to practise for six months by renting a flat and saving up – that was a bad move. We started off with £50 and by the time we left the flat, we'd £25. We set off hitch-hiking and got to London, and spent a week flitting back and forth across London, because none of the people we knew could put up with us for more than one night. One of my friends was a member of CND; in fact, he was a member of the Committee of One Hundred and he'd been on a march six months previously to Aldermaston. He'd passed through Bedford where there were some well-to-do, intellectual Lefties who were quite well-disposed to wild Scottish CND folk. We'd just enough money left for the bus fare, so our trip round the world actually consisted of six months in Bedford.

'I arrived back in 1960 with an air of having done something wonderfully exciting, without having done anything very much at all, just as the Folk Music Revival in Scotland was starting. There was only one club, the Howff in Edinburgh, started by Roy Guest and his wife Jill, and there was Archie Fisher and John Watt. It was about the time Ewan MacColl summoned various people to a famous series of weekends in his house, people like Bob Davenport, Geordie MacIntyre from Glasgow, John Watt from Fife, Pete Shepheard from St Andrews, Arthur Argo from Aberdeen. They were sent out to spread the word, which is why, almost simultaneously, you got St Andrews Folk Club, Aberdeen Folk Club, Glasgow Folk Centre, Kirkcaldy Elbow Room all opening within months of one another. Dunfermline's was called the Howff because it was modelled on the Howff in Edinburgh. It was started by John Watt, as Social Convenor for Dunfermline Hockey Club, in the cellar of an optician's shop. It was very middle-class – very much the ties and flannels and sports jackets and double-breasted blazers. The folk scene when it started was very much like that.

'I came into it through the jazz club, which met on a Tuesday night in the same cellar. Part of the money for the jazz club went to help the folk club. John Watt was more interested in folk music and the jazz club eventually got the bum's rush because – horror of horrors! – someone saw a half-bottle being produced from someone's pocket. I'd definitely fallen in love with the folk club and music of artistes like the Weavers and Pete Seeger. John Watt was ahead of his time because, at the opening of the Howff, he had Willie Scott there. He was clued-up enough to know that people like him should be there. Willie was working as a shepherd in the Cleish Hills and used to drive down to the folk club in a tractor. I was singing in a group called the Tarriers, until we discovered there was a world-famous American group with the same name. We'd had cards printed and we decided Farriers would be a better name, so it was very easy to change Tarriers to Farriers. 'The Alamo' was one of our big songs, and stuff like that, straight off records.

'Then I remember going to St Andrews Folk Club and hearing Pete Shepheard and Jimmy Hutchison and that guy that was killed, John Walton, and Maurice Frankel singing Peter, Paul and Mary songs and stuff I later discovered was Ian Campbell group material. It was a bit like when ye first heard the Watersons – it was revolutionary, it was phenomenal! It really was eye-opening! Archie Fisher and Ray were singing as a duo and they were singing traditional songs but also songs by Tom Paxton and Bob Dylan. Archie was the first person I ever heard singing, 'Don't Think Twice'. That was a tremendous time – it was a golden age. There was a lot of rubbish as well, of course, but you forget all the awkwardnesses and you just remember it like a great party.

'That led on to the first Blairgowrie Festival. There'd been a Federation of Clubs set up and I was involved in the committee. It didn't do anything for the folk clubs, but it did organise the first Blairgowrie festival, out of which the Traditional Music and Song Association developed. To me, that's the point at which the general appreciation of a Scottish tradition really started. It was no accident that Blairgowrie was chosen, and it was clear that, from the start, the idea was not to have a festival like they were having down in England where you invited big names. The TMSA is the best traditional music organisation we have; that's the best way to put it. A lot has flowed from that and there were a lot of people around then, and still are, making good money out of folk clubs, that owed more to that time than they have really given credit for.

'What got me performing round the clubs in a semi-professional way was singing with Barbara Dickson, who was just leaving school and working in the clerical department at Rosyth dockyard. We started singing together and began concentrating on more traditional material and listening to traditional singers, like the Stewarts of Blair. On the sleeve notes of the record 'The Berryfields of Blair', Hamish Henderson says that going recording to Blairgowrie that particular summer was like holding a tin can under a waterfall. Between 1964–7, Barbara and I did a lot of touring and we reached the point where we were singing too much. We didn't have the time to listen any more, and though we were making a considerable amount of money, we'd no time to learn new material and, for me, it became incredibly boring. In 1967, we were given the offer of a tour in Denmark. I was single, although I was fairly closely involved with Aileen by that time, and I had a job I enjoyed, so Barbara went to Denmark and I didn't. I dropped out of the scene for about four years, and I completely lost touch with what was going on.

'In 1972, Aileen had learned to play the melodeon and we played around just for fun in the house or at parties. I began to get to know Davy Lockhart, the fiddle player, and Colin Stewart, who had helped run the Aberdeen club before coming to teach at Queen Anne School in Dunfermline, where there was a club running at the City Hotel, run by the Causeway Folk. Lyndsay Porteous was with them and big Jimmy Dunn, the box player. I'd been impressed by groups like the Marsden Rattlers and the Rakes in the Sixties and I thought if I ever got involved with a group again, it would be one like that, with a singer who encouraged the audience to join in, and the rest being a band playing instrumental music.

'Then Aileen got involved in a radio series for schools called 'Scottish Magazine', which featured the kids' own poetry, and we ended up making a sort of junior radio ballad on the effects of the closing of the Valleyfield pit, bringing in folk song and narrative links and based on their listening to their dads and their brothers. It was quite different from what Barbara and I had been doing in the Sixties, which was very much a matter of 'personalities' getting up to entertain the audience. That's what I regretted about the way the Seventies developed. Whereas in the Sixties there wasn't too much of a barrier between the performer and the audience – it was all very much everybody together in this wonderful new

world and if you weren't too great a singer, it didn't matter too much
– but by the time the Seventies came, you're on television and folk had
images of what 'good folk singing' was from that and the professionals
started coming round the clubs and it broke up into audience and
performer. I can understand *why* it happened and the need to aim for
quality, but it's sad that it lost the sort of camaraderie of everybody
together. People shouldn't think about folk music as some sort of rarefied
thing that you observe but don't actually become part of.

'It was after the City Club packed up and the Causeway Folk split and
instrumental music began to sidetrack the singing a bit, that an informal
weekly meeting started that was regular, but no money was taken and it
moved around to different places and these informal sessions still do carry
on to this day. It's become almost a tradition in Dunfermline *not* to have
a folk club!

'It was out of those early sessions that the group Heritage grew, dating
from about 1976. In fact, when it started, Heritage was not the name of
a group but the name for all those people that went to the initial dos, like
a village-hall concert party. Then it sort of rationalised itself into seven
or eight people who were gallus enough to do it professionally and work
out a repertoire of songs and tunes. The original Heritage was based on
Jimmy Dunn's unobtrusive accordion playing, with its simple bass runs
that other musicians could fit in with easily, unlike the average normal
accordionist who works as a one-man band and doesn't need anyone else.
We started as a group for all sorts of strange reasons, like being invited
to do foreign tours, and that opened our eyes to how our music related
to the music of other countries. Our repertoire widened considerably too
and now we always include something French or Italian. On the other
hand, while I used to sing everything from Bob Dylan to English and Irish
songs, now I sing almost entirely Lowland Scots tradition, simply because
I feel I can't convincingly sing anything else. 'The Band O' Shearers' can
be found on Heritage's 'Some Rantin Rovin Fun' album:

THE BAND O' SHEARERS

5 Hei - ____ land ____ hills.   There's   yel - la corn   in

7 yon - der   fields ____ and the   Au - tumn   brings ___ the _____

9 shea - _____ rin.

CHORUS: Sae bonnie lassie will ye gang
Tae shear wi me the haill day lang?
O love will cheer us as we gyang
Tae jine yon band o shearers.

2. Noo, if the thistle, it be lang
An if it jag yer milk-white hand,
It's wi ma heuk, I'll cut it doon
When we jine yon band o' shearers.

CHORUS: Sae bonnie lassie . . . etc.

3. An if the weather, it be hot,
I'll cast my gravet an my coat
An shear wi ye amang the lot
When we jine yon band o' shearers.

CHORUS: Sae bonnie lassie . . . etc.

4. Aye, an if the weather, it be dry,
They'll say there's love twixt you an I.
But we'll slyly pass each ither by
Tae jine yon band o' shearers.

CHORUS: Sae bonnie lassie . . . etc.

5. Aye, an when the shearin, it's aa dune,
We'll hae some rantin rovin fun.
We'll hae some rantin rovin fun
An forget aa the toils o' the shearin.

CHORUS: Sae bonnie lassie . . . etc.

'The Merchant's Son' is on my 'O Lassie, Lassie' album:

THE MERCHANT'S SON

1. Oh hae ye heard o' the mer-chant's son? It's tae the beg-gin he has gane. He's moun-ted on his no-ble steed and a-wa for plei-sure he did ride. Fal-al-a-doo-ral-aye-do, Fal-al-the day.

2. A beggar wench he chanced tae meet,
   A beggar wench o' low degree,
   And he's taen pity on her distress,
   Sayin, 'Faith lass, but ye've a bonnie face!'

CHORUS: Fal al . . . etc.

3. They baith inclined for tae hae a drink.
   Intae a public hoose they went.
   They baith drank wine, aye, brandy too,
   Till the baith o' them, they got roarin fu.

CHORUS: Fal al . . . etc.

4. They baith inclined for tae gang tae bed.
   Below the blankets they soon were laid.
   Strong wine and brandy went tae their heid
   Till the baith o' them lay as they were deid.

CHORUS: Fal al . . . etc.

5. Noo, in the mornin, the maid arose,
   And she's pit on the young merchant's clothes.
   Wi his hat sae high and his sword sae clear,
   O she's awa wi the gadgie's lowie.

CHORUS: Fal al . . . etc.

6. A little while later, the merchant rose,
   And lookin round for tae find his clothes,
   There wis naethin there intae the room,
   But a ragged petticoat and a wincey goon.

CHORUS: Fal al . . . etc.

7. Noo, bein a stranger intae the toon,
   It's he pit on the auld wincey goon,
   And doon the street he did strongly swear,
   He'd never gang wi a beggar nae mair.

CHORUS: Fal al . . . etc.

Sandy Watt

SANDY WATT

One of the delights of going to Glenfarg Folk Club in the late Seventies was hearing Sandy Watt sing. Sandy was a well-known local character and a great favourite with everyone. He had a wide repertoire of songs, from old ballads and sentimental love songs to music-hall songs and present-day comic songs. He died in 1981, and the folk club still commemorates him in an annual singing competition for a quaich named after him. I recorded him singing, but he always declined to speak into the recorder. His son, Peter, tells his story.

*****

'Sandy, as most people knew him, was born in 1907 on a farm called Dallachie, just above Burntisland. They didnae stay there long, because ma grandad just shifted, as a lot o' fermworkers did in thae days, virtually every six months or every year, and they moved roon aboot. He was doon at Dunfermline, Cairneyhill, Crossgates, and by the time ma dad was seven, they got their wey along to a place along at St Andrews. Then he went away back through the West again, where ma grandad originally cam fae; it was through at Carstairs that ma grandad was born. So he headit back and, at one stage, ma grandad actually worked wi ma great-grandad roon aboot Carstairs at Kilmet.

'Efter that, ma grandad worked wi a man, Barr, at Western which is, I think, between Forth and Carstairs. I mind ma dad telling me at one stage there was a wee tin school at the ferm road-end, and there were eight pupils, five of which were Watts. Ma dad was actually the auldest son: there were eight o' a family. One unfortunately died when she was very young, but it'd be him and his two sisters, two younger brithers and a younger sister who made up five-eighths of the total school population. Ma grandad was actually the dairyman there, and when ma granny just cam oot tae the end o' the close and gave a shout, that was time for school tae get oot and the bairns just took the coos up the road. In actual fact, there's a hoose built where that wee tin school was, because when I was oot along that wey wi ma dad, he used tae point oot Western and where this wee tin school was.

'Eventually, they cam back tae Fife and cam up tae Glentarkie above Strathmiglo there, but by that time, ma dad was nearing fourteen years auld, so he didnae actually go tae the school roon aboot. He just left the school and helped roon aboot the byre, and so that was him actually started in fermwork. He didnae spend a lot o time in fermwork because, thinking back, that was 1920–1 when they were at Glentarkie, but ma grandad moved away through the West to Girvan, and ma dad actually went intae service roon aboot the Carstairs area again, Forth and such like, and that was when he cycled the seventy miles fae Carstairs through tae Girvan just tae spend the weekend there. Ma grandad then moved fae Girvan to old Kilpatrick, and that would be aboot 1926, because ma grandad actually bought a bus. In thae days, there was nae companies, it was just individuals, so ma dad seemingly went tae a driving school and he actually drove this bus when he was seventeen. A lot o' folk used to think he was telling stories when he said he had his PSV when he was nineteen, but he was right enough because he was actually driving a bus when he was nineteen. I think it was in the early 1930s before they insisted that they had to be twenty-one, so he actually had his PSV at nineteen years auld and he was a bus-driver for aboot twenty-one years.

'Then ma grandad moved fae Old Kilpatrick through near Carluke and he took a wee ferm there, but by this time, I think the bus had been in a fairly bad smash. In fact, ma dad was very badly injured and it was touch and go whether he pulled through or no, and the bus was badly mauled, so they never put it back on the road again. But ma dad had the driving bug by then, and he worked wi a Gala [Galashiels] company. I think it must have been in Lanark, ken, it was aa wee private companies, and he worked wi anither wee company, MacDonald and something, and then everything was kind o amalgamated and he started wi Central SMT roon aboot 1930. He was still biding at hame and helping ma grandad oot on the ferm as well. In thae days, everyone got rigged oot for work, ye ken, there was nae leisure. So he must have driven the buses for aboot fully twenty years fae 1926 tae 1947.

'During the war, he actually had a job as a sales rep, but they wouldnae allow him tae leave because during the war, it was very restricted in thae days. I think driving in the blackout really put him against driving, because it was horrific driving in the blackout. In fact, he reckoned at one stage that there was mair folk getting killed wi buses in Glasgow than wi the bombing. He actually knew a driver on the road intae Glasgow and he killed a pedestrian, and he killed anither yin on the road oot, so that was two in one night. As I say, he got anither job but he wasnae allowed tae leave the buses, and he still kept in agriculture – that was, I think where his heart really lay.

'Ma dad mairried a miner's daughter, and they were very keen on music, every one o' them, and I can mind as a laddie, that was ma dad's only entertainment because at that time, he wasnae much o' a drinker. Now, a lot o' folk find this very hard to believe, but at that time, if ma dad went oot for a couple o' half-pints, that was the limit. Can you mind o' the go-as-you-pleases? They wasnae sae popular through this wey or in Fife, but through the West and the mining areas. But that's where ma faither and his brithers-in-law hung oot. He'd two brithers-in-law, Arthur and Peter, and they were awfy keen, and that's what they did on a Saturday night, either that, or wi some o' their ither cronies went tae sing-songs, which ma dad was always very keen on. That was his social life in thae days; of course, they were a lot more restricted than they are nooadays, but that was how they enjoyed their spare time, ye ken, at the go-as-you-pleases and their sing-songs.

'1947, that's when we cam through tae Letham in Fife and he worked for ma uncle there for seven years, but there again, just so as tae go doon tae Ladybank tae sing, as singing was really his only hobby and relaxation, or intae Cupar. He liked naething better than when ma two uncles cam through fae Wishaw, and ma grandad, who was a great friend wi his father-in-law, and that was their relaxation, gaun intae Cupar or Ladybank or wherever the buses were handiest for getting back and forrit. It was only in pubs the likes o' these sing-songs took place.

'In 1953, ma dad went through tae Houston, near Paisley. He was a ferm manager through there for six months, and the only time he ever went oot in thae six months actually was when his brithers-in-law cam through fae Wishaw, and then it was just intae a hoose or wherever there was a chance tae have a sing-song. Then in 1954, we cam up tae Glenfarg and I dunno how long he'd be at Glenfarg. He was virtually unknown in Glenfarg, and then one New Year, he used tae deliver the milk. He had a wee van and I worked doon at Burley at the time, and on New Year's morning, ma granny phoned me aboot eleven o'clock. Ma dad had went oot wi the milk at the back o seven o'clock and he hadnae returned. What had actually happened was he'd went in and folk had insisted on New Year's morning on gien him his New Year, and he'd gone roon the length o' Hayfield Road and he'd went tae Geordie Patrick and by this time, everywhere he went, he was giein them a song. Up until that morning, naebody even knew that ma dad sang. He was even in the local bobby's giein them a song that morning, and by the time he got tae Hayfield Road, he was fleein. Geordie Patrick had actually taken over the driving so that let him drink as much as he liked. Ma granny was up tae high doh so efter that, he used tae deliver his milk on Hogmanay; I went roon wi him and that left him tae enjoy his New Year.

'It was efter that that he began to come oot a wee bit; that morning did mair good for ma dad in Glenfarg because, as I say, he was virtually unknown, and then he got friendly wi Davy Scott, of course. Davy and him used tae go to the sing-songs thegither because Davy was anither great lad for the sing-songs. Just efter we were mairried, they used tae go doon tae a lot o the miners' clubs doon in Fife, like Lochore, Kinglassie and Thornton on a Saturday night. That was afore the sing-songs at Glenfarg started. It was Jim Hunter who started that, ye ken, because previous tae that, the man wasnae sociable. I can mind when we first cam tae Glenfarg, some o the men had tae travel along tae the Bein Inn tae get a pint. If you ask some o the aulder inhabitants o' Glenfarg, they'll mind o' that because, at that time, the Lomond didnae hae a licence; it wasnae a licensed hotel at aa. In fact, if must hae been aboot the late Fifties or early Sixties afore the Lomond got a licence, and the folk that were in the big hotel, they were mair interested in bringing auld folk in for holidays, and I mind seeing the men waiting for the six o'clock bus at the cross on their way tae go doon tae the Bein Inn. It was only certain nights the beer was on, so Jim Hunter was the best thing that ever happened tae the Glenfarg Hotel because he was a great lad for encouraging folk in and, of course, the sing-songs, and I imagine it was simply because o' the sing-songs on a Saturday night that the encouragement came for the folk club tae start.

'In later years, ma dad took an interest in the fitba when Glenfarg started up, and there again, Jim Hunter and Davy Meldrum were the two who, wi ma dad, used tae go and they never missed a match. There was a time when Willie Ormond was the manager up at Muirton, he became very friendly wi ma dad, Davy Meldrum and Mrs Hunter and such like, and he used tae organise the young schoolboys along at the park. That was a big social event in Glenfarg, and anything like that was always a great excuse wi the Glenfarg lads for a guid booze-up.

'Until the day he died, ma dad never considered himself as a folk singer. He kept saying, ''I'm no a singer, I'm no a singer!'' He sang purely for enjoyment which is the best way tae sing, and he'd hae the three o' us sitting roon the fire – ma sister, ma wee brither and I – at night, sitting singing his songs and telling us aa the escapades he'd had as a young fella in service wi the maids and such like. I didnae realise until I started thinking back, that he in actual fact was driving a bus at nineteen, and that only gave him five years in ferm service, but then again, wi a lot o them, it was just six months. There was one place he went tae as orra horse and helper wi the milking; that was the terms o' his contract. The first day started early when he got up and helped wi the milking and then he was away oot working wi the horse aa day, and maybe at half past five at night, he got his tea. Then efter his tea, he'd hae tae go oot and dae the milking at six o'clock at night. So one night, he decided six months was gonna be too long because he thought he was finished for the day when he had tae go away oot again, and he thought some other work would be better. So although he was only five years in ferm service, he probably had seven or eight jobs within that time, which was quite normal in thae days just for the one term. In actual fact, I think that was the place where he got an auld motorbike and he broke his shooder on it, because his brither, who was only eleven months younger than him, had tae come and take ma dad's place while ma dad was recovering at hame, and his brither, Willie, couldnae get oot o' there quick enough. But as I say, I didnae realise how little time he was in ferm service until I started thinking aboot it. He liked the land up until the late Forties and then, of course, it was aa agriculture efter that. It was common to be oot milking the coos at ten or eleven years auld in thae days.

'One o the songs he used tae dae went:

> Eil flask, tea flask, piece box an aa,
> A hutch in the bottom ready for tae draw,
> A hutch in the bottom ready for tae draw,
> And I'll no be hame until the morning.

That was a song that a miner would sing, and one o oor favourites was:

> The night we took Agatha tae the ball,
> She said she really couldnae dance at aa.
> When we asked her tae rehearse,
> She fell an skint her erse . . .

'To us, wee ditties like this were real fun, and wi him mairrying intae a mining family, these are just two that he got fae them that springs tae mind.

'Anither yin he used tae sing at Glenfarg was 'Mush, mush, mush Toodle-aye-amy'. Ma brither had been mairried quite a few years and we happened tae be in the hotel that night and ma dad sung that yin and ma sister-in-law thought it was hilarious. It was just one that he'd dragged up fae his memory, because it was anither o oor favourites and I was quite surprised that she hadnae heard it.

'Another yin he used tae sing was called 'The Whole Damn Family' or something like that. They were just silly wee songs which amused us

— especially that one about her that fell and skint her bum, because we werenae allowed tae say words like 'erse', ye ken, but we thought it was so funny him coming away wi these 'wee ditties' as he used tae call them.

'There was one night, I canny mind what folk did it one night; maybe it must hae been a folk programme on a Friday night and we were heading uptae ma brither's in Alyth, and this group came on and said, "This song we're gonna sing now, we got it talking wi an auld man in Glenfarg one night, and it's called 'Roon The Stooks o' Barley Neuks, Jinkin You Johnny Lad'." When that song came on, I said tae ma wife, "I bet you that man was ma dad!" and that doctor boy fae Glenfarg, Colin Campbell, was wi me that night and he was quite annoyed that they hadnae mentioned ma dad's name in their preamble, we aa were, because that was one o the ones he used tae sing and one o' the ones we heard aa oor days:

JOHNNIE LAD

2. For the sheep are in the clover an the kye are in the byre,
   An aa the lads an lasses roon a rattlin roarin fire.
   But there's yae gleekit lassie is like tae gaen mad
   Roon the stooks o' barley neuks, jinkin you ma Johnnie lad,
   Jinkin you ma Johnnie lad,
   Roon the stooks o' barley neuks, jinkin you ma Johnnie lad.

3. It was in aboot the harvest time, the towns were in a steer,
   There was plenty for yin an aa o baith breid an beer.
   For I gien tae him an I modestly did say,
   'If it's e'er gaun tae be, tell me noo, Johnnie lad,
   Tell me noo, ma Johnnie lad,
   If it's e'er gaun tae be, tell me noo, Johnnie lad.

4. O gin that I were mairried in a hoose o' wir ain,
   I wad whisper in his ear what he wad tell tae nane.
   If treasures were but pleasures, although 'twad mak me sad,
   It's in Heaven I'd be grievin, wantin you, Johnnie lad,
   Wantin you, ma Johnnie lad,
   It's in Heaven I'd be grievin, wantin you, Johnnie lad.

'One of the songs he was aye requested tae dae at the folk club was 'The Jolly Barber':

THE JOLLY BARBER

2. There was a fine young lady who dresses up sae fair.
    She asked the jolly barber tae come and curl her hair.
    Wi his curlin tongs and scissors, his soap box and his razors,
    He went away tae shave her!
    Don't ye know then what I mean?

3. Next mornin, very early, the barber he arose.
    And tae make himsel look tidy, he put on his Sunday clothes.
    Wi his curlin tongs and scissors, his soap box and his razors,
    He went away tae shave her!
    Don't ye know then what I mean?

4. He walked up very proudly and gladly rang the bell.
    There stood the haughtiest servant that ever stood in Hell.
    'Is the Mistress at her leisure? Tell her I've come tae shave her!
    Tell her I've come tae shave her!'
    Don't ye know then what I mean?

5. 'If that's the jolly barber, send him up tae me,
    For I want tae be united, and united I must be!
    For ma husband, he's a yeoman, and he might as well be no man,
    For he's awfy like a woman
    When he lies in bed wi me!'

6. And so the jolly barber strippit intae the pelt.
    And so, the jolly barber took a span below the belt.
    The beds, they went a-squeakin and the maids, they went a-peepin.
    'Hey Mistress, are ye waukin?'
    'What the devil dae ye mean?!'

7. After the night was over, after the deed was done,
    She gave the jolly barber five sovereigns and a crown.
    And he always went tae shave, but he never took his razor.
    Twas the barber's pole he gave her!
    Don't ye know then what I mean?

Belle Stewart
Photo: Ian F. MacKenzie

VOICES FROM THE
STRATHS AND GLENS

In contrast to the romantic picture of the travellers' life that is often painted, the stories that Belle Stewart and Willie MacPhee have to tell of their families' circumstances have been of a harsher nature. To hear of the hardships and tragedies which they and their forebears have endured is a humbling experience: the hard physical work they have done, to a well-organised annual pattern, adapting to changing circumstances, how they have traditionally loved and cherished their children and their old people; and how little regard they have for property and material things, preferring the more precious riches of family and social life. Settling in houses, going to school and coming under the influence of the mass media does, in many cases, destroy these old values and often make travellers resemble the settled community. But most of Belle's and Willie's generation still treasure the songs, stories and family history that they have inherited.

Singing and storytelling, along with piping, were always part of their way of life as with the rest of the farming community, before wireless, films and television came along and before travellers attended school and were told they could not sing unless they sang in classical style. Traditional singing went on however in the family circle or round the camp-fire, and there was always busking to make money round the doors, particularly with the pipes.

BELLE STEWART

Belle's husband's family, however, were good pipers, particularly the father, John Stewart, who won medals at Highland Games for both ceòl mór and ceòl beag. Members of the family still make a living in the summer, playing for the tourists in beauty spots like Glencoe and Aberfoyle. Belle's husband Alec died in 1980, and in 1986 Belle received the BEM for services to folk music.

*****

'I was born at a place – a stretch called Stenton, on the River Tay at Caputh on 18th July 1906. I was born in a wee, wee bow tent; the wee-est, auldest-fashioned thing a tinker can build. My father was pearl-fishing at the time. I was registered at aboot eleven o'clock in the morning, same day as I was born. My father walkit fae Caputh and he went and registered me and he come back to the camp and my mother got up when I was aboot four or five oors auld; she got up and walkit wi him tae the minister. I was baptised in that kirk because long ago, ye got a good piece at the minister's, or a hauf-croon.

'I was seven month auld when my father died an my mother took a single end in Blair. After that, my mother hawked aboot, my uncle made baskets, and my brothers made heather reenges, the heather scrubbers they clean the pots wi, and heather besoms. Donald and my Uncle Jimmy made these things at night when they cam home fae their work, so as my mother could hawk them during the day. She always had her own customers. She went around hawking in the toon o' Blairgowrie and Rattray, she cam owre tae Alyth where she was very weel-kent and weel-liked, or she'd go tae Coupar Angus.

'School was pure hell – and I was only there for aboot eighteen months altogether – but we always got away from school in the beginning of April and we didn't have to go back until the beginning of October. It was away up to Speyside for the pearl-fishing, maybe Glen Esk way or, down at Brechin, there's a place called Justinhaugh – there's a good river down there as well. That was the main living in the summertime away back; pearl-fishing for the menfolk and for the women, hawking. If the men did get a couple o' pearls, they got two or three pounds each for them, which was quite a lot o' money at that time. The women were allocated a certain amount of the money to buy stock to put in their baskets.

'When I was sixteen or seventeen, I wasnae just the worst-lookin in Blair, and I thocht a gey lot o masel, 'cause I was the only lassie in the hoose; and I've seen my puir auld mother many a day, when she could hae done wi the few bob, she used tae go an leave it on a frock or dress for me and pey it up an get it oot when it was peyed – and I really did think a lot o masel when I went doon the street dressed in ma finery!

'Noo when the War came, the tinker people said, "What in the name of God are we gonnae fight for? We've got no country." They were hunted aboot, naebody wanted them, they were a despised race. So Ireland was a free country and they wouldnae be called up for the army there. Now that was the reason Alec's family went tae Ireland. Then a letter come fae Alec's mother tae us in Blair: "Why dae ye no come tae Ireland . . . it's a great country for pearl-fishin." I left my job at Lindsay and More's jam factory in Dundee tae go wi ma brother Donald and my Uncle Jimmy. We went tae Ireland and we went tae a place just above Derry, called Carrigan. It's on the borders o' County Donegal. That's where we met the Stewarts for the first time in years an years. That's where I met Alec.

'It was at McGuire's Bridge, in Omagh, on oor next time over, that my brother Andy got a huge pearl. We decided tae come back tae Scotland to sell the pearl, tae get a better price. Alec said tae his father and mother the night afore, "I'm gaun tae Scotland wi them." 'Cause it was *me* he was gaun wi richt enough! So we came here, and it wis jist aboot berry-time and Alec stayed a fortnicht wi us, wi ma mither and Donald. And he says, "I think me an Belle's gettin married. Have ye any objections?" But they said, "No." What angered my mither was, she thought wi me bein the only lassie, I should hae been married here. Instead o' that, we went back tae Ireland, got married in Ballymoney in the County Antrim on the 17th August 1925.

'What with my mother bein a widow and I so much attached to her, I got fed up wi Ireland after only five months and went back to my mother in Blair. About two weeks after I got back, Alec followed and we got a job spreading flax. We just werena gettin on; he couldnae get on wi my mither – she thought I shouldnae hae left her 'cause I was her only lassie. I was never brought up tae the travellin life. I didna want tae travel. I didna like it. But Alec thought I was bein unfair, as I knew exactly what was involved when I married him. Then on 26th April 1926, my first son, John, was born. I never saw Alec again until my John was five month auld. Then I went over tae Ireland tae try an patch things up. We finally decided tae let my mother bring up the bairn. The same thing happened when I had Cathy and Andy. I would say we were two stubborn young people and neither one would give way to the other. The first ten years o' oor married life was just a case of – he was wi his folks and I was wi my mither, and it was jist a-comin, a-goin, a-comin, a-goin, an we never really settled doon to life until two year after Sheila was born. My mother

said to me, ''Now look, Belle, ye'll hae your man when ye'll no hae me.''
So after that we got on better.

'As for songwriting, what started it off for me anyway – I used to make
up wee silly things talkin tae the bairns, but they didnae maybe even
rhyme – but Donald had a lot o' illness in his time an he lay for weeks
wi very bad bronchitis. Well, he couldnae read an write, so he couldnae
lift a book tae amuse hissel, an so he wad compose verses. By this
particular time, I wad be aboot five years married tae Alec, and he wad
be five years married, an this was verse for hissel:

It's five years and more since I took the door an started on my own,
But luck was aye against me an caused me many a frown,
But I wish that I was hame again and I wad settle down.
Noo my sister was the youngest an she tried the same aul game,
Five years and more since she took the door to sail across the main,
Twas over in aul Ireland she tried tae mak her hame,
But nae doot she's wishin she was back tae be caaed her mammy's wean.

'It just sort of set me off an we started from there. My mother was a
great auld body for listenin tae songs. My father had been a really good
singer. She couldnae sing, unfortunately, but she wad sit an listen tae
Donald and Andy and me singin the auld sangs or makin up verses. We
always had a sort o' thing atween us, that on Hogmanay night we'd aa
make up something different. It wad be aa aboot just what happened tae
wursels. It concerned oor ain family:

O we went up by Fortar or maybe the Linns
Lookin for rags an a wee puckle skins,
And naebody kent what we had tae bear,
Or the hardships and cauld till we got back tae Blair

But me and ma mither we aye trauchled through
And we aye got the price o' a wee taste o' brew.
And Donald and Jimmy they baith did their share
And that is the reason we never left Blair.

'One day, it was one o' those very, very bitter cold, keen, frosty days
at tattie-liftin time, an till about eleven o'clock it was real caul, you
know, liftin tatties, wi the frost, but it came out the most beautiful day
ye ever saw. In the efternoon at three o'clock, we got a piecie time and
I jist looked owre an twa fields' breadths away was this plooman, sleeves
rolled up and he'd twa white horses, real white horses, and he was
whistlin. I said to Alec, ''Can I get a page oot o your book?'' Ye ken,
the book for takin doon the names o' the fowk for their peys an that, and
these are the few verses I wrote:

WHISTLIN AT THE PLOO

1. Noo, I'm just a com-mon ploo-man lad that whis-tles at the ploo. The sto-ry I'm a-boot tae tell will seem gey queer tae you, for I'm no keen on skif-fle groups or o-ny-thing that's new, for I am quite con-ten-ted just gaun whis-tlin at the ploo.

2. Noo I'm workin wi a fairmer and he bides no far fae Crieff
   But if he'd hired a teddy boy I'm sure he'd come tae grief.
   Wi this new-fangled rock and roll and ither things that's new,
   Naw, he wouldnae bide contentit jist gaun whistlin at the ploo.

3. Noo jist take a common plooman lad that works among the neeps
   I'm sure he wadna feel at ease in a pair o' yon ticht breeks.
   Nor wi his hair growin owre lang and hingin owre his broo,
   Naw he wadna be contentit jist gaun whistlin at the ploo.

4. But we canna blame the teddy boys that's jist their way o life
   So I think that I will settle doon an tak masel a wife.
   We'll bide in oor wee cottar hoose and she'll ne'er hae cause tae rue
   O the day she wed her plooman lad that whistles at the ploo.

5. Noo I think ma story's ended but I'm shair that you'll agree
   There's nae life like the plooman's life as far as I can see.
   We rise content in the mornin an we work the haill day thro'
   And we never seem tae worry when we're whistlin at the ploo.

'My two brothers died just a week between them. Donald died at a quarter past five on the 20th of December 1964 and Andy died at quarter past five on the 27th December, the same minute o' the clock as Donald died the Sunday afore. I mean there was nothing wrong wi Andy. Donald was an ailing man wi bronchitis for years. We knew he was goin. That was understood. Maybe Andy caught a cold at the graveside. Maybe Donald came back for Andy. But, oh my God, Donald and Andy was all I had! It was my auldest brother, Andy, wha learned me that song 'The Twa Brithers' that ma father had sung. That's why it means sae much tae me:

THE TWA BRITHERS

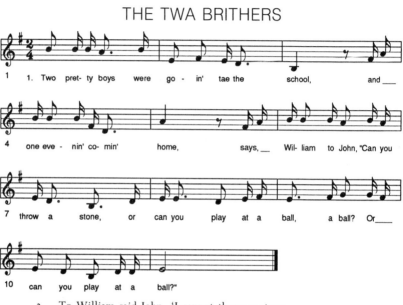

1. Two pretty boys were goin' tae the school, and one evenin' comin' home, says, Wil-liam to John, "Can you throw a stone, or can you play at a ball, a ball? Or can you play at a ball?"

2. To William said John, 'I cannot throw a stone
   Nor little can I play a ball.
   But if you'll go down to yon merry green wood,
   I'll try you a wrestlin fall, a fall,
   I'll try you a wrestlin fall.'

3. So when they came to yon merry green woods
   Beneath the spreadin moon,
   The little penknife slipped out of William's pocket
   Which give John his deadly wound, wound,
   Which give John his deadly wound.

4. O you'll take off your white Holland shirt
   And you'll tear it from gore to gore,
   And you shall bind my deadly wound
   That it shall bluid no more, no more
   That it shall bluid no more.

5. O he took off his white Holland shirt
   An he tore it from gore to gore
   An he did bind his deadly wound
   But it bled ten times more an more,
   O it bled ten times more.

6. 'O what will I tell to your sister dear
   This night when I go home?'
   'You can tell her I'm away to a London school
   And the good books I'll bring home, home,
   And the good books I'll bring home.'

7. 'And what can I tell your father dear,
   This night when I go home?'
   'You can tell him I'm away to a London school
   And the good scholar I'll come home, home,
   And the good scholar I'll come home.'

8. 'And what shall tell to your sweetheart dear
   This night when I come home?'
   'You can tell her I'm dead and in grave laid
   And the grass is growin green, green,
   And the grass is growin green.'

9. 'And what will I tell your stepmother dear
   This night when I go home?'
   'You can tell her I'm dead and in grave laid
   For she prayed I might never come home, home,
   She prayed I might never come home.'

Willie MacPhee
Photo: Aåse Goldsmith

WILLIE MACPHEE

Willie MacPhee, last of the tinsmiths and cousin to the Stewarts, was born in the West of Scotland although he has spent many years in Perthshire now. His mother, Nancy, was known in the family as Perthshire Nancy because she came to that area and married John Stewart, who was father to Belle's husband Alec and his two brothers and five sisters. Willie and Bella now live on Doubledykes Caravan Site at Inveralmond on the outskirts of Perth in a well-cared-for and comfortable trailer. Even in his eightieth year, he is a tall, strong, handsome man, able to play his pipes, sing and tell stories, very much respected and liked by other travellers and also by the many settled folk who are his friends. He is regarded by farmers, policemen and locals as a man of integrity and honesty, a gentleman in all his dealings and a representative of all that is best in the travelling people.

In his younger days, when he had to take his father's place in the family and be able to stand up against any aggressor, he was known as 'the best man in five counties' and one could picture him as someone few would care to meddle with. In an account of a famous affray on the berryfields of Blair, I learned something of Willie's prowess when under provocation, but I have never seen him show violence to anyone.

For many years, he and Alec Stewart would go up the Perthshire glens during the summer months to play their pipes for the tourists and wayfarers. After Alec died however, Willie was too heartbroken to get the same enjoyment out of their old occupation.

It is a striking feature of traveller life that work and play are not rigidly differentiated and neither is an end in itself. As well as the ancient Highland virtues of hospitality and strong kinship ties, the traveller lifestyle has preserved other aspects of life in the past that are based on a non-materialistic set of priorities. While travellers may trade and bargain, move around to get whatever work is available and like to make money, family life and social life remain supremely important.

One of the greatest pleasures of Willie's life is ceilidhing and, since the campfires of his younger days have become a thing of the past, he is delighted to discover the informal music of the Folk Revival in clubs and at festivals. Willie is a king of storytellers, with a wonderful repertoire and a prodigious memory that makes his illiteracy through inadequate schooling seem quite irrelevant. It also makes him excellent company round the fireside, and his views on current affairs show what a wise insight he has into the hearts of men.

*****

'I'll tell ye some crack o' where I was born. It's simple – I was born in a village ootside the toon o' Helensburgh on the 22nd o' September 1910. My father was born aboot twenty-five miles awa fae there an my mither was born twenty-five miles in another direction. So the whole family belongs to Dunbartonshire. My father was a farm worker, of course, a tinsmith, a piper, a basket-maker and also of course my mither could make baskets. There were five brithers on ma father's side and six brothers on ma mither's side. There were four sisters on ma father's side and one sister on ma mither's side. 'Course they're aa dead noo, every one o' them. My father was Andrew MacPhee and my mither's maiden name was Maggie Cameron. They haunted and travelled Dunbartonshire, Perthshire an Argyllshire. They both o' them died in Dumbarton. My mither died at the age of eighty-four, an my father was thirty-nine when he died. I was eleven year old when my father died. It's a long time ago. I learned to do everything. Of course, I *had* to learn, for there was naebody there fur tae act as a bodyguard fur ma mither. I was the oldest o' the family, so any wee charge that had tae be done, I was the one that had tae dae it. I had tae learn tae make baskets, an ma mither sellt them. I learnt tae be a tinsmith an I was also a blacksmith for two year, at Bowlershaugh near Dunfermline. Two year there. An also a mechanic. There was a blacksmith's shop an a garage all in one, ye see. The old man ran the blacksmith's shop an the son done the mechanicking. I done the mechanicking too, an I'm a very good mechanic, although I say it maself.

'Makin tin wouldnae pey ye noo. Ye couldnae make this tin an make a profit o't. Tae mak a thing like a pea-strainer the day, ye'd get aboot a pound for that, an it wouldnae be worth it, because it wad tak ye an oor or maybe an oor an a half tae sit an make that, if ye had the material. But it's strong enough. It'll last for years an years, that. Faur better than the plastic stuff they're makin. I do still make baskets. Big yins for haudin waste paper. I also mak smaller sizes, an yins wi a hannle for message baskets, square an oval shape. When I started makin baskets at first – ye're maybe no gonnae believe this – fourpence was the best you could get for them. But it would get ye a lot in a shop, fourpence, then. They're made o' wild willow. Ye can cut them an peel the bark aff them in the summertime. An they're white when ye tak the bark aff them. In the wintertime, when ye cut them ye have tae steam them in a big long tin hauf fu o' water, standin straight up, then ye wap plugs or anythin ye can richt roon aboot a bit o' canvas tae haud the steam in, for aboot an oor. Then ye tak one oot tae see if it's ready. If the skin comes off, ye know it's ready. The steamed wand is the strongest an the best for makin baskets. They lest far longer an through the years, a boilt one'll turn brown-coloured. They last for years an years.

'Tae mak a heather scrubber, ye tak a bunch o' heather an walt it owre a stane tae tak aa the wee sma heids aff it. Then when ye've got it bare, ye catch it aa thegither an tak a wire an wap it, wap it canny. They're tremendous things for cleanin pots an pans. They'll last for years tae.

'I used to go pipin up the glens in the summer with Alec Stewart, to pipe by the roadside. We'd go to Glencoe, Fort William, Inverness and Ullapool. It was twenty years, we were going up there. Then when he died, I never bothered so much. I lost ma best pal. He was a great old man.

'We used tae get moved on a lot at one time. We were up in Scone Woods once for eighteen months, then the polis chased us oot o' there and I got fined £20. It had been a campin place for years an years. I was also fined off the Doubledykes, for campin there [that was before the caravan site was made] – I was fined £50 or £60! But the man at Redgorton, he was a real Christian, a real man, this one. Even when there was nae work on the farm, he let us stay there, he never bothered us. When the quarry was there, we used tae lock the gate an no one got in past us. We watched the quarry. Then there was some people stealin diesel doon there. We reported them twice to the farmer. When ye've got a freen like that it's as much as ye can dae tae help him. He's helpin you, ye see. We were helpin each ither.

'When I first learned stories, ma father and mother was alive. My father wasnae much o' a storyteller, he was a silent man. But my mother used tae tell stories, and also her brothers, ma uncles. I had an oul aunt. She was very, very good at storytelling. That was her hobby. At night, she used tae gather all the weans roon into one camp an tell them stories, an that's where I first learned a lot o stories.

'Some o' the stories were aboot Burkers. An I've been threatened wi Burkers. Oh aye! No sae very many miles fae here! It wis at Crieff, aboot the back-end o' the year, late in October, at the tattie-liftin time, an I came tae Bridgend at Crieff. I'd only a push-bike and a wee bow-tent. The tent wasnae broad enough for me tae lie across it, so I had tae lie wi ma feet at the door. An it wis one o' thae kin o' tents that ye laced up an fastened wi a pin at the bottom o' the door. I wis lyin sleepin when I wakened up wi something workin at the door. I said, "Hoosh, get away wi ye!" It went away, an I dovered owre tae sleep again. But then it came back, an it was at the door again. I says "Hoosh, get away wi ye!" again, an it went away, but this time, I stayed awake an waited. After a wee while, it wis back again. It was very difficult tae get the door opened because o' this pin on the inside but in the end, it got the door open. I wis lyin there in ma troosers an ma shirt wi ma feet jammed right up agen the door an two hands came in aneath the blankets an grippit ma ankles. He must ha been a big man, tae grip me richt roon the ankles. Then I wis bein pulled oot the tent an as I wis bein pulled oot, I heard some ither body drop a sheet on the grun, I heard it fallin on the leaves. So I shouted, "Hoosh, get away wi ye!" an pulled ma feet back as hard as I could an I rolled oot the side o' the tent and scooted away intae the bushes. There were two or three o' them but they jist stepped back intae the shaddies — they didnae try tae rush me. I ran awa up the road tae some ither friends I had, an aboot twenty minutes later a big car drove by the tents, an it went away up the road to a farm — ye could hear the dogs barking. Next mornin when I went back tae my tent, it wis aa ransacked and knocked doon. I hadnae seen the car at the time — I was rinnin too damn fast!

'This is a song in the Cant language:

BIG JIMMY DRUMMOND

1. Oh my name it is Big Jim-my Drum-mond,
   my name I will ne-ver de - ny._____
   I will mou-lie the gan-nies in do - zens,
   there'll be nae - bo-dy there for to tell._____

2. O last night, I lie in the cauld granzie,
   The night, I lie in the cauld jail.
   My mort and my kinchens are scattered
   And I dinna jan where they may be.

3. But, if ever I dae bing a-choring,
   I'll be sure for tae gang by masel.
   I will moolie the gannies in dozens
   And there'll be naebody there for tae tell.

'Here's a sang I've kent for a long time caaed 'The Maid o' The Sweet Brown Knowe':

THE MAID O THE SWEET BROWN KNOWE

1. Oh come aa you lads and lassies, aa come listen to me a while. I will tell you of a verse or two that'll cause you for to smile. For it's aa about a young man and a maid and I'm gaunna tell you how, sure, the fellow found the courting at the fit o' the sweet brown knowe.

2. 'Oh come on, my pretty Catherine,
   Come on along with me.
   For we'll both run off together
   And a-married we shall be.
   We will join wir hands with wedlock bands,
   I'm speaking to you now.
   Sure I'll do my best, whatever I can
   For the maid o' the sweet brown knowe.'

3. 'Look you down in yonder valley
    Where my men are at the plough,
    Look up in yonder green fields
    Where my crops sae gently grow.
    Look down in yonder valley
    Where my men are at the plough
    Sure they're at their daily labour
    For the maid o' the sweet brown knowe.'

4. 'Then if they're at their daily labour
    Then, kind sir, that is not for me.
    I've heard of your behaviour,
    I've heard indeed,' said she.
    'There is an inn where you call in,
    I've heard the people say
    That you rap and you call and you pay for all
    And come home at the break of day.'

5. 'Then if I rap and I call and I pay for all,
    The money is all my own.
    I will never spend your fortune, dear,
    For I hear you have none.
    But you've raved and you've spoke
    And my poor heart's broke
    As you spoke to me just now.
    But I'll leave you where I found you
    At the fit o' the sweet brown knowe.'

Jock Lundie
Photo: Ian F. MacKenzie

JOCK LUNDIE

Another great character and singer who, at the age of eighty-four, still does a day's work, does his own housework, drives a car and dances at ceilidhs is Jock Lundie, who was born on Blacklaws farm between Blairgowrie and Alyth.

Jock was fifteen years-old when he first made a stand against authority, but it seems to foreshadow a good deal of his life in which he always resisted attempts to push him about and, no doubt, led to the years of active service which he gave to the wages sub-committee of his local union branch. Jock has a clear and orderly memory of the farms he worked on as a ploughman, including the names of the people he worked for, the names of the farms themselves, which are richly evocative and poetic, the length of time he served and the pairs of horses he worked. His expertise with horses is illustrated by the tales he tells of his working life.

*****

'I was born on 10th April 1907 near Blair, at Blacklaw Fairm, one o' the cottages. There's a little church alang at the end o' the road there, an I joined the church there an it was the Rev. Andrew Wylie Smith that was minister at that time. In fact, he christened me, he married me an he christened aa ma family. I was wi Jim Fleming at Aberbothrie latterly for twenty years, an he bocht some o' that ground there off Blacklaw. An there was the two cottages on it. I was born in one o' them an we went back an we pit them aa doon. An he wis alang wan day, an I said, "Well, I didna think for a minute I wad ever come back an haul doon the hoose I wis born in!"'

'I left Rattray school at fourteen year auld an I was workin a wee while at the berries at Pictfield Farm. It was Adamson, the ironmonger, that had it at that time. After that I was workin wi Grant at the Thorn, an ye speak aboot bein hard! I was among the sheep. We had seven hundred hoggs an we'd twa hundred lambin ewes an there was the shepherd an maself. Oh, a big capable man, but he jist had one hand: he'd a thing at the end o' his yairm an could screw a cleek or ring intae it. He could lift a barrow or hang up the nets or onything wi this cleek.

'We startit in the mornin aboot half-past six an I was there at six o'clock at night. I mind once we shiftit along tae the Burnside at Alyth an that day, we come an shiftit aa the sheep back tae the Thorn. We'd jist tae snip twa–three minutes for wur midday meal an we never stopped for six o'clock. So they come oot – it was jist aside the big hoose, I mind – and the maid come oot wi tea at the back o' five o'clock. She said, "Come on, Jock, an hae some tea." I said, "I'm no takin tea at this time o nicht. Ma tea's sittin waitin on me at hame. If it had been earlier on in the efternoon," I says, "I wid hae taen it, but no at the back o' five o'clock. I'm finished at six o'clock." I'd never stopped a minute the haill day, puttin up nets an sortin the troughs an that for feedin. As I was fixin up the last net, I could hear six o'clock ringin in the steeple at Rattray. I said tae him, "Donal," I says, "ye can bide aa nicht if ye like, but I'm gaun awa hame. For," I says, "if they think they're gonnae get me tae potter aboot amang the sheep till nine o'clock at night, for a drink o tea," I says, "they're far mistaken!"

'On another occasion, I wanted away tae the market, Blairgowrie Market, the feein market. The farmer's wife came oot an she said tae me, "He says, if ye get the troughs filled by dennertime, ye can get awa tae the market." So the market day came an the pit we were on was finished an I went hame for ma denner an come back. I carried aa thae troughs masel tae feed thae sheep. I struck the earth an aa thing aff the pit an gied him a hand wi the cutter. An I says, "Now, Donal ye can dae onything ye like. I'm gaun away tae the market."

'I was getting three shillins a day, an when I got ma pey on the Saturday, there was one and six for aa the time I was off at the market – taken off. Yes! The fairmer at that time wanted me tae bide again an I said, "No, no. For three shillins a day? I couldnae think aboot it!" He said, "Ye ken, I hiv a man doon at Bruntie?" He had the fairm doon aside Burrelton. "He'd mak twa o' you." "Well," I says, "I dinna ken what he is at Bruntie, but I dinna think he's a man at aa. He'd be mair o' an eediot, workin for less than three shillins a day!" He said, "I never thocht ye were sae damned cheeky." I says, "I'm no cheeky. I'm just tellin ye the plain truth."

'The first farm I got was Thorn Green; there were four pair there an

I went there for the fourth pair. I left there and went to Burnside of Marlee an there was jist the farmer, his wife and masel there; wasnae a big place. It was a Mr and Mrs Kemp had it at that time. She was a schoolteacher before she was married. They were very good. Ye couldnae hae got better! A funny thing – I used tae laugh aboot it – my younger brother went to Burnside o Marlee in my place and he could not stick it! Didnae suit him at aa! I was there a year an I went to Gormack for the fifth pair; there were five pair there. I left Gormack and I went to the Braes o' Carse at Guardswell. I was there six month and I came back tae Blairgowrie and I was at the Hillbarns. I was at Hillbarns six month and I left an went to Balbrogie. I was in the bothy there for six month and I left there and went to Bridge Farm, that's at the Beech Hedges at Meikleour. I was there a year and a half an I left there tae get married. That was 1928; I was twenty-one at the time.

'I left there and went to Blackcraig, that's ten mile north o' Blairgowrie. I was there a year. The Forestry Commission took it owre at that time. I left there and went to Perth, to the feein market at Perth, Little Dunning, and I went tae Woodend, Ballathie. It was a Mrs Alexander that had it at that time. I was there two year wi her an she sold oot an it was a Willie Pullar that took it owre. There wis three brithers; they had Kirkhope, Bishopshaugh and Willie had Woodend. I was three years there and I left an went to Innernytie and I was three years there. I left there and went back to Balbrogie for the third pair. I was three years on the third pair, three years on the second pair and I was eleven year on the first pair. I lost my first wife there. I left there and went up tae New Alyth, tae stay in a cooncil hoose. Ma sister was up there an she did quite a lot o' ma washin. Then I was twenty years wi James Fleming o Aberbothrie.

'When I was at Woodend, I was oot wi ma horse a few times at different ploughin matches, an there was a man caaed John Taylor, a fairmer, o' Honeyhole, an he said tae me, ''What aboot gaun oot tae the match yersel?'' I said, ''No.'' He said, ''If ye can mak a job like that wi a cellar ploo, I'd like tae see ye wi a swing.'' ''Oh,'' I said, ''I've used a swing afore.'' ''Well,'' he said, ''I've ma ploo there. I'll gie ye it ony time ye like.'' But I never taen it, 'cause I hadna time tae practise. I was too busy workin! Och aye, I was oot wi ninety acre there and I was masel. Mr Duncan, Mrs Alexander's brother who had Greenhead, he often cam owre, but I was as often back wi them. Hard times, but happy times!

'I was aye gettin the new horses an once they were startit, some ither body was gettin them, an I was gettin ither yins that were comin in. In this case in particular, I went oot tae yoke yin tae the cultivator. I'd the awfiest job keepin a haud o' 'im, before I got the cleeks in him. Damn me, when I got the cleeks in him he wadna start. Then, when we yoked him tae the binder, oh, he created hell! It was the noise o' the binder. I'd a job keepin a haud o' 'im an my grieve was there. I said, "Look, Andrew, the best thing you can dae is go oot the road an leave me masel till I see how I get on wi 'im." I thought it was the noise that was daein it — right enough! I took ma hankie an tore it in two an stuck it in his ears, an he went away, like that!

'The gaffer's son once said tae me — I was seventeen year auld, couldn't care less at that time — an he says, "I'll bet ye hauf a croon, ye'll no get a horse workin withoot a bridle." I said, "Och, that's nae bother! But if I was tae dae that, I wad need tae get the hauf-croon first, because," I says, "if I waited till after, I'd never get it." "All right," he says. We were in tattie dreels, ye see. So I says, "I'll ging twa roons first, then I'll loosen it an go withoot a bridle." So I went twa roons, turned him at the end and jist went forrit, took off the bit, took off the bridle and hung it up on the heims. I spoke tae him an he went awa an I was whistlin away, ye see. The horse is first lookin roon at one side, then lookin roon at the ither. It was really laughable! But two or three roons, an he was walkin away quite the thing.

'I used tae laugh at one beast. We used tae go alang tae Burrelton for tattie bags. Goin along the Perth road, if she heard a train comin behind her, she would put her ears flat on the back of her neck and she would go as hard as she could travel on that road. You would think she was tryin tae race the train! And when the train passed, she would jist slow doon back tae her normal pace again. I wondered what was wrong wi her the first time. An I said, "Well, ye can carry on! Ye'll get tired afore I will."

'Oh but that was a bad job, that fire when the horses got burned at Balbrogie! When I went doon, it was jist like a furnace. The beams were aboot that thickness, big steel beams. When I went doon, the heat had the beams bent doon, meltit doon. An the water tank an everything was burst. So I said to the vet, "It was bluidy bad we couldnae hae gotten the horses." He said, "It's a damn good thing ye couldnae get in tae the horses, because ten to one, you'd hae landed in there an no got oot. When ye brought them oot o' the fire intae the fresh air, they'd hae dropped an ye'd be damn lucky if ye got oot. So it was maybe the best thing that could hae happened."

'That time the horses were burned, we had some Italian prisoners an some o' them said, "I bet it was that Italians!" "Nut for a bluidy minute!" I said. "I'll tell ye, dinna let me hear ye say that again unless ye're askin for trouble, because," I says, "thae lads has a damn sight mair respect for the horses than they hae for you." In fact, there wis one lad — he was workin a black horse — an he was jist cryin like a bairn. Aye, oh God! He was cryin like a kid that had lost something. I said, "Look, ye canna dae nothin aboot it. It's past."

'They were tellin me it wis time I stopped the work. I says, "Well, I dinna see whit I'm gaun tae stop workin for," I said. "There's nothin wrong wi me." But I left an went alang tae Bankfoot, tae the kennels in the back o' Waterloo. Lady Ramsay o' Banff had the kennels an Miss Macleod helped her tae rin them. My son had the transport cafe at Bankfoot, an I was helpin oot in the cafe in the forenoon an then wis workin at the kennels in the efternoon. Wir name was in for a cooncil hoose in Stanley, Bankfoot or Luncarty, but there wis young couples gettin married an they were walkin intae some o thae new hooses. So I says, "Oh'm no gonnae stick this any langer." I seen this advert in the papers an I came across here tae Auchtermuchty. The fairmer asked me what I did. "I've been workin on a fairm since I was fourteen year auld." He said, "Well, that's the kind o' lad we're needin here. Who were ye wi?" "I was with Jim Fleming at Aberbothrie. I was twenty years wi him. I was last to work horses wi him." So he laughed – he obviously kent him fine. I came here fifteen years past, July."'

'I heard 'The Banks o' the Nile' in the bothy when I was at school. Mony's a time I got a swearin for bein in the bothy. I used to go in tae listen tae the songs. My brother-in-law and I was at the Thorn at that time:

THE BANKS O THE NILE

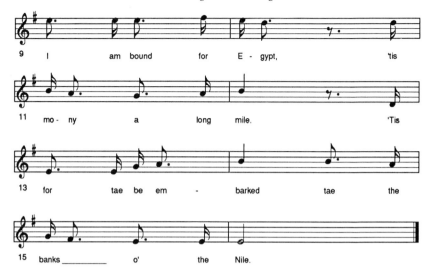

9   I   am bound   for   E - gypt,   'tis

11   mo - ny   a   long   mile.   'Tis

13   for   tae be em - barked   tae   the

15   banks _____ o'   the   Nile.

2.   O Willie, dearest Willie, these words do break my heart,
      O come let us get married before that we do part,
      For parting wi ma Willie is like partin wi ma life,
      O stay at home dear Willie an make me your wedded wife.

3.   O Nancy, dearest Nancy, but that would never do,
      ****[Line missing]****
      The government gives orders and the king he gives commands
      And I am bound by oath, my love, to fight in foreign lands.

4.   O I'll cut off my yellow hair and go along with you,
      I'll volunteer my service and go to Egypt too,
      I'll fight under your banner; kind Fortune yet may smile
      And I'll be your loyal comrade on the banks o' the Nile.

5.   Your waist it is too slender, your complexion is too fine,
      Your constitution is too weak to stand the hot campaign,
      The sultry suns of Egypt your precious health would spoil,
      On yon hot and sandy desert on the banks o' the Nile.

6.   O cursed, cursed be the day that ere the wars began,
      For oot o bonnie Scotland they've ta'en many a pretty man,
      They've ta'en away our lifeguards, protectors o' oor isle,
      And their bodies feed the worms on the banks o' the Nile.

7.   Let a hundred days be darkened and let maidens give a sigh,
      'Twould melt the very elements to hear the wounded cry,
      Let a hundred days be brightened, and let maidens give a smile,
      And remember Abercrombie on the banks o' the Nile.

    'The Rattlin Ploughboy' is one which ma brither an I used tae sing thegither when we were at the berries:

THE RATTLIN PLOUGHBOY

1. Oh I'm a rat-tlin' plough-boy an'
Jock it is ma name. It's ca-rin an vex-a-____ tion that
bo-thers ma broo, an' aa my de-light lies in
hau-din' the ploo.

[VERSES 2 & 3]

2. A-ri-sin' tae the mor-nin' an' the
lark's sing-in' gay. Be-tween my twa hor-ses, I
whis-tle them a-way. I clean them and clap them an'
corn____ them sae fu, then on wi' the ta-ckle an' it's
aff tae the ploo.

3. If I get a chance for tae ging in tae the toon,
The lasses aa miscaa me for a roch country loon,
But their silks and their satins, there wad be but few
If it wasnae for the laddie an his haudin o' the ploo.

TOMMY BONTHRONE

Tommy Bonthrone worked at Woodside of Marlee on the picturesque road from Blairgowrie to Dunkeld in the late 1950s and early '60s and died in Auchenblae in the late '70s. Although he remembered his mother, father and sister, when Maurice Fleming recorded him in 1957, he had apparently been orphaned early on and, as many orphans were in those days, put out to a farm to work for his keep. By some quirk of circumstances, he was labelled 'mentally defective'.

Mr Reg Forsyth of Mains of Ardblair remembers Tommy, who used to come along from the farm where he worked to have his tea with the Forsyths and sing a few songs: "Tommy was at Woodside of Marlee, working for Tom Goodall, a tenant farmer on the Blair-Oliphant Estate. He must have been there from about 1955 or 1956, and I would say he was in his forties then. He lived in a wee bothy at Woodside. I think he had been in a home of some kind before that. I don't really know exactly. But he was working for sweeties there – just his keep. He was well-known for singing and diddling all around Blairgowrie."

In the late 1950s, something happened which radically altered the course of Tommy's life. It became apparent that Tommy was able to take quite a lot of responsibility on the farm, even being left in charge at times when the farmer was away, and certainly appearing to be anything but 'mentally defective'. His case was investigated and Tommy was declared to be a person of normal intelligence – 'certified sane', as he put it humorously. This meant, of course, that he had henceforward to be paid a farm servant's wage, and Reg Forsyth believes that at this point he left Woodside of Marlee. Having suffered years of injustice, Tommy should have been able to claim compensation, but he never did. Having met him and heard him talk about it, I know that it was not lack of education that made him unwilling to attempt this. He simply was not interested in money. "I've aye been weel looked after," he said. "I've aye liked ma work, an I've been weel-treated. I've nae complaints." He was one of the most contented and cheerful people I have ever met.

Tommy divided his song repertoire into 'Straight' Songs and Comic Songs, and he was a champion diddler. 'Straight' Songs included 'Dark Lochnagar', of which he gave an almost operatic rendering, 'The Bonnie Braes o Airlie' and 'The Flower of Strathmore', two Victorian songs that manage to miss a good deal of the affectation and sentimentality that often mar such songs. 'Straight Songs' tended to be in standard English and in as close an imitation of art-song style as Tommy could manage. Of 'The Flower of Strathmore', he says that he got it from a lady who used to work up the glen. "She wrote it down for me. I put the air to it myself. She didnae just know the air."

The other song, 'The Bonnie Braes o Airlie', appears to have been composed by a Scottish exile who talks of the Cam and 'the pure classic fountain', (Cambridge University, perhaps?). As only the sons of the gentry went south for their education at that time, it is a possibility that this song was composed by some scion of the nobility or, at least, the son of a local laird. Tommy got the song from a man called Charlie Finlay:

THE BONNIE BRAES O' AIRLIE

1. Bonnie sing the birds in the bright English valleys,
Bonnie bloom the flowers in the lime-sheltered alleys,
Golden rich the air wi perfume laid on rarely,
But dearer far to me are the bonnie braes o' Airlie.

2. Winding flows the Cam and it's no [*indecipherable phrase*]
Rosy deck the mead but it's no like Glenisla
Cloudless shines the sun but I wish I saw it clearly
Sweet blinkin through the mist on the bonnie braes o' Airlie.

3. Searching for a name I left my native mountains
Drinking here my fill at the pure classic fountain
Striving hard for fame I've listened late and early
And oh, that I might rest on the bonnie braes o' Airlie!

4. Yonder gleams the prize for which I've been longing
Darkness comes atween my struggles sad prolonging
Dim has grown my een an my hairt is breaking sairly
Wae's me! I'll never see the bonnie braes o' Airlie.

Tommy's repertoire included the standard favourites of the bothy chiels, 'The Soor Milk Cairt', 'Nicky Tams', which could be classed as the bothy anthem, 'The Road and the Miles to Dundee' and this fine version of the transportation ballad 'Jamie Raeburn':

JAMIE RAEBURN

1. My name is Ja-__ mie Rae-_____burn, in Glas-gow I was born. My___ place and ha-bi-ta-_____tions, I'm forced to leave with scorn. From my place and ha-bi-ta-_____tions, I now must gang a-wa far frae the bon-__ nie hills and dales of Ca-le-do-ni-a.

2. 'Twas early one mornin, just by the break of day,
   I overhead the turnkey and unto us did say,
   'Arise ye helpless convicts, arise ye ane and aa,
   This is the day you are to stray from Caledonia.'

3. We aa arose, put on our clothes, our hearts were full of grief.
   Our friends, they all stood round the coach, could grant us no relief.
   Our friends, they all stood round the coach, their hearts were broke in twa
   Tae see us leave the bonnie braes of Caledonia.

4. Fareweel, my aged mother, I'm vexed for what I've done.
   I hope none will upcast to you, the race that I have run.
   I hope you will be provided when I am far awa,
   Far frae the bonnie hills and dales of Caledonia.

5. Fareweel, my honoured father, he is the best o' men.
   Likewise, my own sweetheart, it's Catherine's her name.
   Nae mair we'll walk by Clyde's clear stream, nor by the Broomielaw,
   For I must leave the hills and dales of Caledonia.

6. If e'er we chance to meet again, I hope 'twill be above
   Where hallelujahs will be sung to them who rise in love.
   Nae earthly judge shall judge us then but he who rules us aa.
   Fareweel, ye bonnie hills and dales of Caledonia.

Among his repertoire of Comic Songs were those like this wildly absurd music-hall song 'The Whiskers Of My Grandfather's Grave', a parody of 'My Grandfather's Clock', which he rendered with hilarious mock-solemnity:

THE WHISKERS OF MY GRANDFATHER'S GRAVE

2. My grandfather's whiskers were too large for his face
   They grew round the neck of his hat.
   And they were many a hue, they were red, white and blue
   But my grandfaither painted them black.
   And the whiskers they did shave and they placed them round his grave
   When the old man died.
   And the McGees and the McPhees, the McDougalls and McCuskers
   Were invited tae the burial o' my grandfaither's whuskers,
   And the seagulls came as guests to get stuff tae build their nests
   From the whuskers of my grandfaither's grave.

The last four lines of the song were punctuated with heart-rending sobs, which Tommy effected by sharp and dramatic intakes of breath that reduced his audience to hysterics, especially as they were accompanied by facial contortions of the most Gothic character.

When it came to diddling, Tommy had one firm rule about it. 'There's nae "dums" in diddling!' he said, with the air of a man who had established himself as an authority on the subject by winning local diddling contests, where he competed with another local champion, Davey Glen, a kenspeckle figure with his long beard and climbing boots, who was also noted for another old-fashioned entertainment – dancing dolls on a wooden springboard. Tommy had a most rich and powerful voice and a great sense of style. If the circumstances of his life had been different, he might have become a trained concert artist. As it was, he sang with all his heart and loved singing. The only unhappy times of his life were when he was working in places where there was no opportunity for singing. His mother and father had been singers, so he and his sister inherited a family tradition. It is a tribute to the strength of tradition that Tommy kept it up, even when his family was broken apart. He learned the two music-hall songs, both by James Curran, while he was working in Broxburn and a concert party from Glasgow was performing for a week in the local hall. He went every night they were there, in order to learn the songs – not by writing them down, but by listening to them. He also spoke about a Sandy Mitchell, the grieve at Pittendreich farm, whom Reg Forsyth also remembers as a fine singer. No doubt Tommy learned songs from him too.

Charlie Murray
Photo: Aåse Goldsmith

VOICES FROM THE FERM TOUNS

CHARLIE MURRAY

Charlie Murray was born at Wester Suddie in the Black Isle on 30th August 1916, youngest of a family of ten. He talks of the first two Banffshire farms he worked on as a boy, Nether Dallochy and Easter Whinty. He sings songs about the conditions met on the farms like the meals served in some farm kitchens, like the one where the bread was 'baked as hard as hell', or the other where the soup had 'three seeds o barley an the smell o a leek'. But those farmworkers who were 'chaumered' [put up in rooms on the farm] may well have done better in most cases than those who were 'bothied'. The bothy lads lived and ate in their own quarters, and these could be very rough. Charlie has experience of both of these systems and observes, 'I never had a very good stomach when I was in among the bothy stuff'. In the Forfar area, where Charlie eventually worked for twenty-four years, the bothy chiels were reputed to be very fond of cold porridge, made a week in advance, some say in a drawer, and eaten in hunks as required. Charlie's friend and fellow bothy ballad singer, Adam Young, has eaten such fare, but Charlie says, 'I don't think I could hae stomached it'.

Charlie's father was a cattleman on farms in the Black Isle, Banffshire and Aberdeenshire and moving about meant that Charlie's schooling was frequently interrupted.

When he got married in 1936 to Irene, a girl he met when he came to Nether Dallochy a second time, he was only nineteen – too young, his mother thought. But things turned out very well, a fact that Charlie, with typical modesty, attributes entirely to a wife who to his mind has been all but perfect. As Charlie's family grew, they flitted from farm to farm, from Munlochy in the Black Isle to Tain in Easter Ross, down to East Lothian, where he worked with top shorthorn breeders and eventually to West Drum and then Craigeassie, near Forfar.

It was when he was at Craigeassie that singing began to play a large part in his life. The farm was not too far from Justinhaugh Inn – Charlie became one of the regulars and soon acquired a reputation as a singer. As a result of his singing Charlie came to the notice of the Traditional Music and Song Association, an organisation founded in 1967, with the aim of giving a platform to such authentic tradition-bearers as Charlie and his friend Adam Young, Belle Stewart and a host of other singers and musicians, who did not fit into any of the musical categories of the time.

He now lives in retirement in the village of Justinhaugh with his wife. With the superannuation from Charlie's years with the Boots' Estate, they feel very comfortably off.

*****

'Ye'll maybe hae heard the rhyme:
> Doon at Nether Dallochy there's neither watch nor knock
> But porridge time and brose time and aye yoke, yoke.

'That's where I started working! Then I went til a farm just a bit further up the road caaed Easter Whinty. It was rather a tight place, a bit bare. We just lived in the chaumer, as we caaed it, and got wir meat in the kitchen. It was pretty rough stuff; jist the meal an the tatties, that was the height o' it, pretty bare livin, like. At Easter Whinty, I never seen beef. I was there a year and a half and I seen – *wance* – I seen a bit beef in it, aa the time I was in it. That was aa. That was what they used tae caa beef brose on Bannock Day – that's Pancake Tuesday. We got stovies on a Tuesday from the leftovers o' what was ben the hoose. Brose is all right if ye can make it right. If the milk was good, it wasna bad, ye know, and if ye could judge your salt and your pepper and you had good bit of cream, there was nothing wrong with a bowl of brose.

'My mother had a rough time o' it, bringing up ten o' a family, and my father was pretty fond o' the drink and he couldn't afford it, and with one thing and another, it left a mark on her; she got sort o' soured o' life.

'The first feeing market I was at must have been aboot 1932. That was the first time I seen Jimmy McBeath and heard him and the crowd was aa around him then. He really was a great turn, until he got too much to drink. But he really was a great attraction to everybody, Jimmy

McBeath, and then there was one or two more worthies roond him aboot
Banff, yonder, too. Most of the songs I sing, I heard Jimmy McBeath
singing. I didn't actually get them from him, but I got them. I've heard
him sing, ye ken, 'I've seen the hairst o Rettie' − well, that place was
jist next door to that Dallochy I was speakin aboot. So I knew aboot
Rettie − it was a seven pair o' horse place, a great big farm. I always heard
bits o' it, then Jimmy McBeath got it put out in a book, so I got the
words. It's a lovely song, nae question aboot it. According to John
Strachan, it was the best bothy ballad that was ever written:

THE HAIRST O' RETTIE

1.   I hae seen the hairst o' Ret-tie lads an' twa'r three aff the throne. I've heard for sax or sei-ven weeks the hair-sters girn an' groan, For wi a co-vie Wil-lie Rae a mon-thie and a day, syne aa the jol-ly hair-ster lads gae sing-in' doon the brae.

2.   In a monthie and a day ma lads the like was never seen;
It beats tae sticks the fastest strips o Vickers' best machine!
The Speedwell it brings up the rear, the Victory clears the way
An twenty acres' daily yield's laid doon tae Willie Rae.

3.   He drives them roond and roond the field at sic an affa rate
Yet steers them canny oot an in at mony's the kittle gait,
An wiles them gently owre the steens and many a hidden hole,
An he'll come tae nae mishanter if ye leave him wi a pole.

4.   He sharps their teeth tae gar them bite, he taps them on the jaws,
An if he sees them dowie-like he'll brawly ken the cause,
A boltie here an a pinnie there tae keep them aa in tune,
He'll quickly stop their mad career an bring the cleishach doon.

5. He whittles aff the corners an maks crooked bitties stracht.
   He likes tae see that man and beast are equal in the dracht,
   An aa the stages neat an square and nae a sheaf agley,
   For he'll coont wi ony dominie fae the Deveron tae the Spey.

6. He's no made up o' mony words nor kin tae puffin lee,
   But just as keen a little chap as ony you will see,
   An if you're in search o' hairvest wark upon a market day,
   Tak my advice, be there in time, an look for Willie Rae.

7. Noo, we hae got it in aboot an aa oor things be ticht,
   We'll gaither roon the festal board tae spend a joyfu nicht,
   Wi Scottish songs an mutton broth tae drive oor cares away,
   We'll drink success tae Rettie an ma bandster Annie McLean.

8. But before I end my hamely screed, I canna weel forget
   The gentle dames that gaird the hoose an keep the folk in meat.
   Lang may they bile the kale an stir the porridge weel
   An may they never need or want for nail tae keep the timmer haill.

9. Here's a health tae aa ye Rettie blades, a ringin cheer, hurrah!
   A band o' better workin chaps a gaffer never saw!
   They're aye sae eager for tae pairt an ready for the fray;
   It was them that made the boatie row that was steered by Willie Rae.

'I was first fee'd at Brandon Fair at Banff, and then there was Porter Fair at Turriff, but the real, the real market was Aiberdeen, the Friday before the term, Muckle Friday:

MUCKLE FRIDAY FAIR

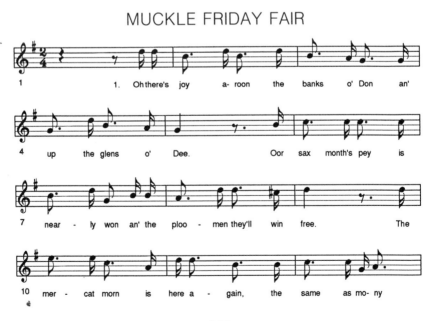

1. Oh there's joy a-roon the banks o' Don an' up the glens o' Dee. Oor sax month's pey is near-ly won an' the ploo-men they'll win free. The mer-cat morn is here a-gain, the same as mo-ny

13 mair, an' we'll dirl a - wa in the mor - nin' train tae

16 Muc- kle Fri - dy Fair.

2. Gin ten o'clock the Castlegate was in an unco steer
   An ilkae minute as we wait mair billies dae appear
   Doon Union Street an roon the Queens great crowds assemble there
   For hunners come tae Aiberdeen tae Muckle Friday Fair.

3. The fairmers stand ootside the croods wi topcoats owre their airms
   Tae pick an chise amang the loons tae suit their different fairms.
   Some o' them are in their prime an some are auld an sair
   But deil o'm ony ever missed a Muckle Friday Fair.

4. But noo, the maisters an the men they're aa thegither mixed,
   The siller's socht, the arles taen an mony a peer loon's fixed.
   Some tae bailie stirks an stots an some tae caa a pair,
   And some were gettin nineteen notes at Muckle Friday Fair.

5. Noo, the toon can boast, as weel she may, her pictures, music halls,
   An palaces o' grander grace but it's enclosed in walls.
   But gie tae me the countryside, grey skies an caller air,
   Nae muckle than a day we'll bide at Muckle Friday Fair.

6. Noo, the maids we met in Union Street were clad in bright array,
   Like butterflies in sunshine feed upon a summer's day.
   Wi gaadie dress an poodered face, but yet ye'll nae compare
   Wi the rosy-cheekit country lass at Muckle Friday Fair.

7. Noo, here's a health tae aa ye country lads an dry ye weel your sark
   An if your maisters use ye weel, I'm sure ye'll dae your wark.
   An may your hairt be licht an free frae ony warldly care
   An I hope ye'll get a dacent fee at Muckle Friday Fair.

'The week after Muckle Friday, there was the Rascal Fair for them that gave up the job. They'd maybe fee'd to go somewhere and they never went hame. When ye fee'd, ye said, ''Oh I'm gaun hame tae sic and sic a place.'' Well, they never went hame, an then they went tae the Rascal fair an they got anither job there. They'd broken their contracts. Oh ye were a rascal if ye did that! They'd jist take a tummle, or heard something that wisnae richt aboot it – the pair o' horses, or the food – some o' them was very tight, ye know.

'The wife really was a manager, you know, she was something special. I would never have struggled through as she did – I mean, when we started, when we wis married first, we had £50 a year, that's what we had. However, my wife was lucky enough. She was wi this mistress for a good while and she gave her a good bit when she left. She furnished the house not me. She did all this and then we brought up this big family and they all turned out pretty well. Well, she struggled on an she brocht them up. They were always the speak o' the district, the way they were turned out.

'I did land wi a stroke o' luck when I came doon tae Boots' farms; that was a really good job for me. I was there wi them for twenty-four years. What ye didn't get in many farms, they had a pension scheme, so it's left me a lot more comfortable noo wi ma pension. That Aiberdeenshire farming was really rough: wi anything from eighty to a hundred cattle, ye'd tae feed them three times a day, ye know; ye'd a long, long day. Wi two of us, when ye got in among the pedigrees, it was a different story. At Craigeassie, we had aboot forty pure-bred Aiberdeen Angus.

'One bull I sold made £8,100 and another made £8,000; top prices. I never was the champion at Perth – I was champion at the Highland and I was champion at the Royal, but I was never champion at Perth. Perth is the place for the bulls, all the good ones. I was reserve Champion at Perth with a shorthorn. He was called Proctor of West Drum and he went to Australia. The next one I had, that got £8,000, I've never seen a bull wi hair on like him! Everybody was round him, for the hair. He went away to the Argentine. He was first in the class all right. He was called Proud Jeff. An Aiberdeen Angus – he had hair on him like a Galloway! Whether he was a throwback or what it was – I don't think anyone ever seen hair on a bull like him!

'But it was a slippery stone. It was all right as long as ye were doin all right. Ye couldnae depend on havin it every year. I was with the McGillivrays – that was *the* shorthorn men at that time, the really top ones – I was second cattleman wi one o' them, up aside Tain. He was wiped out wi foot and mouth disease at the end o' the war. Then I come doon tae be head cattleman wi them when they shifted doon tae Pitkethin in East Lothian. I went doon there wi him and oh, he was alright when he was gettin the reserve champion, things like that! But when things went wrong – well! That was that! Ye wis out!

'But it was when I was at Craigeassie and I had a few extra shillings that I started goin to Justin pub with mates, and I was in there singin an I was surprised how everything gaed doon – it went doon really well. Then I got in wi the TMSA and started singin at festivals.'

(Sadly, Charlie Murray died while this book was in preparation.)

WILLIE BARCLAY

Another character I was fortunate to meet and record before he died in 1986 was Willie Barclay, an outstanding cattleman and singer. By the time I got to know him, Willie was deaf, partially sighted and in a wheelchair, but remained a cheerful and entertaining personality, with a delight in songs and singing.

Willie's daughter Barbara, who worked with her father until he retired, enlarges on some of his comments to show what an often hard life he led and how determinedly he overcame the challenges that faced him. At Castle o' Fiddes near Stonehaven, where most of Barbara's memories of her father stem from, one of Willie's successes was with a cow called Fairy, who won the Scottish milk record. Willie was always singing in the byre: he said it helped the milk down, and he swapped songs, on occasion with the well-known North-East character, John Mearns.

When his days as a cattleman were done, Willie retired to Scone, having worked latterly at North Ballo, Coupar Angus. After his wife died, he spent his remaining years in Catmoor House in Scone, 'the best place in the world', he said, a cheerful and comfortable haven where 'they won't let you do anything!' This was said not in complaint but in wonder: if one tries to imagine what it must have seemed like to Willie to be so well looked after when all his life, he had toiled so hard to take care of his family and his cattle, one can glimpse a little of his feeling of being in paradise.

*****

'I've been aroon Perth aa my days. I was brocht up wi a step-auntie. Ma faither was killt in the First World War and the auld wife gane aff her heid and I'd nobody. But the auntie *made* me. She had a dairy, ye see. Mony a nicht, I gret for ma mither. My auntie *made* me.

'When I was up at Dunkeld there and auld Mrs Roberts was livin, there was pipes an aathing, ye ken. Aa the sheep men wid be there an there wis tumblers o' whisky sittin at every corner o' the place. It wis only nine bob a bottle at that time! I've seen us at five o'clock in the mornin, an some richt sangs tae – an the pipe boy wi his pipes:

THE NICOLLS O' CAIRNEY BRAE

1. O Mair - tin - mas is cam a - gain, oh boys I'm glad tae say, it's when I be - came a ploo - man chiel tae the Ni - colls o' Cair - ney Brae tae work a se - cond pair o' horse an' fol - lae yon big man. His name wis An - dra Bar - lass an' he's ca'ed an' ex - cel- lent hand. He blaws a - boot his pair o' horse an' aa his dan - dy fee, but I can sing o' ma wee broon mare, she's the li - ly o' the lea.

2. We gang tae drive the dung ma boys that comes frae Perth canal
**** [line missing] ****
Three rakes a day, that's what we dae, an that richt speedily.
An wi oor graips an shovels boys, we spread it owre his ley,
But if we meet a bonnie wee lass, it's untae her we'll say,
'Oh bonnie lassie, neebor us tae the Nicoll's o Cairney Brae.'

3. Noo Little Dunnin's near at hand an again we're aa tae fee.
We're aa gaein doun tae bonnie Perth toun jist tae hae a pairtin spree,
An as the glasses they pass roun, we'll sing some bothy lay,
An we'll ne'er forget the happy nichts we spent at Cairney Brae.
It's now we've been three lovin lads, it's a pity that we should pairt,
Our equals again will never be fund in the Nicoll's o Cairney Brae.

'Craigie Farm is at Kinnesswood, comin the back road tae Pitscottie. It's a ten-pair place an there wid be ten men on it. There'll be some mair history – it's a braw, big place. Whether they'd been stealin the tatties or whether they'd been sellin them, I dinna ken, but the sang says:

TATTIE JOCK

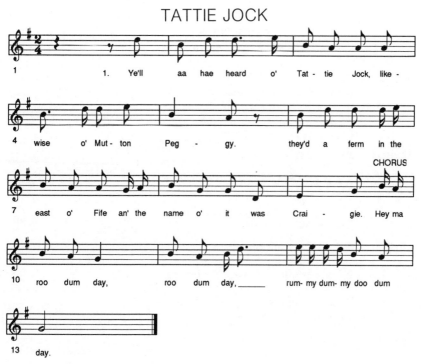

2. They had ten pair upon that place
Likewise ten able men
But five went oot tae scrange the shed
An five tae steal the hens.

CHORUS: Hey ma roo dum day, . . . etc.

3. Three months we sair'd Tattie Jock
   As weel's we did agree,
   For we jist noo broke the tattie shed
   Wi the bothy key.

CHORUS: Hey ma roo dum day, . . . etc.

4. We werena lang in the tattie shed
   Oor bags were hardly full,
   When Tattie Jock behind the door
   Says, 'Ye'll all stand still.'

CHORUS: Hey ma roo dum day, . . . etc.

5. Ten polismen were sent for
   But nine there only cam.
   And it bate them aa tae tak's that nicht
   We bein ten able men.

CHORUS: Hey ma roo dum day, . . . etc.

6. But some o' us went tae the dung
   Ithers tae the mill,
   But better had we aa been plooin
   Upon Pitlowrie Hill.

CHORUS: Hey ma roo dum day, . . . etc.

7. For Donald Gray oor hinmost man
   He was the best man o' us aa,
   He jined a man o' war at Leith
   And couldnae stand the law.

CHORUS: Hey ma roo dum day, . . . etc.

8. When we got oor sentences
   We aa stared round an round.
   The judge says, 'It's fourteen years
   Ye're in Van Diemen's Land.'

CHORUS: Hey ma roo dum day, . . . etc.

9. When Tattie Jock he heard o' this
   He roared an grat full sair
   'A hunner guineas I'll gie for them,
   If that will pey the score.'

CHORUS: Hey ma roo dum day, . . . etc.

10. He says, 'A bag o' gold I will produce
    If that will clear my men.'
    But the lawyer only told him this
    'Money would never clear his men.'

CHORUS: Hey ma roo dum day, . . . etc.

11. As we were comin up through Perth
You could hear the post-boys cry
'It's sad to see such able men
All bound for Botany Bay.'

CHORUS: Hey ma roo dum day, . . . etc.

12. When we arrived in Botany Bay,
Some letters we did send,
Aa aboot the hardships
We endured in a foreign land.

CHORUS: Hey ma roo dum day, . . . etc.

PLOUGHMAN'S TOASTS

Here's tae ma bridle and brecham
And here's tae ma harness an heims
And here's tae the bonnie wee lassie
That lies in the plooman's airms.

Here's the rose that buds and blows
When ye've pu'd it as your own
The rose shall fade an so shall the maid
That lies too long alone.

A FRAGMENT

It's porridge, brose and tatties
They feed me wi their pigs,
While they gae jantin roon aboot
An drivin in their gigs.

[Barbara recounts her memories of her father]

'Dad was born on the 21st March 1906 at Capledrae, Auchterderran. He was about five years old when he was boarded out to an auntie who already had thirteen kids. She was very cruel to him. He was beaten often and slept on an old sack in the corner of the kitchen. He used to make us cry at the thought of how they used him, but the funny bits would come through to make us laugh, like when he found a golf ball and set it on the fire and it exploded and stuck to his cousin's nose.

'He was well-known as a bit of a character in Dunkeld, when he worked with the MacDougalls of Fiungarth. It was there a horse kicked him on the head, just above the hairline. The story goes that he picked himself up and kicked the horse back! He used to show us the dent he always had there.

'He delivered milk to the Mill Inn, and at the back of the Mill Inn were huts and caravans that really poor people lived in during the last war. It was there he found my mother. She was a war widow with a son and baby daughter. Her two older daughters were in a home. Dad was delivering milk this day and he heard the bairn greetin and went to find out what was wrong. He found mother, almost deaf, nearly blind and starving. He gave her some milk and started bringing her tatties, meal flour and milk from the farm. He took pity on the poor woman. So one day, he went to Nell, his fiancée, and said, 'Marry me now or I take someone else that needs looking after'. Nell was too cosy to give up her lifestyle and Dad went to Mum, asked for her birth lines and went and put the banns up. Poor Mum didn't know what was happening. He was so good to her, it was unbelievable. There wasn't any room on the farm for a married man, so he moved to Mains o' Myrtle near Peterculter, where I was born.

'When we were at Castle o' Fiddes, there was aye a ceilidh in the cattler's hoose! There was Sandy and Alec from the bothy at Clocknahill, where Rabbie Burns' father is reputed to have lived before his move to Ayr. Sandy played the moothie and Alec the melodeon and there was the carpenter from Drumlithie, locally known as Skite — I can't recall his real name now! He played the fiddle, Dad the Jew's harp and spoons. Who could ask for a better band? The fiddler taught me a version of the Highland fling and a jig and these were my party pieces. I also sang, 'I'm No Awa Tae Bide Awa'. They would all come round to our house. It was a cup of tea and Mum's baking (which was awful). Our ceilidhs didn't go on late because Dad always had to be up for 4:30 a.m. to milk. The Rosses from upstairs would come down — there were five of them and seven of us; sometimes some of the fourteen Walkers, the five Laurences and the three Duncans would come and the farmer, Geordie Munroe, his wife and daughter and auld Babbie. Bent at the waist from her years of slavery, she never managed to stand up straight. These were all the people of the Castle of Fiddes, its two out farms, the East and West Bendings.

'We were all taught to lead cattle for the shows. All the cows had proper names, exquisitely drawn in wee books. Dad aye wore his nicky tams, braces and flat cap, turned worn back to front when he was milking. I'm sure he didn't lose many beasts, as his pure will-power kept them alive. My sister got stuck in Aberdeen when there was a foot and mouth outbreak — Dad didn't let her come home till a long time after the scare was over. He took no chances.

'Show days were high days. Sometimes up all night brushing, polishing and making sure nothing was missed. There was a special kist with all our brushes, powder for whitening, combs and halters. The bull even had a pole specially for the shows. We got a row if we didn't get a ticket! I was leading cattle in the ring from six years old. The day a calf was born, Dad had one of us bairns with it on a rope leading it round and round the close, so as it'd learn to walk properly. We also had to teach them to stand. They were all posers. I bet that was the secret of his success at shows. He took all the big prizes and, of course, he got a back-hander – the only money he kept to himself. He drank it, I'm afraid! But what a merry drunk – singing his head off and everybody got a bag of sweeties!

'We were always very poor. He used to go to the local roups and bring back sixpenny lots. What fun we had, raking through the junk. I used to moan about always having cast-offs, being the wee-est. The jumble sales was where our togs came from, or the big hoose. The first time Dad got a new suit was when my sister Muriel was named. He'd never had new clothes in all his life. Mum didn't keep well but Dad was aye there. He always managed to feed us. He'd go out and do the cattle, come in and get us ready for school, make our porridge, then be there at night for us to come home to. We'd a two-and-a-half-mile walk to the school and back. We lived off milk, tatties, neeps, pheasant, salmon, crabs and cockles. Dad swapped pheasant and salmon for shellfish at Stoney [Stonehaven] – all poached. Rabbits, of course, were common fare too. I remember him getting up in the night if one of us was ill; it was aye in his sark tails, not pyjamas.

'Once, he took us camping to Milltimber; we went away on the Saturday and were to come home on the Sunday. All we had was a tarpaulin sheet. As it got dark, a storm got up. Dad had fixed the sheet up and made a fire; he fed us porridge, tatties on the fire and singed bread and marge. We all crawled in on the bare ground. Well, our sheet took off and so did the pony. We were all soaking, but Dad kent where the bothy was, so took us there to spend the rest of the night! He'd to hunt high and low for the pony and we got back home late on Sunday. The only other holiday we ever had was one week in the bothy at Fiungarth – the holiday of a lifetime! We set out on 15th July 1955, my birthday, in a taxi all the way from Castle o' Fiddes. I wonder where the money came from? I honestly don't know. One memory I have of that holiday is of Dad taking us outside and there was this great boulder. He told us to sit by it and listen hard and the boulder would say awfy slowly – NAE-THING! I sat for hours!

'Dad saw the advent of the tractor as marking the beginning of the end of farming as he had known it. Dad and I stood at the stable door and watched the first 'Fergie' come home. I'll always mind the sadness in his voice as he looked at the horses and said, "Well, lads, we've had oor day." Dad predicted a long time ago that there would soon only be the farmer and his sons, working on a farm. In our byre, there were three milking ninety-six cows, two carrying milk and one in the dairy cooling. It was a lot of work scrubbing, cleaning, mucking, feeding and bedding, and then you'd all the calves, heifers and bullocks. Draff was the big feed. We got the job of tramping it down. It was hot and steamy on a cold day. Dad used to let us eat the locust beans in the cattle feed, also sup the treacle.

'I've seen him struggle to milk a heifer for the first time. He was so gentle, no matter how hard she kicked. One split his nose with her horns, but he never gave up till she was quiet, then he attended to himself. Didn't believe in beating his cattle. We all carried sticks to bring the kye in, but don't let Dad catch you giving them a thwack!'

MABEL SKELTON

Of course, it was not just men who worked on the farms. One of the most important members of the workforce was the housekeeper, or 'kitchie deem'. As Charlie Murray showed us, on those farms where the men ate in the kitchen, it depended largely on the housekeeper whether what was served up was palatable or not. Food was plain and often sparse, so she would often have not much to work with — mainly brose, kale and potatoes. On farms where the men lived and ate in the bothy, the poor women would often try to keep the place tidy and clean. This was no easy task, for while the bothy billies might know how to 'cairt and harrow and ploo', they were mostly ill-versed in the niceties of housekeeping.

The late Mabel Skelton of Arbroath was one such woman. She worked on a local farm in her early twenties and had a habit from an early age of making her own songs, as well as picking some up from her great-grandmother and her grandmother and from any others she heard singing around her. The song she wrote at Peasiehill has a distinct bothy-ballad style:

PEASIEHILL

7 dig - ger, at me he aye was win - kin'

10 Di - rum - a - do - a - di - rum - a - day, di - rum - a - do - a -

13 dan - dy, di - rum - a - do - a - di - rum - a - day, the

16 fair - mer's life is dan - dy.

2. Washin oot the milkin cans, cleanin oot the bothy
   Biled tatties, mashed neeps, cauld brose an coffee.

CHORUS: Dirrum-a-doo . . . etc.

3. Cottar wife was affa clean, she was affa neat O.
   Hung her washin on the fence, the fairm horse ate her sheet O.

CHORUS: Dirrum-a-doo . . . etc.

4. When you're workin on the land, my advice to you, sir,
   Always wear your nicky tams when spreadin fertiliser!

CHORUS: Dirrum-a-doo . . . etc.

Another of her own compositions is 'Awa Wi Ma Laddie', which mentions the old name of her home town:

AWA WI MA LADDIE

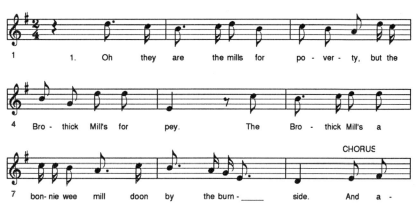

1 1. Oh they are the mills for po - ver - ty, but the

4 Bro - thick Mill's for pey. The Bro - thick Mill's a

CHORUS

7 bon- nie wee mill doon by the burn-_____ side. And a -

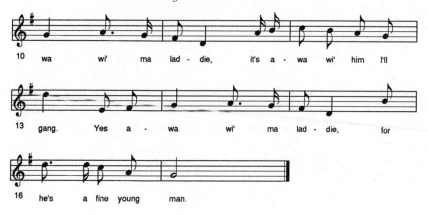

10 wa wi' ma lad-die, it's a-wa wi' him I'll

13 gang. Yes a-wa wi' ma lad-die, for

16 he's a fine young man.

2. I tuik him doon tae the Brothick Mill
Tae see them aa gaun in,
Rosy cheeks and curly hair,
That's the wey they rin.

CHORUS: And awa wi ma laddie . . . etc.

3. Maybe I'll get mairried yet,
Maybe no ava.
Maybe I'll get mairried yet
Tae ma laddie far awa.

CHORUS: And awa wi ma laddie . . . etc.

Mabel's song repertoire was wide and varied and ranges from ancient ballads like 'Lord Randal', 'The Beggarman' and 'Oor Guidman cam Hame at Een' to old songs learned from her mother and grandmother like 'The Bonnie Lassie's Answer':

THE BONNIE LASSIE'S ANSWER

1 1. Now, it's for the want o' poc-ket mo-ney and

4 for the want ___ o' cash maks mo-ny a bon-___ nie

7 lad-die leave his bon-nie lass. "But _____

2. 'Bide at hame, my bonnie laddie, dinna ging sae far!
   For little, little dae ye ken the dangers o' the war'.
   'The Queen is short o' men, my love, I for one must go
   And for the very life of me, I darenae answer, "No".'

CHORUS: It's aye, 'Oh no, my love'! . . . etc.

Other old songs included 'Happy We've been Aathegither', 'The Braes o' Strathblane' (which she got from her Irish great-grandmother as 'The Braes o' Strabane'), 'The Corncrake amang the Whinnyknowes', 'The Braes o' Balquhidder' and 'The Hielan Soldier' to Irish songs like 'She Moved Through the Fair', 'The Pride o'Lagimore' and 'Where the Shannon Flows'. Mabel knew lots of the popular songs of the time like the jingoistic music-hall songs used on recruiting drives in the First World War. As a cook at Barry Camp near Arbroath, Mabel had a great deal of admiration and affection for Highland regiments and wrote more than one song on this theme.

Her voice was strong, clear and very expressive, and she suited her style and expression to the kind of song she was singing, ranging from a certain grandeur for the old ballads, to a light, dancing lilt for what she called the 'fun' songs. Mabel's cheerfulness and interest in collecting songs remained with her all her life.

*****

'It was called Peasiehill: I fee'd on that farm. I had tae clean the bothy. The first day I was there, I says, "Ye know this, Mr Wilkie, I dinny ken hoo I'm gaun tae get on, because I've never lived at a farm". He says, "Ye needna worry. Once ye get on yer nicky tams an get in that bothy wi thae boys, ye'll be aa richt!" There were some guys there that widna lea' me alone, 'cause I was young, I was jist aboot twenty-two. I had two babies an I wis a widow. I had to clean the milkin cans an everything, aa the gas jets, as the cows' udders, aa the electric mixers an what have you. Every time I went tae clean the bothy, the [potato] pit men were there, five o' them on tap o' the pit. I went over tae open the bothy door an they were beltin me wi tatties! I got the place aa cleaned up, went through aa the old socks – what a mess! – it was awful! Aa kinds o socks, football papers, magazines – I cleaned the whole lot oot. The guy comes for his denner, says, "Whit hae ye done wi thae guid stockins that wis lyin doon there?" I says, "Guid stockins? They were aa sweat. I've thrown them intae the bin!" He says, "Whit aboot the newspapers?" I says, "They were jist rubbish! I've thrown them oot!" he says, "But we *need* aa them!" I says, "Well, ye'll need tae get them oot yersel. An dinna leave them lyin aboot. Pit them in a corner."

'When I tried tae come ooi the bothy, that boys is aa standing on tap o' that pit an I'd tae defend masel frae tatties. But one day, I'm in washin the milk bottles – there wis millions o' them – an I hid jist washed the fleer, when I hears them speakin ootside. I wis jist gaun tae gie it anither rinse owre, when I thocht, "That's them swines at that tattie pit. They're gaen awa tae get their denner an they've ducked oot ahead o' me again. They'll be in here askin fur a drink o' milk." They always did that. Then they chased me roon the milk hoose an I'd tae run screamin. I'd say, "I'm gaun tae tell the fairmer," an they'd say, "He's awa tae the mairket!" So I hears them – an the water wis dirty tae – an I turn roon an threw the haill lot o' water on them. An ye want tae hae seen them! They said, "Whit did ye dae that for, wifie?" I says, "Well, that's whit ye get! Jist stop throwin tatties at me!".

'They're standin ootside eatin their pieces an aa their claes is steamin on the biler. Alang comes the foreman – he made them sweat blood when they were workin – an he says, "What in hell's gaun on here?" I says, "Well, they're aye throwin tatties at me, so I jist threw a bucket o water on them!'' He says, ''Some cairry-on! Wait till I tell the fairmer. An you're jist as bad.'' I says, ''The fairmer's no here. He's awa tae the mairt.'' He says, ''Well, when he comes back. An weet or no, get them so-and-so claes on an get crackin on thae pits!'' It wis great! I had a lot o' fun on that fairm. I really liked it, ye know.

'One day, my neighbour asked me in for a cup o' tea an she told me, 'I was standin oot there, while you were in the bothy, when doon the road came the four ploomen wi a horse an cairt an their bunnets across their chest, an their heids doon, walkin slowly. My man was there an when he passed me, I says, ''Hi Ed.'' He never answered an naebody answered. They went on to that field there an they went right to the middle o' the field an they lifted something oot o' the cairt an they buried it, an they sang, 'There is a Happy Land'. They come oot wi their bunnets on, an I says, ''Here, c'mere, whit's aa this, 'There is a Happy Land,' an aa thing?'' ''Well,'' he said, ''we've been cleanin oot the byre, an ye ken the fairmer goes an messes in the byre, an we picked up a turd as big as that [indicating a large size] an we pit it in the cairt an took it tae the field an buried it an gave it a funeral service!''

> Boys in khaki, boys in blue,
> Here's the best of jolly good luck to you.
> You're all right in love and war,
> You'll get there just the same as you done before.
> Boys in khaki, boys in blue,
> It's no idle boast or brag,
> When both of us get together,
> There's gonna be dirty weather
> For anyone who tramples on the flag!

'These recruiting songs I have were sung in the music hall because they were getting very stuck for recruits in 1914. So the women always sang songs about soldiers and sailors to entice the men to come up – the recruiting sergeant was up on the stage. The singer always kissed the man to try and invite him up. So any young guy who was hungry, didn't have a job and wanted to kiss a beautiful woman, he went up and joined the army and got hissel killed in France! He went up and wrote his name and got his shillin from the sergeant and he was in the army.

'Ye know how son-in-laws are with their mother-in-laws? My granny was aye sayin things to my father and tellin him what to do. For instance, my mother had another child and another child and she kept sayin tae ma Dad things like, ''Jock, dae ye no think it's time ye stoppit haein bairns?'' An ma father used tae get real wild. So when ma granny had a hot stout, she used tae sing this song because she wanted him to know she wouldn't be livin forever:

1. Happy we've been aa thegither
    Happier still we'll be an aa
    Come lads an kiss your lasses
    Auld wives'll wear awa.

2. Happy we've been aa thegither
    Happier still we'll be an aa
    Aye drunk an never sober
    Happier still we'll be an aa.

'Some of my granny's songs have words of advice to young girls:

> When I was a wee thing I lived wi ma granny
> An mony's the advice the auld body gied me,
> She telt me 'Beware an take care o' your riches,
> And ne'er lift your petticoats owre your knee.'

'Another of my granny's songs to the tune o' 'The Laird O' Cockpen'
is about other things grannies did!

1. I'll no ging hame tae ma granny nae mair
    I winna ging hame tae ma granny nae mair
    She skelpit ma dowp an she made me greet sair
    An I'll nae ging hame tae ma granny nae mair.

2. I'll awa back tae ma mither A wull
    I'll awa back tae ma mither A wull.
    She'll gie me a maik if A run for a gill
    I'll awa back tae ma mither A wull.

'I remember the Temperance woman called Carrie Mason. She was
always shouting and shaking her fist, "Down with drink! It's the curse
of the nation!" Then someone wrote:

1. O Carrie, stop your carry-on!
    O Carrie you're mad to look upon!
    It's sad for to think,
    We must do without a drink,
    Carrie, Carrie, Carrie stop your carry-on!

2. Jocky Bendy's lyin seik, guess what'll mend him?
    Sixty kisses in a cloot, lassie will ye send him?
    I've a pot and I've a pan an I've a kale ladle
    If I never get a man, I'll never get a cradle.

'This was a wee song sung by the fisher folk:

1. My Mammy says that I must go
    Wi ma Daddy's denner O
    Chappit tatties, beef and steak,
    Twa reid herrin an a bawbee bake.

2. Went tae the river, I couldnae get across
    I peyed ten shillins for an auld blin horse.
    Jumped on its back an its banes gae a crack,
    I played on ma fiddle till the boatie came back.
    The boatie came back an we aa jumped in
    The boatie capsized an we aa fell in.

'These are some wee songs we used to dance to when we were children:

[To the tune of 'Oh The Shearin's No For You']

Tak the buckles aff your sheen, ma bonnie lassie O
Tak the buckles aff your sheen, ma bonnie lassie O
Tak the buckles aff your sheen, for your dancin days are deen
Tak the buckles aff your sheen, ma bonnie lassie O

O the lad that canna kiss his lass
Is no the lad for me
O the lad that canna kiss his lass
Is no the lad for me,
O the lad that canna kiss his lass
Is no the lad for me,
My bonnie laddie's kissed twa or three.

First a heel and then a toe,
Lassie can ye dance the polka O?
I can dance and I can sing,
Lassie can ye dance the Hielan Fling?

Ma mither sent me tae the well
Better had she gone hersel,
Broke the bowl an fell masel
Dance Katie Bairdie.

Annie Bell
Photo: Aåse Goldsmith

ANNIE BELL

Anyone who has attended TMSA Festivals at Blairgowrie, Kinross and Kirriemuir will know Annie Bell: singer, melodeon and mouth organ player, whistler and diddler extraordinaire. Born in Kinross-shire, she worked in service all over Tayside, married a ploughman and cottared with him in Perthshire and the Borders. The story she tells is of hard work, long hours and little money, but the recurrent theme of her story is of happiness, contentment and enjoyment of all forms of music. Told off by judge Alec Green at Kirrie festival for stamping her foot while she was whistling in the whistling competition, she told him, 'All the best musicians do it'. Alec felt it was taking over from the melody, but she retorted, 'Well, I've one bad leg. If I'm not to stamp my foot, I'll just have to cut the other off.'

*****

'I was born in Milnathort in 1916; that's where I first saw the light of day. My father was a serving soldier. He was in the Argyll and Sutherland Highlanders and I didn't see him till he came home from France when I was about three years old. I didnae like that man! Didn't know him, ye see. He had a moustache and I just didn't know who this man was who had invaded my mother's home. However we soon got to know each other. I went to school in Milnathort, until I was about seven. I had rosy cheeks, like rosy apples, the teachers told me. I can remember very vividly the nurse coming in every week to bone-comb the hair and pick the lice oot and put them in the fire – not *my* hair, thankfully. Scarlet fever, diphtheria, tuberculosis, all these things were very prevalent in these days – consumption as it was known, and cancer was just 'a growth' – 'the auld body deed wi a growth'.

'I had plenty o' wholesome food, plenty o' porridge, soups, eggs and rabbits; they killed the pig and made potted heid. We had herrin an saut fish and aa these kinds o' things. Chickens – ye can get a chicken any time now, but you couldnae get a chicken then, except at Christmas, your chicken or your auld hen. If you were working wi a fairmer and he decided to give you your Christmas, it was an auld hen, hung on the back o' the door. Ye jist plucked it and cooked it in the big pot beside the fire – nae electricity – we used coals and sticks. When we went oot wi the bairns in the pram, we aye come hame wi a load o' sticks for kinnlin. An paraffin lamps, of course, an the cannles. We bought our cereals – they were aa sold loose. Ye could get two ounces of tea and a quarter o' butter and half a pound o' sugar, a jar o' treacle or syrup for a penny. Ye took your jar an they filled it up at the grocer's oot o' the barrel. There was no teabread or fancy cakes the way ye see them now in the baker's shop, but there were plenty o' tattie scones, treacle scones, bannocks and oatcakes. I can mind on my mother making tablet and toffee and greasing her hands and she'd pull the toffee and I pulled, and she pulled and I pulled, and it twisted and twisted and then we cut it off into bits and made rock. She was a marvellous baker, a marvellous cook. She could make a rabbit pie into a feast for a king. The shopkeepers were kindly folk and at Christmas you would maybe get your box o' sweeties, a quarter o' tea and a calendar. The baker would gie ye a cake o' shortie.

'I went to school, as everyone else had to do in these days, and played aa the usual games in the playground: London Bridge is Falling Down, Bee Baw Babbity, Jing-a-Rings, Stand Up and Face your Lover, roonders and tig, hide-and-seek, skipping games. I used to sing a lot in these days. You know, there was the modulator on the wall and the teacher used the pointer and we'd sing, 'Doh-mi-soh-doh' – I was really quite good at that. I went through school and qualified at eleven and took a bursary for Perth Academy at twelve. It was valued from Glenfarg and we actually moved to Kinross and my parents would have had to pay the difference, which my father wasn't really prepared to do. I wasn't very happy about that, but I *was* quite happy to leave the school because we lived on a farm at that time and I was quite happy among the beasts and things like that. My father played the fiddle and my granny played the melodeon, so I guess it was on the cards that I would be musical. My brother was also musical, and he got the first melodeon that came into the hoose and when he was finished and moved up a grade, I got the leftover. I went to step-dancing classes and paid a shilling a time, and did the Highland Fling and the Sword Dance and the Sean Triubheas. That's when I think I started to diddle, because I had no music and so that I could do it properly when I went back the next week – that's how I started diddling. I didn't know I was diddling in these days, but that's really what diddling is all about.

I also got a mouth organ, and the teacher took it from me when she found me playing it when I should have been working. I actually used to play the mouth organ and dance the Highland Fling at the same time – can you imagine it?

'There was a time we lived in this really eerie house, which I've never forgotten. My father had engaged this elderly man, who had a bit of a heart problem, to go round about and empty the snares for him. He'd been away home for a weekend and had come back, and on the Monday night, when my mother opened the wall press and father spied this black pudding and says, "Oh good, a black pudden! We'll hae that for oor supper, Jess." She says, "No, no! You're not gettin that the night, it's for the morn." This old Bob piped up and said, "Och come on, Jess, let's hae the black pudden the nicht. We'll maybe nane o' us be here the morn." Well, do you know this, the strangest thing happened. There was the most awfy scratching and squealing at the window, the like of which I've never heard before. There was no explanation for it. It was about eight o'clock in the evening and it literally sounded like someone scratching a nail down the window pane and rattling at the window. Well, do you know this, the old man took ill and he died at midnight, and if that wisnae a sign of foreboding, I don't know what it was. I've certainly never forgotten it.

'I left the school at fourteen with a good education, which is something ye always carry about wi ye, really. I've done various things in my time. One of the jobs I had to go to was in a castle and I arrived just as the other cook general was leaving, so I didnae really know what to do. She said there was partridges to cook for the dinner at night and there was other things to do as well. So I got set to and I cooked the partridges and whatever else there was to cook and it went up the stair. When the plates came back down again, there was wee tickies o' corn and grass on the side of the plates. I'd forgotten to take the gebbie oot! The partridge's crop.

'I spent some time as a probationary nurse in 1932–3. They were taking in young girls with a good education, at sixteen and it was a sanatorium where there was tuberculosis and patients were dying like flies. Most of them came from the mining villages. Maybe the farmworkers were poor, but the miners were even poorer. We had the fresh air up above; they were down in the bowels of the earth. When they got their pay at the weekend, it was just a big splash out in the frying-pan. There, I encountered some very peculiar people that were inclined to be envious if you were a young lass with a sparkle in her eye and you could get the wrath of the sisters and the old matron doon on your neck for nothing at all. It was a terrible job and I wouldn't want to go back to that again! I was round by Glenalmond not so long ago, they're building houses there now and I said, "There must be hundreds of ghosts round here." I remember the sick blocks – the buildings were known as 'blocks' – where the worst, most ill patients were and I'm still there in my dreams! I was only there about a year when I decided it wasn't for me, and I just went back to domestic service.

'Ye just went where ye could find work. Immediately before I got married, I was a clippie on the buses. That's where I left at eighteen, coming up for nineteen and I married Harry Bell, a plooman laddie. I've got a wee song about that:

THE PLOUGHMAN

1. Ere I was se - ven - teen, I had coor - ted mo- ny's a yin, an' ma hairt it was as rest - less as ma ee, Un - til a sim- mer's day in the mer- ry month o' May, a fair ploo- man lad - die cam a- coor - tin' me.

2. Though his pooches were near timm there was never anither yin,
    We focht at times and then we would agree,
    We would pledge oor love anew and promise to be true,
    An e'er lang we wed, ma plooman lad an me.

3. Well, when feein time came roon, nae mair the orra loon,
    But a mairried chiel's position his intent,
    Wi his arles in his pooch, we thocht that we were rich,
    An we settled in a hamely but an ben.

4. Fae on the Border lands sae fair tae the valley o' the Tay,
    Fae the hills and glens o' Angus we hae roamed,
    An wi courage, faith and love and blessings from above,
    We hae shared the joys, the laughter and the tears.

5. Tho noo we're gettin grey, I ayeways bless the day,
    The plooman laddie socht me for his bride,
    Through troubles great or sma, I'll gledly face them aa
    Wi ma handsome plooman laddie by ma side.

'We've had a hard life; fifty-four years, we've been married. Harry did quite a lot of hill shepherding and a lot of weekend work amongst cattle. He was a plooman when we were married; he was an orra horse and then, of course, he got a pair of horse. Then he wanted a bittie more money and he had tae work a whole weekend for about four shillings more than the plooman got. The plooman was finished on Saturday at twelve o'clock, but the cattleman and the shepherd worked the whole weekend and maybe the horseman's wage would be twenty-eight shillings a week and the cattleman's wage was thirty-four shillings. You didn't get overtime in these days; you got a 'harvest pound' – one pound at the end of the harvest. The first place we were ever on was Lower Tarsappie, just on the outskirts of Perth, and the farmer there just gave us two pounds a fortnight and kept the five shillings a week till the end of the term. This was in case you would break your bargain, you see. So that was the first five-pound note I ever had at the end of the term. Oh that five-pound note bought an awfy lot – a kitchen dresser, a bit o' carpet for the floor, and bed and dressing table for the bedroom, boots for him and shoes for me. That five pounds was elastic! I thought it was just a delight, me walking through the streets of Perth with a five-pound note in my hand. It was really something!

'We started off our married life in Perthshire and we went into Fife and from there, we went back to Kinross, where we both belonged. After that, we went to Kelso and I had a third child there which didn't live. I never really cared for the Borders. From Kelso, we came up to Banchory, just on the outskirts of Meikleour, and from there, we've just been around this area for a long time: Harry working on farms and I was just working for other people like farmers' wives, scrubbing oot the kitchen on hands and knees and doing odd jobs and working in the fields. Then, however, a grand-uncle from America died and left me a wee bit o' money, not a lot by today's standards, but enough to buy us a small but-and-ben in Jessie Street in Blairgowrie. When we bought it we shared a toilet, then we converted a walk-in cupboard into a toilet with a wash-hand basin. From there, we went into the council house and that's it. It's been a very chequered life and I've seen and done a lot.

'It was hard when you had your washing and your bairn's nappies to dry and nae washing-machines, tumble-driers or anything like that, no even a pulley or a wash-house. You just put the big pot upon the fire and your tub in the middle of the floor or on the tub stool – a three-legged wooden contraption with a bar on top for the hand wringer and ye got on with the job. You filled up the big pot with a pail fae the water outside, then you heated it up and put the washing in to bile, then ye took them out tae sine – a long, hard business. Ye usually just got corned beef on a day like that.

'We always laid stuff by for the winter. When you had your garden, ye took up your tatties, carrots and whatever ye could and stored it. You sauted herrin in a barrel and ye could also buy in these dried salted fish – a big piece of cod which were as hard as a brick and you kept it hanging on the back of the door. You'd take about six inches off it each time and soaked it aa night, then ye threw away that water and then ye biled it up. Then ye threw away that water and biled it up again and then you could start to cook with it, because it was *really* salty fish which was very tasty. You never see that nowadays.

'There were feeing markets, like Little Dunning in Perth. Little Dunning was a general holiday and the streets were lined with stalls, right from the top of the High Street to the bottom. If you didn't have a job, ye looked in the Courier which took adverts. If you hadn't got fixed up with a job by the time the feeing market came roon, ye just went into town and the farmers approached you if you looked a likely lad, but if you hadn't contact with the farmers, you went to the saddler. He had names on his books and he'd get in contact with a farmer on your behalf and he took a fee from the farmer. For your arles, if you were lucky, you got five shillings, the main thing was about half a croon. Half a croon changed hands and that was you bound to the farmer for six months or a year.

'Oh but they were hard devils! No wonder a lot of them died and left a lot of money – they wouldn't part with it! In these days, you paid something like half a croon a month into the Prudential, or the Ancient Order of Foresters, or the Ancient Order of Shepherds, and when you were sick, they gave you approximately five shillings a week, and you gave all of that to the farmer and he gave you your pay. But that only went on for a week or two; if you went on longer than that, it was just get on with it the best way you could. That was before the National Health, of course, and I don't know how folks nowadays would get on if they had to live like that because there was absolutely no security. There was no such thing as a union in these days: it was just the survival of the fittest. We always had itchy feet, Harry and I, and we never liked to settle long in one place. You thought you might improve your lot a bittie, but it didn't always work out that way.

'When we were on the farms, we all got together. Ye were always getting invitations into somebody's house – if it was mine this weekend, it was somebody else's next weekend and there was always a fiddle, melodeon, mouth organ or something like that. We used to get a good-going band wi a melodeon or an accordion and I got a couple o' sticks to hit pot lids and we had some good rattling times! Oh yes, these were very happy times! We've been *really* poor, down to our last ha'penny, wi just the meal, the milk and the tatties, but I've never asked, borrowed or begged and we've just got along well together. I've kept up my singing. I *love* to sing. If I hear anybody else singing. I want to join in. It's just a way of life wi me. As far as the whistling goes, I've whistled aa my days – I just *love* to whistle. I picked up songs on hearing other people singing them and going to the TMSA festivals. I've heard a lot and I was singing Scottish songs, the ordinary ones that are in the books, but then I'd heard some o' these awfully bonnie songs like 'The Bonnie Moorhen' and things like that, which I liked very much:

THE BONNIE MOORHEN

2. My bonnie moorhen has feathers enew,
   Lots o' fine colours but nane o' them blue,
   She's red and she's white and she's green and she's grey,
   My bonnie moorhen, come hither away.
   Come up by Glen Dui and doon by Glen Dee,
   Roon by Kinclaven and hither tae me,
   For Ronald and Donald are oot on the fen
   Tae brak the wings o' my bonnie moorhen.

Jock Duncan
Photo: Aåse Goldsmith

VOICES FROM THE NORTH-EAST

The North-East of Scotland has retained its traditions longer than most other regions, and is rightly admired for doing so. Now that the oil boom and the decline of fishing and farming are transforming the character of the area, many people will wonder if the vigour of the language and music and song traditions will continue. These were forged and sustained by the land and the people who lived on it.

Ian Olson, writing about the state of North-East society around the turn of the century, dispels the myth that it was an area with an uneducated and declining rural population, and declares: 'there were probably fewer illiterate rustics per square mile than anywhere else in Europe'. [*History of Scottish Literature* Vol. IV. (ed. Cairns Craig, Aberdeen University Press, 1987).] The songs that Gavin Greig and James Duncan collected about that period were not the last gasps of a dying culture, but the rich flowerings of a thriving one.

JOCK DUNCAN

Certainly, Jock Duncan, with his rich Buchan tongue laced with occasional equally expressive English phrases, is an intelligent, imaginative and articulate chronicler, who can make you feel his pride in his heritage. His recollections include songs that relate to the daily work and play he shared in and he sings them in the same natural and warm-hearted way that he talks.

*****

'I wis born in New Deer district, Gellybrae wis the name o' the place. There wis six o' us born there. My father had that farm afore he wis mairried an the wey he met my mither wis — she wis a school teacher at Culter Cullen School, an she wis born an brought up in the Bogenlea o' Byth. This Sunday nicht, she wis bicyclin hame tae Culter Cullen — aboot twenty miles — an it came on fit ye caa blin drift an she wis overcome wi exhaustion at a place they caa the Dam Brigs, which wis only half a mile fae ma father's place. An she struggled through till she saw a chink o' licht an this wis the fairm kitchen licht, shinin through the windae fae Gellybrae. So she knockit at the door an ma father's sister, my Aunt Lizzie, took her in, an there she hid tae stey oot the storm. She renewed acquaintance wi ma father an romance must hae blossomed 'cause they were mairried within three month. She cam hame as mistress o' the fairm toon at Gellybrae. The First World War had finished an she lost her sweetheart in it, ye see, an mairried him on the stot.

'My father wis an affa big man — he wis an affy strength, an strong men at that time hid tae cairry one-and-a-half-hundredweight bags o' corn or two-hundredweight bags o' barley at thrashin mulls. He did that at Royston for two days an suddenly collapsed and my mither hid an invalid on her hands for two years — he wisna allowed tae dae a hand's turn. Then he come aa right. They said he'd strained his hert. I never kent him tae lift onything heavy again. He fairmed at Gellybrae a fyowe year until my grandfather gid oot an he gid in an took owre the ferm at South Faddenhill. It wis a hunder acre an we'd fower acre o' moss. I wis jist three year-auld fen they moved. I wis born twa month owre seen an Dr Craib out o' New Deer said, ''Och no, the baby's nae gane tae lest long. He'll be deid ere mornin.'' So my father said it wis kill or cure an he gave me a gweed tablespeen o' fusky. He aye says it wis the accoont o' that that I come better. I had several maladies in my youth an double pneumonia wis een o' them, but sin that time, I never hid a day's illness.

'He wis a great man amang horses, a great horse-breeder, an they were aa that, aa roon that kintraside. I aye mind the names: Yvonne was one that come fae Gellybrae tae Faddenhill, and Gyp wis anither, and Big Bess. They were aa prolific an studded really guid foals every time. We hid a shelt, a big beast, an she wis in a gig, an she wis in the sledge, a proper sledge for the job, wi luxury seats for gan tae the kirk an aa thing. This shelt hid a great speed aboot her. I mind ma father gane awa tae Keith, an comin hame, it cam on thunner and lichtnin and she took fleg an she never stoppit aa the wey back, an that wis thirty-something miles. I wis at the pitten awa o' her, when she wis twenty-seiven year auld awa back in 1941. She wisna deein heavy work by that time, jist an easy job, rollin the ley corn park. She jist fell doon deid efter she wis roon a bittie; it wis a hert attack. It wisna worth phonin the vet so ma father phoned the knacker. But he hidna the hert tae see her awa himself; he jist couldna face't, so he gave the job tae me. It wis a gey hard job for me tee, tae see awa a shelt that did twa generations an twa ferm touns, an seein the First World War an this wis the second een. I helpit the mannie load her, an it wis gey hard tae look at her empty staa that nicht.

'There were aye plenty o' foals an I used tae help oot at the Foal Sales. The first time I wis there, I wis only eight year auld. I hid that job every year until I left the school, an it wis a great enterprise, the Foal Sales. Ye rose at something like three o'clock in the mornin an I'd hardly slept that nicht — I thocht this wis a great adventure. There wid be something like five hundred foals an it wis in Aiberdeen. It wis a great adventure an a thing ye never see nooadays, sic an amount o' foals.

'My mither died fen she wis forty-six. I think it wis somethin like meningitis. I wis fourteen year auld at the time. She wis awfy musical, the Lambs were famous as musicians. There wad hae been a lot o' musical evenings in the wintertime — nae ither time. The fiddle players used tae come roon aboot an there wis a young lad caaed Charlie Taylor, an Willie Fowlie — Willie Fowlie wis famous as a fiddler. He wis hidin his light below a bushel, because he'd great hands on him, an this wis a man that hid never been fae hame farther than Aiberdeen in his life! He learned aa these joinery skills at hame, jist himsel, an it amazed me. The nicht Willie dee-it, he wis only fifty-two, his nephew, of whom Willie wis affa prood o', wis playin a viola in a philharmonic orchestra in a programme that Sunday nicht on TV. This instrument wis the second een Willie had made for him.

'I mind at Faddenhill, we hid oor first radio in 1939, fen the war started. I aye mind, we wis cuttin the crap [crop]. It wis an affa brilliant day efter this terrible storm that hid flattened aa the crap, an wis an affa tyave to man and beast, an ma mither wis comin doon wi the pieces an scones an she wis greetin. I aye mind fit she said. ''I hope we're nae gaun tae see mair o' that again.'' She'd heard fae the wireless hoo serious things were an nae doot she mindit aa her relations that wis wipit oot in the First World War an folk 'at she'd kent. But we *did* see aa that again, but nae wi sic a loss o' life in the North-East there, nothin like it.

'It wis in 1943 I wis bein called up intae the Gordons an I decided tae jine up as a wireless operator/air gunner in the RAF an they took me doon tae Edinburgh. They said ma left eye wisna sae good as ma richt, so they askit if I wad consider goin intae the Forces as a wireless operator only. I did nine months trainin an the war wis owre aboot nine month efter that. I wis abroad as far as France, settin up stagin posts there. I wis at Lyons when the war finished in August 1945 an I got oot in Spring o' 1946.

'Jock Strachan, he aye likit tae cairry on the Ferm o' Crichie at Fyvie as lang as he could. Johnny wis an affa couthy character; affa weel-likit, a prolific storyteller and a renowned horseman. His son, Derek, wha had Bruckleseat next tae Faddenhill, wis anither character. I mind my brother Fred got mairried an Derek got in touch an said, ''Here, we'll organise a feet-washin''. He cam owre wi a tractor and a bogey an he'd a puckle lads an quines, includin masel. We captured Fred an had a gey wild time an landit up in the dam at Faddenhill. We used horse-bleck on him and on aabody else tee – it wis easy tae get at that time. Back owre we went tae Bruckleseat an we got mairchin ben the hoose an he'd aa this fine records o' Jock Strachan to listen til an the place wis fu o' folk. An there wis this pile carpet – if ye set doon a beer, it fell owre an spilled aa the contents – an it must hae been a terrible scene when we left there. We drunk aboot aathing under the sun. There wis naethin left but this green-lookin gin. I dinna ken fit it wis. He took it oot an we startit tae drink it an mechty, there wis a lot o' lads sick on't! It jist cowpit them up. In the mornin, that fine room wis covered wi black bits aa owre't. Derek said, ''Ach never mind! I'll get a servant tae clear it up.'' Nae wey wad she clean thon! His wife wis in London, ye see. She wad never hae allowed the like o' that. That's maybe fy Derek disappeared fae human society for a filie! Went aboot wi a hantit luik on his face at the kirk. He wis under severe petticoat government! Feet-washin wis really a common thing when somebody was gettin mairrit. In fact, I got it deen twice. It wis a tradition ye'd tae cairry on.

'Fen we gaed tae dances, there wis naethin much in the modern line, although we had dancin classes every year at Millbrex. I gaed as a bairn an fen we wis growin up tee. We gaed every year jist for the sake o' entertainment. This man that hid the class bikit somethin like six mile there an six mile back an ye peyed sae mony pence for your class. It wis one wey o' gettin your airm roon a quine, of course it wis! That's the place I met my wife aboot 1946. That wis in the Millbrex Parish an the Parish o' Fyvie. It wis a wee hallie that wis an ex-army hut an wis acquired efter the Boer War. They still had the pictures o' 'Kilted Redcoats Saying Goodbye to their Sweethearts'. In this small hall, they had magnificent plays like 'Mains Wooing' by Gavin Greig, and folk came especially for that home-made kin o' entertainment. They had a Gala every year an that wis for kirk funds tae, an they had bairns' races an there wis aye this fantastic marquee dance at nicht. At the dance, we had the Bill Rennie's Cornetty Band. Bill played best fin blawin the whisky through it. He likit a dram.

'Of coorse, the two great characters that entertained in those days in oor locality wis George Morris an Willie Kemp. Morris wis mairrit tae Willie Kemp's sister an they baith competed against each ither, composin songs. The last time I heard Willie Kemp wis in 1947 or '48, in a concert in New Deer. Morris had a slightly different approach. He composed songs as tho' he wis the farm servant himsel an it wis a magnificent success. I think he wad hae been a hotel-keeper maist o' his life. He wis born in Aiberdeen, but spent most o' his life in Oldmeldrum. The Kemps had the hotel afore him. Then young Bill Morris, he wis the vet. The last time I saw young Morris, he wis judgin us as The Fyvie Loons an Quines against the Kingseat Bothy Billies an the Belnagoakers fae Methlick against the famous Kennethmont Loons and Quines in the toon hall in Inverurie, an I'm afraid we didna come up tae standard: he placed us last in the Final.

'I've been a singer maist o' my life. I enjoyed singin. At that time, we'd no wireless, but we'd a gramophone and Morris's records wis the rage o' the day, an Willie Kemp, an ye'd Curly Mackay on the melodeon with 'Bogieside' an a 'Ythanside' mixture. Then ye'd strains o' some orchestra. We bought nothin, ye ken, but at a roup, ye'd maybe get a gramophone for a few bob, an ye passed the records round tae ither folk when ye got tired o them. Or a lot o' them wis connached! The first een I mind wis by Morris, caaed 'Sleepytoon':

SLEEPYTOON

1. Come aa ye lads that fol-lae the ploo, a
    sto-ry true I'll tell tae you a-boot the
    on-gauns we gang thro' fen we get up in the
    mornin'.

2. At five, oor foreman jumps like a shot
    An he cries, 'Lord sakes, fit a sleepy-heidit lot!
    Are ye aa gaun tae lie there till ye rot
    At sleepytoon in the mornin?'

3. We hae a great muckle kitchie deem,
    I'll swear she's gey near achteen steen,
    The auld cat kittled in een o' her sheen
    Afore she got up in the mornin.

4. Oor bailie's sober thin an sma
   Sideweys he's hardly seen at aa
   But he'll pu neeps wi ony twa
   'At ever got up in the mornin.

5. A keen bit birkie is oor loon
   His mealtimes cost him hauf a croon
   His claes is as ticht he's fleyed tae sit doon
   For tearin his bricks in the mornin.

6. She's a hungry hun the fermer's wife
   Her een says fiddle an the ither says Fife
   A face like a decanter an a nose like a knife
   Wad hash Swadish neeps in the mornin.

7. The missy she is nae sae bad
   It's jist aboot time she had a lad
   I wis eence thinkin o' speirin her Dad
   For his dochter some fine mornin.

8. I've been writin this screed on the cornkist
   I'd better awa or I'll seen be missed
   An I'll get a wallop o' the foreman's fist
   Ta-ta till some ither mornin.

'The Guise O' Teugh' is another great bothy ballad; Jock Strachan sang it:

THE GUISE O' TEUGH

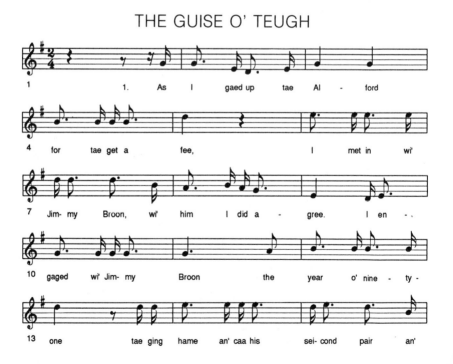

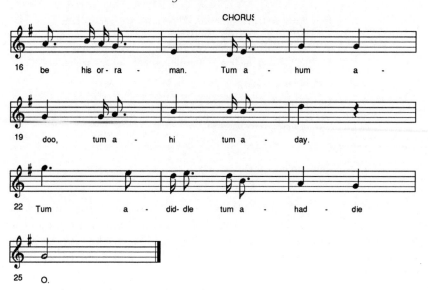

2. I gaed hame tae Guise o' Teugh upon an evening clear.
   Fae aboot an orra hoose, the gaffer did appear.
   'I'm the maister o' the place an that's the mistress there,
   Ye'll get plenty cheese an breid an plenty mair tae spare.'

CHORUS: Tum a-hum a-doo, . . . etc.

3. I sat an ate the cheese an breid till they at me did stare,
   An then I thocht that it wis time tae ging doon an see ma pair.
   Fen I gaed tae the stable, ma pairie for tae view,
   Fegs! They were a dandy pair, a chestnut an a blue.

CHORUS: Tum a-hum a-doo, . . . etc.

4. On the fallaein mornin, I gaed tae the ploo,
   An lang, lang ere lowsin time, ma pairie gart me rue.
   The ploo she wisna workin weel, she widna throw the furr
   The gaffer says a better yin tae the smiddy tae ging fur.

CHORUS: Tum a-hum a-doo, . . . etc.

5. I wrocht awa a month or twa wi unco little clatter,
   Till I played up some nesty tricks an broke a tattie chapper.
   The gaffer he got word o' this an orders did lay doon,
   If I did the like again, he'd pit me fae the toun.

CHORUS: Tum a-hum a-doo, . . . etc.

6. We hae a gallant bailie an Wallis is his name.
   He can fair redd up the kye fen he taks doon the kaim.
   We hae a little bailie an Jamieson's his name.
   He's gaen owre tae Alford an raised an affa fame.

CHORUS: Tum a-hum a-doo, . . . etc.

7.   He's gaen doon tae Charlie Wood's for tae get a dram,
    An lang, lang ere I got doon, the laddie couldnae stand.
    We hae a gallant kitchie lass an Simpson is her name,
    For tae tell her pedigree, I really would think a shame.

CHORUS: Tum a-hum a-doo, . . . etc.

8.   She dresses up on Sunday wi her head above the level,
    Wi twa raw o' ivory wad scare the very Devil,
    An noo ma sang is ended, I won't sing ony more,
    If ony be offended, ye can walk ootside the door.

CHORUS: Tum a-hum a-doo, . . . etc.

'We hade fower [acres] o' peat moss an this wis the third cuttin doon, ye wis richt doon tae clay and there wad be a few generations lookin back tae ancient history, aboot ten thoosand year. This mighty oak trees and ash and hazelnut, they were absolutely solid till ye touched them; then they just fell tae pooder, ye ken, an they became peat years ago. I enjoyed the peat fen I wis a loon. There wis a certain method o' cuttin – unlike the Hielanders – maist o' them cut the peat from the top. This yins wis aboot fourteen inches long by six inches wide by five inches deep. Ye cut it in the face, that high, five feet deep ye gaed doon. Ye cut it aff intil a barra, of saxteen peats, rowed it in the barra till it's standin fifty till a hundred yairds awa, intae raws. The next stage efter a wick wis to spread the raws. The neist wis tae put them up intae fit ye caa rickles, like stooks. There'd be eight tae ten peats in a rickle, jist sit them oot supportin each ither; that let the wind clean through them. The sun dried them till they were hard like coal. Then ye waited maybe anither wick till they were really winned and they could stand the rain fen they were hard like that. We'd a hundred yards tae rowe them in big barras intae a heap, where the horse cairts could come with shelvens an transport them hame. My Father wis a magnificent bigger o' a peat stack. It wis an art, jist like buildin a roof. It wis somethin like fifteen feet wide, onythin up tae thirty tae forty feet long – it wis a hell o' a length. Ye built them like roofin slates, wi a slight hang then aa the rest o' the peats were filled intae the centre. It took somethin like a week tae tak hame the peats an build a peat stack. Oor open kitchie fires took a barra load of peats at a time.

'We had a water thrashin mill, worked by an undertakin in the moss made a hunner years afore by oor forefathers; they'd some sense. The water cam doon intae this dam an then doon this sluice an drove a magnificent water wheel, somethin like twenty-five feet in diameter, with an immense amoont o' paddles. By means o' various transmittin wheels and an overhead cable an pulleys the mill wis driven fae the steadin. That system went oot o' use in 1947 when a tractor drove the mill. The whole magnificent array, even the dam in front, provided great vistas for the women tae hae picnics in the summertime and us young bairns tae skate across the dam in wintertime. We had hame-made boats, adapted horse troughs, that we careened owre the dam in the summertime as well. An ducks – we'd wild ducks, we'd a hell o' domestics ducks, we'd geese, and up the lade there, wis a water hen an ye'd aa the waterfowl richt up the moss as far as ye could see. Fit dae ye see nooadays? Nothing. They've plooed up the whole moss an made it pasture, a wild pasture. There's no wildlife tae be seen, no water hen, no ducks, no dam, there's nothing. Aa that's disappeared. They've lost a lot wi fit they caa modernisation. It's a shame.'

Tam Reid
Photo: Ian F. MacKenzie

TAM REID

Tam Reid, a farmer at Woodside, Cullerlie, near Echt, is very proud of his title of 'The Bothy Ballad King', won in 1979 at Turriff, but otherwise is a modest and unpretentious man. He and his wife Anne are weel-kent figures at traditional music festivals, where he carries on the rural song tradition with cornkisters and comic or sentimental songs. He maintains that, in his experience, people sing these songs far more today than they ever did before, and smiles at the idea that men sang 'at the ploo' – the work was much too hard for that! Singing was a social thing, for after working hours and special occasions. But singers like Willie Kemp were popular, and Tam particularly likes his songs. His favourite character is the rather backward country loon, too shy to kiss the girls and an easy butt for practical jokers.

At the moment, Tam is aiming to turn his 'wee placie' into a working farm museum, to preserve a picture of the North-East's rural past. The countless obsolete implements that he has lovingly collected over the years, and whose uses he knows and can demonstrate, can be seen all round and inside his house and outbuildings. Having been a 'milkie' for fifteen years he has a fund of earthy stories collected en route with which he regales audiences at country ceilidhs and festivals. But he enjoys singing more than anything and always looks perfectly at home standing before an audience with his open, ready smile and comfortable voice, going through a version of one of his favourite songs.

*****

'I wis born in 1929, doon at Craigston at fit wis kent at that time as Countess Wells – I think nooadays it's Kingswells: like a lot o' ither things, it's changed an aa. That's at Westhill. I went to school at Westhill for six months, then we moved up here. Peter my brither, led the coo. We'd jist aboot hauf a dozen stirkies. I aye mind comin intae the hoose here, jist the auld-fashioned kitchen, bare waas, the hole in the waa for the water pails – there wis nae water in the hoose – the saut box, wi a thing for papers hung in front, and the big press. Ben the back, there wis jist a scullery, then intae the milkhoose, wi auld fashioned timmer shelves tae put the basins on. In the kitchen wis a box bed – ye opened the doors and climbed intae bed – but it wis later made intae somethin mair up-to-date. Comin intae the new place, the dykes were aa alang the road; you could walk on them withoot fear o' loosenin a stane, but noo ye can see the deterioration in the dykes – they're aa saggin; ye couldnae walk on them noo.

'I had one brither and three sisters. There's a younger yin, but he's nae actually a brither. My mither just brocht him up. He cam in aboot here in 1947. He wis jist like a brither; he didnae ken ony difference. He wis six weeks old when he cam here and he grew up here jist like a younger brither. Moll, my aullest sister, she's never mairried, an Peter, there's neen o' the twa o' them mairrit an they baith bide owre in a hoose in Banchory, jist aside the brig o' Dee, as ye gae awa roon tae the Brig o' Feugh. My youngest sister, she's mairrit an she's oot at a croftie in Dyce.

'Fen we cam here, ma faither jist had the wan horse, an this aul beast ma grandfaither hid, she cam up here tae mak the pair, tae dae the plooin. This cairried on for quite a while, that he jist had wan horse an got a len o' anither een. It wis a gey bare kin o' existence. I've still got the statement o' the value o' the grain crop on the 8th May 1936 an the grain crop price at the Martinmas term. The amount due at Martinmas for grain was £35-5-6d, less harvesting: echty-three quarters at 4/- a quarter. We've got a box oot there wi aa the accoonts in. I got an accoont in ae day fae a blacksmith an I think it wis 1942, for pittin four new sheen intil a horse, wi taes an heels – 12/6 – for four new sheen intil a horse! Nooadays, I dinna ken if poonds wad dae it.

'Wi the aul swey, the fireplace wis jist the means o' cookin. Wi my mither, the kettle wis bilet, the big broth pot wis pitten on tae mak the soup; if she wis makin a dumplin, it wis aa bilet on the fire. Anither thing I mind aboot, on the side there wis twa ordinary bricks. I'm spikkin aboot the war years noo. Fin there wis a richt cauld kin o' a nicht, ma mither wad hae said, "Ye can tak een o' the bricks tae bed wi ye". The bricks were aye het. We jist got an aul sock an pushed the brick intil't and awa tae the chaumer tae wir bed. The brick wis a great idea. It wis aye het in the mornin; it bade het a lang time.

'At the present day, there's nae a van o' nae description comes in aboot here. There used tae be a van every day o' the week. The grocer fae Banchory, he used tae come on a Wednesday and a Setterday – he come twice a week. That's somethin o' the past. There wis a baker come fae Banchory, the ither baker he come twice a week an aa fae Culter. We'd a baker on a Monday and baker on a Thursday. There's no even a fishman comes roon noo.

'Speakin aboot the big fire, well, the only way ye could keep that fire gaun was wi peats. Every year, there wis a big stack o' peats. Fit took place wis, ye put in aa your grain crop, then ye put in your neeps, then ye jist gaed awa tae the moss. Ye spent aboot six weeks castin peats. Every tenant on the estate got a peat bank alang wi the lease o' the fairm. We had a bank jist tae oorsels an we used a horse an a sledge tae bring them hame. A lot o' the next eens, they had a ditch tae cross an they had tae row their peats in a barrow, they couldna dae't wi a horse an cairt. Every tenant could cut peats doon there, an when it wis in its heyday, it wis great. Aa the different fairmers, they got a chinwag doon there, comin or gaun fae the moss. We wis jist sort o' on wir own. Jist aye afore the hairst startit, ye wad hae haen the peats, or sometimes after hairst. If the hairst wis early, ye jist didnae hae time tae cut peats, ye'd tae wait till efter. Doon here, we jist used an ordinary spade. Oor peat is nae like a lot o' the peat banks where ye jist hid the plain moss – we had a lot o' sticks an tree reets. Well, ane o' thae cuttin spades wis nae use among the sticks. Ye need a spade far ye could use't a bittie like an aix. The sticks wis rotten but ye still hid tae cut them.

'I workit the horses masel, ye see, for a lot o' years, just bein a little placie, money was aye tight. Ye couldnae spend a lot o' money on a horse, an my father bocht horses. Then this grass sickness, it became a problem. That was really the main idea in the tractors gettin in. Efter ye had your hairst aa deen an your rucks aa in the cornyaird, it wis anither thing tae hae your rucks weel thackit an tied doon. Some fowk gane tae an affa hicht tae see fa could be the best eens. We used tae hae them thackit an it wis affa fine fen it cam thrashin if it happened tae be a shoor o' snaa the nicht afore, it helpit tae keep the snaa aff the rucks. Aa the foonds were made wi steens; every simmer efter ye had the crap in an aa thing, ye'd gae awa doon tae the cornyaird an ye pickit aa the weeds oot o' the steens an ye'd hiv aa roon aboot scrapit an breakit, ready for the next crop comin in. Efter the tractors startit, they biggit the rucks in the parks. This wis efter the baler cam on the go. Ye'd the thrashin mill an ye'd an affa problem puttin the baler tae the back o' the mill. If ye had these steen foonds, ye'd tae scramble owre the tap o' them wi a tractor, so a lot o' them jist startit biggin the rucks in the parks. At one time o' day, it wis aa pitten intae the cornyaird wi the three men that wis pit tae cairry the grain intae the steadin and, of coorse, fin they startit wi a tractor and a cairt, ye jist loadit the cairt an cairried the grain in aboot. Ye still had aa the humphin o' the bags, but it wis easier. Latterly, ye could dae the thrashin wi less fowk because o' this bailer. A couple o' lads could handle the strae, where ye needed a dizzen afore. That wis a big advantage.

'On some places at thrashin time, there wis a man for every job; there wisna a spare man. Afore that, when it wis biggin rucks o' strae, there wis aften an extra kin o' body, which wis great. There'd jist be twa men pittin in a fork o' shaves, twa men up on the tap o' the mill tae cut the tows tae lowse, then of coorse, the twa men took turns at feedin the mill. Then they got this thing pit on, a self-feeder, so ye jist needed the twa lowsers, ye didna need onybody tae feed the mill. The twa men jist threw the shaves into this canvas an it fed the stuff intae the mill. So that wis anither man that wis done awa wi. A lot o' places jist had the men coontit an they jist had fit they needed tae keep them goin. I think forkin the shaves wis the hardest job. If there wis a spare man, he wad hae gien ye a hand tae put up the foonds. But otherwise, it wis an eident job. A lot o' the fairms we gaed til, there were maybe twa-three men there, but they were aye among the grain. If there wis onybody hired, they aye got this job o' forkin the shaves. I've forkit shaves for weeks on end! It wis a hard job. Sometimes, ye got a good heat up! But it wis jist the wye o't then. If ye didna dee't, weel, ye'd hae been fair affrontit, if ye wisna able tae dee your wark.

'They sometimes had harvest hames, fen they got the harvest in, but there's mair o' that noo, I think. There's far more than there used tae be. The last shafe that came oot the binder wis the clyack shafe. Fen ye cut the hinmost shafe, fen ye'd finished leadin, that wis you; ye'd winter then. That wis a common speak, "Hae ye gotten winter?" or "Are ye throw leadin? Are ye throw hairstin?"

'At one time, we wis aye goin to Garlogie, Friday an Setterday nichts and we'd aye a good sing there. This competition at Turriff got going an, of course, the local fowk here said they thocht I should ging to it. So off we set. I dinna ken fit I wis expectin tae see that day. There wis a crood of aboot fourteen thousand fowk at the Haughs o' Turriff. It wis enormous! There wis roond aboot thirty competitors for this thing. I dinna ken, I didna think I wis ony better than mony mair I'd heard singin, but however, I competed and I wis successful. I sung 'The Muckle Gackit Gype' which wis a favourite. I've sung for a lot o' years. It wis een o' the best-known eens o Willie Kemp:

THE MUCKLE GACKIT GYPE

1. Noo, aa my life I've aye been thocht a back-ward kin o' chiel, for I was ne-ver kent tae blaw, for I was ne-ver feel. But when I met E-li-za Broon, I took her for a walk. We baith walked on in si-lence for we ne-ver tried tae talk. But when we cam back tae her door, gey bold I must hae been, for I squeezed her um-brel-la tops, syne she said I was green. Her mi-ther kee-kin' thro' the lock, hid fo'an an' shou-ted right, 'til Li-za skelps him on the lug, the muc-kle gac-kit gype.

CHORUS

So I can-na thole the wee-min fowk; they're far owre cute for me. Some-times I think that aa my days a

21 ba - che-lier I'll   be.   But   I   jist crack a - ni-ther   spunk   an'

23 when I   licht   my pipe,   it's   soo- thin' con-   so- la- tion   tae   a

25 muc- kle   gac- kit   gype.

2. Noo ae day doon upon the shore I thocht I'd hae a dook,
   So I took aff my beets an claes an tried tae be a deuk.
   Then I came oot gey shivery, losh! I felt aa forlorn
   For deil a sign o' ony claes were left that I had worn.
   The only thing upon the sands wis just a lassie's shaal,
   So I dressed up masel in it but I wis affa caul!
   Syne takkin aa the back roads hame fen Liza owre the dyke
   Says, 'Here's your claes wi compliments, ye muckle gackit gype!'

CHORUS: I canna thole the weemin fowk; . . . etc.

3. Last year fen on my holidays an waitin for the train
   A bonnie lassie ran tae me an said, 'Dear sir, it's plain
   Ye are a homely sort o' man, will you be good and kind,
   Jist hold my baby till I see if I my husband find'.
   She shoved it in my oxter, syne she turned and ran awa.
   The train cam in and I wis left still waitin for its Da.
   'Twis then I found 'twis jist a dall she'd gien't ma watch tae swipe
   As weel's my cash, so I felt like a muckle gackit gype.

CHORUS: I canna thole the weemin fowk; . . . etc.

'Syne I sung 'The Buchan Vet' which wis, at that time, anither sang
I'd just recently startit singin. This cousin o' mine that came up fae
London, he kent a little aboot bothy ballads and this wis een that he sang
a verse o', so I thocht 'If he can sing it, so can I'. That was my second
sang at the Haughs o' Turriff:

THE BUCHAN VET

1. Noo, it's doon in a wee toon in Bu - chan, I've prac- tised for near for- ty year. I'm the man that's aye socht fen yer horse or yer nowt are loo- kin' a wee bit- tie queer. So if ye see a stirk in the neuk o' a park wi' it's hair up an' his lugs hing- in' doon, ye at eence tell yer ploo - man tae jump on his bike an' get the best vet in the toon.

CHORUS

So if yer auld horse or yer coo is in pain, the du- ty, ye see, is quite

2. Noo ae nicht wi ma gig an ma sheltie
   I wis danderin hame afore dark,
   Oh I'd haen a gween dram, maybe twa, maybe three,
   Fen I saw Main's gang throw's tattie park.
   Oh I cried, 'A fine nicht!' but he never took heed,
   Syne he swore an he caaed me a feel,
   But I fun oot neist day I'd been wastin ma wind,
   'Twis a scarecrow stuck up on a dreel!

CHORUS: So if your auld horse . . . etc.

3. Noo ae nicht as I passit the auld kirkyaird
   I thocht that I heard a queer soun.
   So I stoppit ma shelt, an gaed in owre the dyke
   An I hid a gween look roon an roon.
   Fae a new-howkit grave cam a voice that I kent,
   'Oh,' I says tae masel, 'noo ye're trappit.'
   Says the voice, 'Oh I'm caul!' but I sheelt in the yird,
   'Ye'll be warmer,' says I, 'eence ye're happit!'.

CHORUS: So if your auld horse . . . etc.

'It wis a great event for, apart fae the honour o' winnin the thing, there wis this prize o' £500 along wi it, plus the crown which ye still see sittin there. The singin's non-stop nooadays, as ye can see. It's all go! There's a lot o' fowk that aye says tae me, "Dinna ken hoo ye've time tae dee't." My answer is, "If there's somethin ye're wantin tae dae, ye'll always find time."

'Well, it wis jist shortly efter that we started this milk business. Fermin wisna sae hot and we hadnae jist the best placie here. Fen ma father died in 1967, I thought I'd look for somethin better and I tried to get a few different places and cam verra near on several occasions, but I wis never jist so lucky. I decided we'd jist stay here. My father lived until he was eighty-eight, so I thinks tae mysel that I'll just try an run on his lines: jist work awa some; dinna wint tae stop, must go on. We started the milk business jist as a part-time jobbie. Of coorse, it grew intil a full-time job. It was a trying life, gettin up at three o'clock in the mornin, but we enjoyed it because it wis a slightly different kin o' life.

'One winter, we had an affa hard time. Well, tae begin with, we'd a job gettin oot the roond wi oor motors, but there wis one good thing aboot it. We had a good neighbour here, Bert Mackintosh, and every night at five o'clock, there'd be a digger cam up oor road and made sure that we could get oot ontae the main road in the mornin. He wis verra good that wey. He jist kent that if I canna get oot the road, *he* canna get his milk and his papers in the mornin. There wis probably a method in his madness and he cam eence or twice tae oor assistance that affa winter.

'Then one o' the ither milkies cam in an he says, "Ye needna bother gaen oot in that – the bottles are jist shatterin." He cam in wi a haill load o' milk an the haill lot wis pit awa tae the tip – the bottles wis aa burst! We put oors back intae the stores an we cam hame, and we gaed back again at echt o'clock and we wis too late tae ging tae this dinner an dance at night. It took us fae echt o'clock in the mornin tae efter seiven at night till we got oor milk delivered. That wis one o' the worst days. The eggs were jist jumpin oot o' their shells! Then we started gettin plastic bottles in 1982. Oh, they froze an aa! But supposin they were frozen, ye could still thaa the milk an ye could use it, but wi a gless bottle, if they burst, that wis the finish o' that. Then, of coorse, the last couple o' years, it wis jist completely the opposite and I dinna think there wis ever a frozen bottle.

'We're back at hame again, an still gaun tae fairm a little and we've this ither project in mind if we could jist get a start – this museum collection o' yesteryear implements. I've been collectin for a number o' years. In fact, some o' that things that's sittin there, there's some o' the horse implements that I used tae work masel, fen we wis workin the place wi horse. But it's jist gradually increased, the interest tae aye get somethin mair. I get things maistly at roups an sales. The thing is gettin actual plannin permission tae get the thing goin. I mean, at the moment, aathing's jist sittin here scattert an lyin aboot aawey. The fact is, it's goin tae be a workin museum. We're goin tae work the place wi horse an try tae get people interested in the heritage o' the fermin which is sadly goin, an keep it alive. It has tae be here when there's still a ferm. Otherwise, hoo could ye show the children of today hoo they fairmed yesteryear?

'We went tae get wood tae repair wir thrashin mill on the Garvie road, an he asked fit the wood wis for, an we said it wis for the thrashin mill. And he didna even ken fit a thrashin mill wis. This wis a youth in his twenties an he'd never been on a ferm. So, jist think fit they've lost oot on.'

Elizabeth Stewart
Photo: Ian F. MacKenzie

ELIZABETH STEWART

Apart from the farming folk in the North-East, there were the traveller clans as in Perthshire, with Stewart being one of the pre-eminent names, related to the Perthshire Stewarts, who trace their ancestry back to the patriarchal figure of 'old Jimmy Kate' of Struan. They were gifted musicians, singers and storytellers and in Aberdeenshire, they produced names like Jeannie Robertson, whose mother was a Stewart, and her daughter Lizzie Higgins, and her nephew, Stanley Robertson, names which resound in the hall of fame of tradition-bearers. Not so well-known, perhaps, because of her shy and retiring nature, was Lucy Stewart of Fetterangus, whose niece Elizabeth is now continuing the ballad and story tradition she learned from her aunt, who brought her up.

The older generation of these traveller families earned their living, as did their Perthshire cousins, by a mixture of craftsmanship, farmwork and music. Elizabeth's mother was an accordionist and had a successful dance band, which meant she was out a lot and her unmarried sister Lucy cared for her children. Elizabeth inherited her mother's musical talent and plays the accordion and the piano. Her piano-playing is extraordinary and she was invited to the States in the 1950s on the strength of it. She describes her playing as 'traditional piano', and certainly her style owes more to piping than to Mozart, with a little touch of rock and roll! Her reminiscences of her Aunt Lucy, the family stay-at-home, who tended the children and cooked and cleaned, tell of her singing about the house and, in this way, Elizabeth almost unconsciously absorbed her tradition. (Lucy had also been recorded and studied by Kenneth Goldstein, now a Professor of Folklore in the United States.)

Elizabeth did not emerge as a known tradition-bearer in Scotland until comparatively recently. Before, she played piano in pubs where the demand was not always for Scottish material. She is pretty good at rock and roll and country and western as a result. But she never lost her passion for ballads or her love of Scottish dance music, nor her ability to sing and play in traditional style. Currently, she works in schools in the Grampian area as an 'instructor in the art of ballad-singing'.

*****

'I was born at Fetterangus; that was the family home. My grandfaither had settled down efter comin fae Crichie: he cam fae there. He cam oot o Aiberdeen, I think, and went to Stewartfield, Crichie, and then cam fae Crichie tae Fetterangus, an that's faur the family was brocht up. I dinna mind o' my grandfaither. I mind o' my grandmither though. I was three when she died and I remember her jist vaguely. I remember them burnin her clothes at the back o' the hoose. That was an old custom among the travelling people.

'I remember the hoose we stayed in, the croft at Fetterangus, so vividly. I can jist see the room my Auntie Martha died in, and Jean — she died of tuberculosis, an she was the best singer o' the lot. They were all musicians: there were ten brithers and four sisters and my mither was the youngest. Ned was the second youngest; there wasna much atween them. He was a fiddler and a tin whistler. They all played tin whistles, pipes, fiddles and they sang, my aunts an aa. Patchy played the drums at the Tivoli in Aiberdeen. For years, he was the drummer there. At that time, that was something great, playing at the Tivoli! My mither grew up doing a bit o' music, and my grandmither, before she died, wanted to educate her properly as far as music was concerned, although she was a traditional player. Don't get me wrong, she was a very traditional player. But my grandmither wanted her to be well-educated in her music, so that she'd have something tae faa back on if anything gaed wrong wi her life. An of coorse, things did go wrong wi her life. But I think she was the age o' fourteen or fifteen when her nephew, Curly McKay, had come fae Aiberdeen wi an accordion, an my mither got her hands on it an she loved it an said she was for it. She'd already had a new piano, which cost my grandmither a bit of money an, of course, she kicked up hell tae get an accordion an my grandmither had tae get her it. She got this Cappucino, made for Honeggar; it was banana-shaped wi mither-o'-pearl an rubies on it. I've got a picture of it, fen she was younger, in her heyday. My mither was never a great singer: at the school, she was good at doin harmonies, but she was never a singer like Lucy was. Lucy was my mither's sister born in 1901, an my mither was born in 1911.

'We'd a lot o' faimily in between them. Tam was the eldest; he was a great piper. They were aa in the Gordons: and *their* uncles before *them*, my grandfaither's brithers. Coonted aa thegither, I think there was nineteen. The auld man that's buried at Auld Deer, auld Crichie Donald — they were *his* sons, all Stewarts ye see — they were aa great pipers. His son was caaed Crichie ava. They were aa afore my time, but in my lifetime, I looked up tae them as though they were heroes, because o' their pipin, their playin, their fiddlin, their singin, their storytellin an, of coorse, fit they done in the war. My grandfaither's brither, Robin, this was Sergeant Robin Stewart; he's buried in France and sometime fen I get enough money, I'll get a chance to see across there. This is my dream — just to be at his grave. I heard so much aboot him fae my mither. He was like a hero to her and in turn, he's like a hero to me because he was a good front-line man. He was in Egypt an he wrote 'The Burnin Sands o Egypt' an he come hame an he'd nae money. He was penniless, an he sellt this — or it was tooken from him — an that's known today as 'The Road to the Isles'. That gives me strange mixed feelins fen I play 'The Road to the Isles', because I think this is somebody I dinny ken, but it was my mither's uncle that wrote this.

'But there was a lot mair music in the faimily that my grandfaither wrote an my mither wrote. My mither wrote 'The Maid of Ugie'. She started on this dance band at the age o' fourteen an she did very well. There was an advert one Sunday tae play for Children's Hour in Aiberdeen in the BBC. My mither tried for this job. There were twenty other applicants for the job. My mither went in an she'd a navy blue wool coat, oot o' the pickins, a pair o' shoes wi no soles on them — an she got the job! My mither played on the Children's Hour and ony new piece o' music that came out — she introduced 'The Lambeth Walk' up here. Naebody kent keyboard music like she did. The nearest to her is Bobby McLeod. Fen I hear him, I just think o' her. An of coorse, he's a piper. My mither's playin would have been influenced by my father an her brithers and her uncles, 'cause they were aa pipers. I didnae see much o' her brithers, but wi ma mither playin like this, it come oot in my piano-playin. She was the one that influenced me in ma music.

'Lucy wasna classed as bein a musician at aa. She was the one in the background. She was mair like a slave. She had aa the dirty work to do, for when my grandmither was awa oot, she had to clean the place, get the dinners ready an the washin done. And I suppose she just sung til hersel, picked hersel up that way. She was just an easy-goin type, she was happy tae be at hame, although she was as happy tae ging oot — I've sat on a horse an cart wi Lucy. My sister an I traivelled the country wi her an I wish we'd done even more of it. But I suppose by that time, my grandmither had died, my uncles were married and scattered. Music was very important to my mither, so she settled in Fetterangus. There wasna so much travellin because her life was her music, or her music was her life, whichever way ye look at it. She'd a dance band, she taught, and she'd a lot o' schools in this area over quite a distance. I used to go wi her when she used tae teach in fermhooses. She'd concerts in fermhooses. One o' her biggest classes – an they wad be fermin people at that time – was in Cramond up beside Byth. She'd a big class there an people came from aa owre that area, fermers' sons and people wi their own businesses.

'She was awa quite a lot an Lucy was aye wi us, ye see. Although we had a mither, Lucy was mair o' a mither tae us, because she was aye there. In fact, we took her for granted, to tell the truth, we did. But I mind as a bairn, she was aye singin, and the songs that stuck oot in my mind is 'The lass o Bennachie' and 'I Aince Lo'ed a Lass':

I AINCE LO'ED A LASS

2. The next time I saw my love was tae the church go,
   Wi bride and bridesmaidens they made a fine show,
   While I followed on wi a hert fu o' woe,
   She's awa tae be wed tae anither.

3. The next time I saw my love was in the church stand,
   Wi gold rings on her fingers and gloves in her hand
   Wi gold rings on her fingers and gloves in her hand,
   She's gone tae be wed tae anither.

4. The minister that mairried them he gave a loud vow,
   If there be any objection then let him speak now,
   I thought in my ain hert objections had I
   For tae see my love wed tae anither.

5.   When mairriage was owre an on intae dine
     I fillt up the glasses wi brandy and wine
     I leant owre the table tae kiss the sweet bride
     Sayin 'She is the lassie that ought tae be mine.'

6.   When dinner was owre an gaun intae bed,
     I put on my hat an I bid them goodnight.
     The bridegroom said,
     'Ye've waited owre long for tae get her.'

7.   Ye can keep her an keep her an keep your great pride,
     For the bed that she lies in she canna deny.
     She has lain by my side, aince, twice and thrice
     She's only my old shoes though ye've got her.

8.   O the folk o' the forest they aa laugh at me,
     Sayin, 'How many blaeberries grows in the saut sea?'
     I turnit richt roon wi a tear in my ee.
     'How many ships sail in the forest?'

9.   Ye can dig me a grave an dig it sae deep,
     An I'll turn in for tae tak a lang sleep.
     An I'll turn in for tae tak a lang sleep
     An it's maybe through time I'll forget her.

10.   So they dug him a grave an they dug it sae deep,
     An he's turned in for tae tak a lang sleep
     An he's turned in for tae tak a lang sleep,
     An it's maybe by noo he's forgotten.

I aye mind o' Lucy singin that. It just sticks in my mind. Fen I was at home, she'd just go on and on at them an I didna realise they were bein learnt, of course; they jist went through my heid because I was there too. It was common knowledge. I heard these songs from early childhood; I was brocht up wi them. Fitever else I did in my life music-wise – an the piano was my instrument – these songs was aye in my mind. Efter aa this years, I can still sing remember them and now other people are enjoyin them as much as I'm enjoyin them an that's the most important thing. To me, it matters more than money. To me, it gives a lot o' satisfaction to tell people aboot her songs, and a lot o' people know her name, Lucy, especially as that's who I got them fae. I mean, the memories o' her, fit took place aa these years while she was singin that songs tae me, it aa fits in an gives ye the love for the songs. Of course, she was singin them for the love o' the people *she* got them fae:

THE GALLANT FORTY-TWA

1. It's six weeks come
Sun-day since my love has gaed a-
wa. He's a-wa tae jine the
re-gi-ment o' the Gal-lant For-ty-

CHORUS
Twa. Oh bro-ken her-ted I may
wan-der for the loss o' my true
lo-ver! He's a-wa tae jine the
re-gi-ment o' the Gal-lant For-ty-
Twa.

2. I had only one sixpence and I broke it in twa
   An I gied my love the half o' it afore he wint awa.

CHORUS: O broken-herted I may wander . . . etc.

3. I will sit at my windae an I'll spin at my wheel
   An I'll think o' my laddie an the times we had sae weel.

CHORUS: O broken-herted I may wander . . . etc.

Jane Turriff
Photo: Peter Cooke

JANE TURRIFF

One of the most revered names in traditional singing in Scotland is that of Jane Turriff, born Jane Stewart and related to both Jeannie Robertson and the Perthshire Stewarts. Her late husband, Cameron, a farmworker who went blind, shared her love of singing. Jane has a beautifully clear voice, that she loves to raise in the old ballads and, as she says, singing is her life.

*****

'I wis born in 1915 – I don't worry how old I am – I'm as old as the hills! We're aa gettin older every day, we canny help it. My life wis always a singin one; a housewife tae ma mother an father, to let them get out tae work. I wis the oldest o' the family, an the disabled one. But I wasnae always disabled. I had an accident when I wis a little girl. I wis only four year old. When I wis born, I wis like any other child. I had all my faculties an could walk – *but* I had an accident, I hurt my leg an it never got better. I wis three year an six months in the hospital. I went in walking an came out, I couldnae walk. My father had to carry me home an they had to feed me. I couldnae feed masel because I couldn't sit up, because I wis in stookie right fae ma legs uptae ma chest. So they had to nurse me till they took off the stookie. I got crutches to come home an to try an walk with them an I couldnae walk at all. Ma mother an father shifted from Aberdeen tae Peterhead at that time.

'I had a lot o' cousins in Peterhead. My mother had a few children gin I come home from hospital an when I wis home a few weeks, my cousins took me in the bairn's pram, along wi ma mother's young bairn, an ma crutches too, they took me away to the links at Peterhead. They left me in the pram wi the young bairn an they were rollin their Easter eggs doon the brae an what a great carry-on we were havin! I couldnae get goin because I wis sittin in the pram, so I shouted owre tae them tae pick me oot o' the pram an they got me oot o' the pram an sat me on the grass. The little bairnie wis aye in the pram an she wis wonderin what we wis aa daein. I got oot o' the pram an picked up the crutches an started tae walk wi them. I wis a long time afore I wis on ma feet, ye know, on the cruches, an then I started tae walk wi them an they were surprised! They stared at me an said, ''My God! She's walkin! Oh my, she's walkin wi her crutches!''

'They couldnae get hame quick enough tae run tae ma mother tae tell her. What a cairry-on! It wis great news for her. When they hurried me home ma mother says, ''Noo, where have ye been wi the bairn? My goodness, ye've been away aa day, girls!'' ''Oh wait till we tell ye! She's walkin wi the crutches!'' Oh mother, she couldnae believe it. So of course, I wis frightened tae walk aboot the hoose, because the grun wis hard tae faa an I'm feart o' fallin. I kent I wouldnae hurt masel if I fell on the grass, so it took me a while afore I could really get on ma feet an walkin. We stayed up a little bit o' a stair an I wis aye frightened tae come up an doon that stair for fear o' slippin an fallin wi ma crutches, because I wasnae steady on ma feet. But gradually, I began tae get better an better until I could get goin. My mother always took me up in the pram to go to school – I had to go tae school, ye ken – so she used tae take me up tae school, then when I came home again, I just got the crutches an carried on tryin tae walk wi them an I began jist tae get goin wi them.

'Now my hobby wis housework, an I tried tae help ma mother an let her get oot tae work an ma father tried aa kinds o' jobs tae bring us up. We wis ten o' a family an I wis the oldest one. I tried tae be a good help til her. They could trust me aboot the hoose tae keep it clean. We came tae live in Fetterangus an ma mother an father stayed there for years an years. They were forty-six years in a council house. Ma job wis tae look after the children an ma mother an father got working oot an aboot. I brocht the family up since they wis young till they got a job. I'd tae clean the hoose, get the food, get the girls their dinner made – they aa worked in Gray's, Fetterangus – they aa came in at the same time. Then every time I washed the dishes and got them away and everybody oot o' the hoose, I wanted to sing! I couldn't help singin.

'When my mother would take a day doon tae Peterheid for some messages she'd say, ''Noo, Jeanie, what are ye wantin me tae take back tae ye?'' ''Oh Ma, take a record back tae me!'' ''A record? What kin o' a record?'' ''Oh I want Jimmy Rodgers.'' He wis a great player o' the guitar and a great singer. ''If ye canna get him, get Gracie Fields.'' We'd an old gramophone wi a big horn and I used tae get on these records and

I used tae sing the whole day. I thought it wis great – singing tae records. I used tae copy Jimmy Rodgers – I used tae yodel! An then I started singing like Gracie Fields, puttin the voice away up, 'Red Sails in the Sunset' and all that. That wis my life.

'Then when my father came home at night he would say, "I think we'll hae a tune o' the gramophone." There wis nae wirelesses, ye see. But the spring would be broken. Oh what a cairry-on! My father would say, "I know who did that!" An I got a ragin. But my father could mend the gramophone an put the spring forrard a bit, but it wis aye gettin littler an littler an there'd be no spring left at all! Ilka time it wis me that brak it, because I wis so fascinated wi this singin. I wis the only one in the family that wis like 'at.

'We got an old organ fae somewhere. I don't know who gave it tae us. An my God! I wis wishin it wis afternoon tae get them all away and sit doon an play that organ. That's why I got intae the singin cairry-on. I sung all my life nearly. Then I remember my father got haud o' an auld piano. If we had visitors, he'd say tae me, "Come on, noo, Jeanie, give them a song." If I got a bittie bashful, he'd gie me a wallop. "Come on, noo, throw oot your voice! Ye're grippin in!" So I had tae sing tae them. It wis really happy times in the olden days. I could muse all day aboot it.

'I never used tae sing the auld songs, but I've heard ma folks singin them so often; my grandmother my grandfather and my father and mother. I've ma Dad's fiddle there on the wall, and the bow. It wis a spare fiddle – he'd two others and they had cases, beautiful, yellow fiddles. One day, when ma mother wis left without ma father, an I'd lost my husband, Cameron, she cam owre the road tae me an she said, "Jeanie, dae ye want your Dad's fiddle?" An I said, "Gie me a look o't." It had one string on't, an hadnae a bridge on't, twa pegs aff't. I said, "Oh Mum, I'm not takin that!" So away she gid wi the fiddle again. A week later, she cam back wi the same fiddle. "Dae ye nae need your father's fiddle?" "No, I tellt ye aaready. I'm nae takin it. It's nae use." Then I got a look at the fiddle again. "Gie it tae Billy's bairns tae play wi," she said. "Na, na," I says. "I'm nae daein that." I took it onywey an I hung it on the waa wi the bow.

'Someone told me there wis someone who could sort fiddles, so I phoned up an the man cam doon, an he took it away an sortit it. He polished it up an put two pegs on it an a bridge an strings, an put hair ontae the bow. "That's your fiddle complete, Jane," he said. "It's a good enough fiddle." It wis a good bit tae get it sortit. So I'm happy I took it; I think I wad hae fretted an murned if I hadnae took it. I canna play it. My father used tae play it – jist in the hoose – an I used tae play the piano; we played great thegither.

'We traivelled a lot in the summertime. We gid tae Auld Meldrum, an Inverurie, Deeside wey, Blairgowrie an awa in the hills. We'd a lovely caravan an a guid horse. Ye need a guid horse on the road. It wis an auld-fashioned roond caravan wi a real stove inside an twa-three beds, an we always had a camp an aa, for we were a big family. We'd a great life. I liked the traivellin life. But my Mum an Dad got auld an they werena able. Traivellers like the open air; they feel confined in a hoose. I miss that now, away among the heathery hills an the water an the trees. That's what I loved.

'My Dad played the fiddle an the pipes an he sung too, but my mother wis aye the singer, an ma grandmother. Her name wis Maguire an she wis Irish, but she lived in Scotland aa her days almost. She'd fifteen o' a family and my Uncle Davie, he wis the youngest. He aye cam oot tae see us. He wis a great man, always laughin and happy an singin wi his melodeon. Ma grandmither wisna big, but my grandfather wis big. They were aa big men, my Granda's brothers, bonnie men, and aa pipers. My mother played the pipes an aa; she'd take doon the chanter an play it tae us, if ma father wis oot workin. They're aa musical folk, the traivellin people.

'We used tae hear stories at the camp-fire when we were bairns. The men used tae sit up an hae the news aboot the Burkers. We were in bed an we were listening an we were scared! ''Oh my God! I wish we were oot o' here!'' we'd say. We were in haunted places too.

'When I met Cameron, he wis a farm servant, he wis in the bothy in a place caaed Crimond Meggatt. He wis born in a cottar hoose an he became a cottar man like his faither, but when he come forty, his sight began to go. His mother wis the same. He could see jist a bit when I married him. I wis forty-two an he wis forty-six an we were a handsome couple! He loved singin too. If a letter came in the mornin an it wis for a festival, we were overjoyed. We loved it! We were at Blairgowrie an Kinross. I've been at Keith and Kirriemuir and twice in Edinburgh and in Glasgow – oh, the folk were affa kind tae me there!

'There wis the sort o' song I sang at the festivals:

MY BOY TAMMY-O

1. "Where hiv you been aa the day, my boy Tammy-O? Where hiv you been aa the day, my boy Tammy-O?" "I wis

7 coor- tin' at a - ni- ther young ___ thing, a

9 young ___ thing, a young ___ thing. I wis

11 coor- tin' at a - ni - ther young thing that

13 bides wi' her Mam- my O."

2. 'How old is your young thing, my boy Tammy-O?
   How old is your young thing, my boy Tammy-O?'
   'She's twice six, twice seven, twice twenty and eleven,
   She's but a young thing an she bides wi her Mammy-O.'

3. 'What did ye say tae your young thing, my boy Tammy-O?
   What did ye say tae your young thing, my boy Tammy-O?'
   'I speirt if she wad mairry me an be my little lammie-O
   She said she wadna mairry me, for she couldna leave her Mammy-O.

It's a very auld air fae ma mither an ma grandmither. My mither had a lot o' songs an I should hae learned them aa:

BARBARY ALLEN

1 1. I fell in love with a nice young

5 girl, Her name wis Bar - ba- ry Al - len. I

9 fell in love with a nice young girl, Her ___

13 name wis Bar - ba - ry Al-___ len.

2. Till I got sick an very ill
    I sent for Barbary Allen. [twice]

3. It's look ye up at my bedheid
    And see what you'll find hangin:
    A silver watch and a guinea gold pin
    That hangs there for Barbary Allen. [repeat last line
                                   of verse]

4. O look ye doon at my bedside
    And see what you'll find stannin;
    A vessel full of my hert's tears
    That sits there for Barbary Allen. [repeat last line
                                   of verse]

5. She pulled the curtains from the bed
    And said, 'Young man, you're dying'. [twice]

6. One kiss from you would do me good
    One kiss from you would cure me.
    One kiss from me you shall not get,
    Tho your poor heart lies breaking. [repeat last line
                                   of verse]

7. She hidnae gane a mile or twa
    When she heard the church bell ringin,
    And every word they seemed to say
    'Cruel-hearted Barbary Allen'. [repeat last line
                                   of verse]

8. Oh mother dear, oh make my bed
    And make it lang an narrow
    For my true love has died for me
    And I'll die for him tomorrow. [repeat last line
                                   of verse]

9. Her mother she has made her bed
    And she's made it lang and narrow,
    And laid her down to fall asleep,
    And she died for her true lover. [repeat last line
                                   of verse]

Willie MacKenzie
Photo: Ian F. MacKenzie

VOICES FROM THE FISHING AND MILLING

In the North-East, in the Laigh of Moray and on Speyside and along the coast in the picturesque villages with their harbours and cliffs, were those whose occupations were connected with the mill and the still and others whose livelihoods depended on the sea and fishing.

WILLIE MACKENZIE

Willie Mackenzie was for many years a meal miller and happy with his work. He also helped out in the still during the War and has many a tale to tell of 'the millers and the stillers'. 'We never went to bed the same day we got up' is the telling comment of Willie's wife Freda, remembering how their home was a 'half-way hoose' for those coming and going from Elgin to the country villages round about. Willie is well-known as one of the finest singers of bothy ballads and traditional songs in the North-East. He has sung at clubs, ceilidhs and festivals all over Scotland, always with one foot up on a chair, in typical stance. He has an infectiously cheerful personality, as has his wife, and together they have made a great contribution to the work of the Traditional Music and Song Association.

*****

'I wis born in 1923 on the 6th September, on a bonnie harvest morning, 'cause my father wis ladin corn in the back park, when the wifie hung oot the sheet an he kent it wis aa owre. That's the story that I wis aye telt, onywey. He seen the sheet an he said, 'That's it!' That wis up at Kinnermony farm in Aberlour, Banffshire. I wis there until I wis a loon o' aboot eleven or twelve year auld, when he wis up at Ballindalloch. My father wis a horseman up till then, but he'd an accident wi a horse, so he went on wi the cattle, as it wis a safer kin o' job. He moved up tae George Reid of Lagmore, a great man among black Aberdeen Angus cattle. He wis cattler there for three year and syne we moved down to Manbeen, Wester Manbeen in Morayshire, and I wis there till my father retired. I wis mairrit fae there. That wis my life up until I left the school. I went tae school in Aberlour and at Ballindalloch, I went tae Inveravon School. It wis sic a wide district, they had twa schools. When we went tae Manbeen, I went to Mosstowie School. I finished my schooling there.

'I wis the second o' the family. Ian wis my older brother, syne there wis me, Bob, Alan and Gordon, five o' a faimly. A very happy faimly. My mother wis aye singin an diddlin awa. My faither wisnae musical, but he could aye dunt his feet. The feet wis aye goin if he heard a tune. I aye mind when we wis at Manbeen – we were loons gettin up a bit – he didnae go intae toon every Setterday nicht, but he went in once or twice a month and he aye bocht a record, a Beltona record, either o' Scottish dance music or Willie Kemp or Geordie Morris. He aye bocht the record first, because the record shop shut kin o' early, and then he went tae the pub. The record wis aye stuck intae his jacket an wi the heat o' the pub an the tichtness o' the jacket, it aye cam hame bent! 'Twas aye warped! My mither had tae kin o' lay it oot somewye an pit ither records on the top o' it. She used tae gie it a wee heat at the fire first an pit it on an this kin o' flattened it oot again, afore she could play it. That's what happened an that's what warps records. Folk used tae mak flooer pots oot o' them.

'Syne of course, once I got up a bittie, I used tae gae tae toon on a Setterday nicht. That's when I met Jimmy MacBeath, at the White Horse in Elgin. I wis jist fascinated by him: I thocht there wis naebody like him. I mean, money wis scarce at that time, but I used tae gie him hauf a croon tae hear him singin maybe twa, maybe three sangs. The first yin that I heard him singin that I learned wis 'Grat for Gruel'.

'Efter a spell on a milk cairt, I workit twenty-six years in a meal mill. The work in the mill wis very dusty work and very hot work, because ye'd tae turn the grain in the kiln; ye were jist standin above the fire, and it wis on iron plates. But oh, it wis great work! It wis a water mill, when I started, but then we got in a diesel engine tae help; in the early years o' the War, there wis a big demand on meal, so we got in a diesel engine, and efter the War, they got in the power, the electric. But the wheels wis still there; they could still run free. But it wis a water mill when I started in 1943. I enjoyed the meal-milling. The meal went mainly tae the farm servants, because they got meal, milk and tatties: that wis their perquisites. Every two month, they got a boll o' meal, which wis ten stone at that time. A boll's nae a weight, it's a measure but it wis ten stone all the time I wis there; it never varied. Then efter the War, they put on a big ferry tae Skye, which would take a lorry, and we used tae run over tae Skye wi oatmeal. Before that, it had to go by rail to Kyle and it wis transported across in smaa boats. But aince it got on the lorry, we jist drove richt oot wi't. We took an affa meal tae Skye. There wis nae comparison between it an the oatmeal ye get noo. The grain went ontae this hot plates an ye flavoured it wi the oatmeal husks an it gave it a nutty flavour. Aa this noo, it's dried wi hot air, jist blastin. Ye went in an ye turned it aboot every hauf oor, ten quarters o' corn at a time, which wis thirty hundredweight, an ye turned it three or four times. Ye toasted it actually; it wis toasted. Then of coorse, wi these Porage Oats and Corn Flakes comin in, the millin wis rinnin doon an efter the War, the meal sales jist drappit.

'I think it wis a romantic kin o' job, the mill. I'll sing ye the 'Miller tae ma Trade'. Ye're supposed tae imitate the soond o' the mill wi your hand and airm on the table:

THE MILLER'S SONG

13 meal I've made an' I've coor - ted mo - ny's a bon - nie maid a -

16 mang the bows o' meal O.

2. It happened on a weetie nicht fin I wis in masel O.
   It happened on a weetie nicht a lassie she passed by.
   An as she steppit owre the linn
   She heard the millie's clatterin in
   She sweetly cried, 'Can I come in
   Tae shelter fae the rain O?

3. Says I, 'Ma lass, ye're welcome here, come in an dry your claes O.'
   Says I, 'Ma lass ye're welcome here, come in an dry your claes.'
   Says I, 'Ma lass, ye're welcome here
   For there's some news that I wint tae speir,
   Will ye content tae be ma dear
   Amang the bows o' meal O?'

4. The lachin lassie gied a smile an said she cweedna tell O.
   The lachin lassie gied a smile an said she cweedna tell.
   The lachin lassie gied a smile.
   An she said, 'My lad ye'll wait a while,'
   She said, 'My lad ye'll wait a while,
   Gin ye get me tae yersel O.'

5. Noo that nicht, she named the weddin day amang the bows o' meal O.
   That nicht, she named the weddin day an ne'er will I forget aye.
   The weddin day is by lang syne,
   An noo we hae three bairnies fine,
   An some o' them too we sometimes tine
   Amang the bows o' meal O.

'The fairmers took in their own grain tae be milled – maybe ten quarters o' grain tae be milled an they got back their oatmeal. Sma fairms jist put in a quarter or a quarter and a half o' grain, and we milled it an that wis called a 'melder'. There wis anither word – a 'mouter'. The fairmer put in the grain tae the mill, but he paid no money. Ye kept oot enough grain or oatmeal tae pey for the work done. That wis a 'mouter'. There were aa different grains. Some grains wad gie ye a stone o' meal mair to the quarter, which wis good. Thin-skin grain. An then these modern grains cam in. They'd aa thick husks an they didna mill nearly sae well. The auld-fashioned grain wi the thin husk wis the best.

'We used tae hae a great time pickin the mill stanes when they got aa smooth tae mak them rough. Twice or three times a year, we had tae dae it an there used tae be an affa singin an caperin gaun on. It wis a sittin job wi a diamond pick. Ye inked them owre wi a big ruler an ye picked an picked tae ye jist had spots o' ink. Ye'd tae gae roon maybe twenty or thirty times tae get the flat bits off. That wis the pickin o' the mill stanes.

'I didnae really start singin till I jined the folk club. They started a folk club in Elgin, well, it wis in Fochabers, the first folk club, in the early Sixties, the Speybank Folk Club, 1962–3. I used tae go tae Fochabers on an auld motorbike, but I didna sing at Fochabers. They shifted intae Elgin an I got fu ae nicht an gied them a sang an that started it off. This wis the start o' the singin side o' the business. I never regretted it. I just thoroughly enjoyed it! I wis President o' Elgin Folk Club for four or five years. We'd a great time. The nicht at the folk club wis jist the highlight o' the week, well, every fortnicht. We'd some good nights wi the music – great for haein pairties in the hoose. My mother had often a wee ceilidh in the hoose. When I wis oot stayin at the mill, we'd a wee hoosie there, and oh, there wis some great musical evenings there! It wis a kind o' haufway hoose, haufway between Elgin and Miltonduff, where I belonged tae, an aa the Miltonduff boys came in aboot, ye see, intae the wee hoose. We'd some great ceilidhs there! My brothers aa sing, Bob and Alan and Gordon. They're aa musical.

'My mither wis an affa good singer and an affa bonnie singer. When she wis workin, daein the dishes, peelin the tatties, she wis aye singin away. I used tae cock ma lugs an listen. She used tae be a great one for 'Bogie's Bonnie Belle', an she used tae sing anither affa bonnie yin:

> I'm a lassie broken-hearted an ma fortune's been bad;
> I wis coorted sae early by a young plooman lad,
> I wis coorted sae early, by night an by day,
> An the lad I loe dearly lives far, far away.

She used tae sing that an I used tae think it wis a great thing. I used tae sing it at the folk club an aa, but I used tae sing 'I'm a laddie broken-hearted', I just had a tae change a wordie here an there.

'In the War, I wisnae away. I failed my medical through my eyesight. But I wis in the Home Guard, Dad's Army. We had some good nights. We had a pipe band. I used to go to the camps an I thoroughly enjoyed it! There's some stories fae that time – some I couldnae jist very weel tell! The TV programme [*Dad's Army*] had nae reality at aa, nae wi whit we did. We jist did drilling and out on manoeuvres, but it had some sense in it an it wis very severely disciplined. Ye'd be surprised. They fairly kept ye up tae scratch. But it wisnae a bit like Captain Mainwaring and so on. Just very down-to-earth boys we had at the head o' oors.

'We had call-oots an we had tae go, for we didnae ken if it wis the real thing or no. But it never wis. The call-oots usually came on a Setterday nicht, so ye aye kent it wis a practice; ye assumed it wis a practice. We were called oot aboot eleven o'clock at nicht an did an all-nichter. I wis a fully fledged private! They were affa poor at giein ye claes; they never fittit ye! Ye'd hae tae swap them aroon amang yersels. It wis aa richt if a puckle o' ye jined thegither. But there were only two or three o' us cam in later on, an whit a job! Ye couldnae get swappit wi onybody an ye'd a bunnet that widna fit, an a jacket that widna fit, an troosers. Ye jist had tae pit up wi it. We'd the rifle range and bayonet practice, an aa this stuff. We got the haill whack. So we were ready for onything! We got aboot thirty roonds o' live ammunition. Thirty roonds! It wis supposed tae dee! Efter that, ye'd hae tae run! But there wis never a shot fired in anger; it wis fine. We'd a big standin-doon parade in late 1945. That wis us handed in oor uniforms an that wis my army career!

'I married Freda in 1946. When I met Freda, she wis gaun wi a pal o' mines, when we worked together. I met her in '43 and at that time, ye couldnae get a dram in Elgin. Ye'd tae be bona fide; ye'd tae gae oot so ye'd go up tae Rothes. The pub closed at nine. Ye'd tae go up tae Rothes on a Sunday night an the pub closed at nine, an ye'd come oot an wait for the bus, an ye seen aa this quines snookin aboot, an that wis the start o' it, happily. We were mairried in the Seafield Hotel, in Rothes. Affa gettin mairried in a pub, but I wis mair at hame there onywey. It wis quite common in those days. The minister came tae the hotel an the haill thing wis performed in there. Ye were mairried an your reception wis there an aa. We got a hoosie at the mill, for I wis workin at the mill then. It wis jist the roon stane an the clay waa, a topper o' a hoosie, but it wis damp, that wis the only thing. It wis lyin low an it wis damp an Freda wis asthmatic, an that wis why we got a hoose in Elgin. We moved intil't in 1954.

'In my father's time, there were very few Harvest Homes held at a farm; it wis in local halls an stuff like that. It wisnae the same, for I mind they had a Harvest Home held up at Kinnermony. I wis jist a wee lad then an I thought it wis a great night. One o' the lads wis playin a mooth organ an the dog – every time it heard a mooth organ, it wailed. It wis the dog's party piece; it wis singin an aa! I wis jist a wee loon at the time, aboot seiven or eight. I thought this wis great!

'I've worked a lot at the thrashin mill. In fact, fin I worked in the meal mill, I had three or four o' a family and I used tae go oot at the weekends wi a thrashin mill tae raise an extra bob or two. If the mill owner I wis workin wi bocht the grain, I just got the lorry wi me an taen it home. I mind aboot Jock McRitchie. What a man he wis! He wis jist a tricky devil o' a loon. I used tae wear a bunnet at that time, an if ye put it on a post or onything – ye took aff your bunnet if ye wis sweatin – sure as anything, if ye went tae get your bunnet, it wis nailed on, a big nail maybe three or four inches, richt doon through it intae the post an ye couldnae get if aff! Ye'd be standin an he wis aye gaun aboot checkin his mill an ilin it, an he'd be standin spickin tae ye, an he'd hae this iler in his hand, an he'd pit it in your pocket an he'd be pumpin the ile intae your pocket. Fu o' tricks. Ye jist had tae get your ain back on him!

'Me an ma brither Bob often spick aboot Hogmanay. "It's funny," he says, "Mum an Dad had aa thae Hogmanays an aa Dad had in the hoose wis a hauf-bottle o' whisky". They had thon wee, wee tumblers, an aabody that come in got a dram. That half-bottle did the haill Hogmanay an there wis some left owre for teethache. I think he maybe got the idea fae the five loaves an the three fishes. We had great fun at Hallowe'en an aa. When we were bairns, we were away oot roon the hooses, as soon as ma father come hame an we had oor supper, we were away oot aa dressed up, tae eight or nine o'clock wis aboot the latest we would get oot. Aa the country fowk gave ye aipples.

'The feein markets were busy in Elgin right up until the War. There wis a feein market in Elgin every May and every November at the term. Oh they were busy and aa the quines wis there. They aye got a sweetie, ye ken. The boys bocht them sweeties and I've seen some o' the quines come hame wi eight or nine pun o' sweeties. When boys bocht ye sweeties, they were just hopin!

'When Ake Dunbar wis workin in the distillery, we wis jist doon the road. I had a dartboard there. He used tae come doon dartin. He used tae tak doon usually four in a team; four lads cam doon fae the still an there were four o' us at the mill. It wis a dart match – the millers against the stillers. An he says, "The winners will get a dram. The losers will get one too." Ye never missed oot! It wis happy days at the mill, an I missed the mill for aa that. We never went tae oor beds the day we rose. There wis aye fowk droppin in. It wis a half-way hoose an when the country boys were aa gaun hame, if we'd a light on, that wis it!

'Ake wis a cracker o' a boy an he'd some toppers o' sangs! He learnt me 'As Bella Wis Milkin':

AS BELLA WAS MILKING

1. As Bel - la was mil - kin' ae mor - nin' in May, a - lang came young Ja - mie an' tae her did say, "Oh yer fin - gers fly nim - bly, the milk flows sae free. Oh Bel- la, dear Bel - la, come on an' milk me!"

2. So he laid Bella over an he lifted her clothes
    An what she did get, oh ye may weel suppose,
    Oh there she did milk him, did milk him quite dry;
    Jamie's off tae the mountains amang the dry kye.

3. Now, when Bella had risen from what she had got,
    It seemed tae her mither, she gaed at the trot.
    When tae her auld mither the truth she did tell,
    That Jamie wis tryin tae fill her milk pail.

4. Oh Bella, oh Bella, how oft ye've been told,
    Tae hiv nane o' his money or nane o' his gold,
    Tae hiv nane o' his money or nane o' his kind,
    For his milk is nae good when there's two stones behind.

'When we were loons, we used tae go up tae the dances in Miltonduff. The distillery is just by the hall. Of coorse, the barrels wis oot, ready for fillin an we used tae stop there on the way tae the dances an shake them an we'd hear a swish-swish, swish-swish. This wis aa done in the dark. An we used tae pour it oot the barrels intae a pan or intae a bottle. It wis full up wi chips o' wood an everything. We used tae tip it up an hae a drink. We used tae pit someb'dy's hankie owre the neck o' the bottle an jist sooked it through the hankie. I've seen ma mither often say tae me,

— 246 —

''Fit's that on your hankie?'' It left a dirty stain on your hankie! That's what we caaed billins. That wis when I wis aboot sixteen or seventeen.

'During the War, they were affa short-handed at the still and I worked ma eight oors in the mill, an I used tae work aboot six oors at the still. We couldnae hae worked the way we did if we hadnae had the drams tae keep us going. Ane o' the chaps used tae gie us a lump o' coal hame tae wir mithers. One Friday nicht, I had a great lump o' coal on my shoulder, and on ma bike cyclin, an the damn thing fell aff. I'd to go three times back wi a bucket tae get the coal aff the road. Ye ken the weight o' that blinkin coal – if I hadnae had a dram, no way would I have managed it! I pit it on ma shoulder, jumped on the bike – an this wis aboot three in the mornin – we workit six to two – an here's me wi this great bugger o' a lump o' coal on my shoulder, an it fell off an jist smashed. If I hadnae got that coal hame, someb'dy would have had to answer for that. I wis back an forrit tae pick it up wi this coal bucket.

'Poachin went on, but it wasna too bad. Nearly aabody wis allowed tae tak rabbits. But I mind there wis a new water track cam doon fae Kellas tae Elgin, the Kellas water supply. There wis a wee night watchman on an he wis watchin the shovels an stuff – they were aa left on the track. There were nae huts or onything at that time. This night watchman – if we wis comin hame fae the toon – he wad say, ''Oh loons, gie's a hand tae hale this net''. An we used tae gae doon wi this long net and hale it up this big parks an there were coveys o' paitricks, ye ken. Ye could draw the net right over an they would hardly move till the net wis just right owre them. Ye jist dropped the net an there could be ten, eleven, twelve partridges. He learned us that trick, draggin an ordinary herrin net over an just weighted at the end, an ye walked aboot ten, twelve yards apart. As soon as ye walked owre, they started flutterin an ye drew the neck through the net. An ye picked them up an he wis away intae Elgin wi them tae sell them tae the butchers wha used tae gie him maybe a pan o' sausages. So he'd aye his wee fryin pan o' sausages the next night an he'd say, ''Come on loons, I'll gie ye a sausage.'' I've seen us gettin three coveys in a night, which is over thirty partridges, nice wee plump yins aboot a pun an a half tae twa pun. We never thocht on takin them hame. He jist put them aa intae a bag an intae toon the next day. He wis makin a complete profit, for he only gave us aboot three sausages.

'I went intae the Post Office when I wis aboot forty-five and retired at sixty. Och, I'd be younger than that because I wis in seventeen years. Oh, I'd a lot o' good fun in the Post Office an aa, but ye couldnae get off wi so much there. The last seven years, I wis on the early shifts, so I just loadit my van in the morning and away into the country, an that wis me out there till I come back at the end o' the day. I'd two country rounds and a town een an that wis my rotation o' three shifts. It wis aye my ambition in the Post office tae get on early shifts. I didna like late shifts or split shifts. So I finally got on. It wis aa done by seniority in the Post Office. The senior man got the pick o' duties. By this time, I wis up a bittie, so I got three early shifts — five-fifteen starts — an ye finished aboot twenty-past one. Smashing! Ye jist got your round finished and went home. There wis a few o' us finished at the same time and went for a pint first. Then away hame for your dinner and a wee snoozie in the efterneen. 'Twis fine though,' twis grand to get finished at that time. It wis jist like doin half a day's work.'

Frank Duthie
Photo: Ian F. MacKenzie

FRANK DUTHIE

———

The fisher folk among whom Frank Duthie was born have always been a separate community from that of the land, largely because of the nature of their work and the unsocial hours. Living with the constant threat of storms and loss of life possibly made them more inclined to seriousness and religious faith than country people. The little harbour at Findochty where Frank and his wife live was sheltering just a few pleasure boats when we visited it; the fishing has largely gone from that area. Around about on the rocky steps are clustered the low stone houses that have been home to generations of fisher folk. Frank, a fishery officer, is a quiet man, with a strong sense of duty. He describes in detail the hardships inherent in a fisherman's life but was himself prevented from going to sea by his parents, who would not let him follow in their footsteps.

*****

'I wis born in Peterhead on the 20th o' January 1933, one Friday efterneen, sae ma mither tells me, at aboot two o' clock in the efterneen, jist as the steam drifter Hope PD96 wis comin intae the bay, on the South Bay, Number 3 Charlotte Street. Across the road, there wis a curin yard, and a tee-name the owner had wis Sproulie – Sproulie Reid, and there is a sang that must have been written sometime while Sproulie wis in business. I gather the name for the sang wis 'The Guttin Quine':

THE GUTTIN QUINE

1. Four-teen year auld noo, me an'
Nell will rin nae mair tae the schoo-lie bell. For we're a-wa an' we've tae work in Sprou-lie's yaird fae dawn tae dark.

2. In topper buits, in eilskin cwite
   Wer hair in mufflers, reid an fite,
   In dark o' mornin, we'll sit oot
   Wer fingers aa rowed up in cloots.

3. The cooper cries, 'You, you an you,
   Ye'll mak up a learner crew,
   Nae time at aa, ye'll get the knack
   Wi twa tae gut an ane tae pack.'

4. Fae sax o'clock, we're on wer feet
   An denner time is short an sweet,
   I hear the toon's clock chappin fower
   An still the farlin's rinnin owre.

5. The summer fishin's wearin on,
   Anither week an we'll be gone
   Wi kists aa packit sune aneuch
   We're on the train an hurlin sooth.

6. Ev'ry guttin quine an fisher loon
   That's ever workit Yarmooth toon
   Kens we aa met clicks an freens
   Amang the barrels alang the Deans.

[The 'Deans' is a well-known riverside area of Yarmouth]

7.   Gweed kens far neist we'll hae tae gan
     Tae Ireland or the Isle o' Man,
     Rathmullen Howth or Douglas fair,
     Nae doubt we'll meet auld neibours there.

8.   But lang for hame I never thocht,
     Till aa the boats gaed doon the loch.
     Says I til masel, 'I'm wantin hame,
     Hame aside ma mither again.'

9.   Stronsay toon, we'll bid adieu,
     Fen aa the huts are aye in view,
     If aa gaes weel then aa gaes richt,
     I will be hame some Saturday nicht.

'Ma mither – she wis a Portknockie quine – follaed the guttin fae the day she left the school. She wis wan o' three lassies and younger brither. Ma faither, on the ither hand, wis the aullest o' three loons and wan quine, the exact opposite tae ma mither's faimily, and he drove the drifters. He started to sea as a cook when he left the school at aboot 13, and he progressed tae fireman, and then the driver, and he wis drivin the drifters till the war broke oot, and he jist did his stint like aabody else. When he cam back efter the war, he went back tae drivin the drifters again.

'I stairted school in Peterheid at the age o' five, and went up til the Central and cairried on thro that tae the Peterheid Academy and left as fast as I could at fourteen. I often argued wi ma faither aboot follaein in his footsteps and gan tae the sea. Ma faither put his foot doon and said, ''That ye're nae!'' ''Aw but I am!'' I says. ''Not if I can help it!'' he says, and this would o' been maybe fen I wis aboot eleiven year aul. ''There's nae wey ye're gaun tae the sea!'' he says, ''But I'll tell ye fit, I micht nae be here tae stop ye, but if ever ye div ging tae the sea, ye're nae gyan ignorant.'' So he tellt me as much as he could aboot the fishin and the wey the nets and aathin wis workit, and I could splice and mend a net fen I wis jist gaun twelve. So he wis preparin me, jist in case I did ging tae the sea. Of coorse, he wis still there and so I steyed wi his wishes and I didnae ging tae the sea.

'Instead, I got a job wi the Presenic Stane Company, makkin cement blocks tae start wi for a few months, then I wanted tae be a jiner. That wis ma seicond choice tae gaun tae the sea, but at that time, tryin tae get an apprenticeship wis like lookin for dodo's eggs, and I didnae manage tae get an apprenticeship there. So I had tae find work o' some kind, so I got a job wi the Presenic Stane Company, and fae then, they started tae pey off because trade wis gettin bad. But the foreman seemed tae tak a fancy tae me, so he got me a job in the sawmill and I workit in the sawmill for a number o' years. By that time, there wis an American factory came tae the toon makkin twist drills and I got a job in there, and I workit for them for near nine year. Suddenly, in the fishery, an office job came on the scene and well, that wis nearer tae the fishin than fit the drillin wis, so I applied and wis lucky enough tae get a start there. Noo I'm workin in Buckie and that's far I've ayewis been. So that's the size o' it. I've been married thirty-two years and I hiv twa o' a faimily, a daughter, Shona, an a son, Gordon.

'Fen the summer fishin did rin doon and aa the boats gaed awa tae Yarmooth, the toon jist happened tae be deserted, 'cause there wis nae boats comin oot and in every day. The only consolation wis, for loons like me and ithers like's, there wis monetary remuneration, let's say. We used tae get a penny, tippence, thrippence sometimes; if it wis a big shot o' herrin intae the boatheid, we'd get sixpence even. They caaed it 'rinnin the billie' and that wis gaun doon tae the shore tae the sales offices, lookin intae the windas, and ye wad see a bill posted wi a list o' aa the drifters for that particular salesman's books, wi the shot o' herrin that they had that day and the price per cran that they got for them. Noo, if ony particular drifter had a good shot and a good price, it'd be up tae you tae get on yer bike and caa in the heavy boys and get up there before somebody else did and you wad get the tanner.

'That wis een o' the consolations and the ither consolation wis lookin forward tae the boats comin hame, because fen the boats cam hame fae Yarmooth, there wis aye somethin for aabody. There wis, for instance, Yarmooth rock, pomegranates, sweeties, carpet slippers. These various surprises, aa the bairns, aye, and some o' the auld folk too, lookit forward tae get. Then there's 'The Fisherman's Wife'. I ken it fae my faither and passed the words on tae Bob Massie one musical evening when I heard him play the tune on his mandolin:

THE FISHERMAN'S WIFE

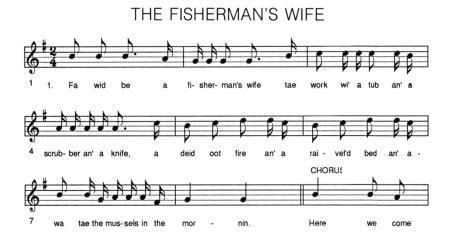

10 scoo - rin in, three reefs tae the fore - sail in. There's

13 nae a dry stick tae pit on wer back, but still wo're aa tee -

16 tot' - llers.

2.   Noo, fa'll gie's a hand tae rin a ripper lead
     Tae try for a coddie in the bay o' Peterheid?
     They're maybe at the Lummies or the clock on Sautis'eid
     Fen we gaun tae the sma lines in the mornin.

CHORUS: Here we come scoorin in, . . . etc.

3.   Ma puir aul father's in the middle o' the flair
     Beatin heuks ontae tippets an they're hingin on his chair.
     They're made wi horses' hair, man, for that's the best o' gear
     Tae be gyan tae the fishin in the mornin.

CHORUS: Here we come scoorin in, . . . etc.

4.   Syne it's doon the Geddle Braes in the middle o' the nicht
     Wi an aul seerup tin an a can'le for a licht,
     Tae gaither up the pullars, ev'ry een o' them in sicht
     So we'll get the linie baited for the mornin.

CHORUS: Here we come scoorin in, . . . etc.

5.   It's easy to the cobbler, sittin in his neuk,
     His big copper kettle hingin on a crook.
     But we're in the boo and we cannae get a heuk
     It's sair hard work in the mornin.

CHORUS: Here we come scoorin in, . . . etc.

6.   It's nae the kin o' life that a gentle quine can thole
     Wi her fingers reid raw wi the scrubbin oot a yole
     An a littlen on her hip, she's awa tae cairry coal,
     She'll be caaed sair deen in the mornin.

CHORUS: Here we come scoorin in, . . . etc.

7.   Still an aa she widnae change for the gran'est o' yer gear
     For she never kens the minute when her hairt'll loup wi fear.
     For he's awa tae the sea an he's aa that she has dear
     She qued be a widow wi his bairn in the mornin.

CHORUS: Here we come scoorin in, . . . etc.

'That's 'The Fisherman's Wife' as I ken it onywey. It's nae the rich fisherman o' the present day. You see, fishermen were verra puir in them days. It wis jist a faimily boat, and maybe there wis three, fower, maybe five brithers, maybe a faither and three sons in the same boat, and if that boat cam tae grief, that wis the haill lot wipit oot. But the interestin bit aboot it is, each verse gies ye a little picture o' their life.

'The seicond verse gives well-known fishing grounds found by being able tae see the 'Lummies' or the muckle kirk clock aligned with Salt House Head. Salt House Head in a headland below Peterhead Prison.

Noo if ye consider:

> Ma puir aul father's in the middle o the flair,
> Beatin heuks ontae tippets, and they're hingin on his chair,

Noo, the heuks [hooks] that he's beatin on — 'Beatin', that means whippin — the heuks were either 'sma line' heuks or 'great line' heuks and they couldnae afford tae hae a breakage, ye know. If a heuk snaggit, they couldnae afford tae loss a line for the sake o' a heuk. So fit they did hae wis a length o sneed — or snood [English], if ye like — and that wis quite valuable itsel, and then, at the end o' the sneed, they'd fit what they caaed a tippet, which is a length o' braided horse-hair, ye see, and that wis whippit ontae the heuk. There wis a special wey o' daein it: ye pit the heuk on at right angles tae the line itsel, and then, just afore the last few hitches were made, ye turned it up and took a few half hitches roon and pulled it through this wey, locked wi a 'whip hitch'. Noo that left the heuks' tips stickin oot proudly. Noo these tippets that the aul man is beatin the heuks on tae are weaker than the sneed and will let the heuk break awa to prevent the loss of line. He had a seat here in the middle o' the flair, and he's got his kitchie table chair here — as he beatit them on, he hangit the heuk ontae the chair and left it tae get the tippet danglin doon, ready tae be gaithered up in bundles, and then attached tae fitever type o' line they were goin tae be usin.

'Anither o' the verses speaks aboot gaitherin in the pullars. A pullar is a kin o' peeler — a peeler crab, a crab which is jist beginnin tae moult and, ye know, a crustacean much like a snake shedding its skin, sheds its shell and expands in its soft state. Noo, the pullar, or peeler if ye like, is verra good bait for aa types o' fish, so ye used as much o' these for the bait as possible.

'"A deid oot fire an a raivelled bed" — ye hadnae time tae mak the bed because ye needed as muckle sleep as ye could get. Ye had tae match yer risin time tae suit the tides. It micht hae been in the middle o' the nicht wi yer seerup tin, or it micht o' been in the oors o' daylicht, as daylicht's comin in, ye ken. And, well, the makin o' the bed and things like that could wait till later, but the gaitherin o' the necessary where-withal tae catch yer fish wis yer first priority.

'Again, the fisherman's wife had tae dae some strange things. For instance, not every port had harbours and fen the boat cam in, she had tae lay off, so she wis jist afloat, 'cause if she'd cam in aground, especially in a fallin spring tide, that wis her until it cam in that far again. So in order tae keep her in a position far she could leave for the sea, she had tae moor it aff a bit, leavin quite a bit o' water atween the beach and the boat. Noo, in order tae get aff til't, she either had tae wade or hae a sma boat or a dinghy. Verra few people could afford tae tie up a boat for this purpose, so fit they did wis: they needed tae keep claes as dry as possible, and ye may believe this or believe it not, but if ye'd like tae come up tae Buckie, ye'll see it in photographs, wimmen wi their skirts hitched up intae their waists like this and their men, big heavy men, on their backs, piggy-backin their men tae the boats, wadin thro the water. Can ye see a modern lassie daein that? And fen the boats cam back, nets hae got tae be mendit, they'd aa got tae be barkit; dried first, then cleaned and barkit and the wimmen had tae faa tae it at the mendin as well as tae the cleanin and spreadin.

'In fact, the wimmen had tae dae jist as much hard work as the men had tae dae *plus* keep their men in bakin breid and clean claes and mend claes and aa the rest o' it. I remember ma faither comin hame jist wi his bag o' fouled claes. Ma mither wad be up lang afore daylicht and the biler wad be on and this wad be aboot fower o'clock in the mornin, every Monday mornin, ma mither wis up at fower o'clock in the mornin, and aa that washin and aathin wis deen lang afore I got up. But onywey, the sheen wis aye polished by her, every fisherwoman did the same, her men's sheen or boots were aa polished. And not only did they polish the uppers, but they blackit the soles tae because ye had tae preserve the stitches far the water wis soakin thro. These things were aa deen withoot a seicond's thocht, ye know, the breid wis bakit – oatmeal oatcakes; that's fit they caaed breid – it wis bakit on a girdle over the fire and roasted on the branner. When Yarmooth time wis comin up, they aa gaed awa wi their tins o' breid an maybe fags or tobacco or fitever. And mind you, though, although money wis scarce, they didnae seem tae grudge their men their fags and made sure that they had their breid wi them tae go doon Yarmooth way. I will say that for them, they were verra, verra carin wimmen and there wis never, that I ever saw fen I wis a youngster, ony jealousy or pettiness amang them. I mean, everybody wis in the same boat.

'But they did hae a system goin at that time jist in case ony drifter or boat came tae grief and there wis loss o' life – the widows had got tae be lookit efter. Wan o' the weys they did it wis, fen the boat cam in tae discharge their herrin, fit they did wis tae pit a sample o' herrin, they took a scoop fae the hold, and pit it in the basket and awa tae the pier wi't, and somebody wad rin tae the saleroom wi the sample. Based on that sample, the buyer wad pey so much for so many cran – efter that, the price draps tae the neist price doon. Aa the boats' samples were then sellt together and the proceeds fae these sample sales aa gaed intae a common fund which wis kept for emergencies like this.

'Anither thing fen the boats were at Yarmooth, for the widows that were in the toon, wi naethin comin fae the Sample Fund at that particular time, the boats would charge or tick their groceries in the local stores, ye ken – the butcher, the baker, the candlestick-maker – they got their stores and they would aa donate so much tae the fund. It wis somethin that everybody contributed til wi good hairt; there wis naebody fa didnae, because it could happen tae them next time.

'Those lines in 'The Fisherman's Wife' that say:

> Here we come scoorin in,
> Three reefs o' the foresail in.

The foresail has been reefed doon because there is a verra high wind and ye hiv tae reef the foresail in because the boat is comin skelpin in, or scoorin in, if ye like. 'There's nae a dry stick' is because there's so much spray flyin aboot that the men are aa soakit. This stems fae the time fen eilskins were aa very weel, but they werenae really aa that waterproof. I've heard ma faither sayin mony times that fresh water jist seemed tae go thro' the eilie nae trouble at aa: salt water wisnae sae bad. I think it possibly wis pourin thro' the wide neck and these eilies were stiff canvas, soakit in linseed eil and they were hard and they made ye sweat underneath, and they chaffed on yer wrists, and haulin herrin nets is nae fun in these conditions. If ye can imagine this emulsion fen it's rinnin doon ontae yer wrists and the eilskin chaffin and rubbin the stuff in, afore ye knew it ye got fit wis caaed 'salt water byles' and boy, were they somethin! They made carbuncles look like pimples, ye ken! I'll tell ye a wee story aboot that which happened around 1912, long afore I wis born.

'This particular day, my grandfaither wis sufferin badly fae salt water byles and it wis a het Saturday efterneen, and he's sittin in the hoose and found a place tae put his airms doon, fen there's a knock gings on the back door. And fen ma granny gings tae the door, there's an aul woman wi a bairn there in her airms and anither at her side, and she says, "I wonder if ye could spare a wee suppie for the baby because I'm dry and he's hungry?". Ma granny says, "Och aye. Come on in." So she gears up a bowl o' broth because they'd had broth for their denner that day and the woman wis grateful and she says, "I see that ye've got a bad case o' byles.

weel, for yer kindness, if ye'd like tae dae fit I tell ye, I'll cure ye and ye winnae be bothered wi salt water byles efter this.''

'So she says, "If ye can ging tae the byre wi a bucket and get fitever the coo deposits, straight away as it's comin fae her and get it intae the bucket; by the look o' it ye'll need een for each airm. Fill sea-boot stockins wi't and put his airms in til't up tae the oxters, richt in as far as they'll ging and ye'll need tae leave him at least owrenicht, for at least twelve oors.'' and she says, ''Weel Frank (my grandfaither), div ye think ye'll want tae dae that?'' and he says, ''Gladly! We'll see if it'll dae ony good!'' so Saturday nicht or no – he wis a meetin man – he says, ''We'll no be able tae go tae the meetin the morn, but I'm sure the Lord will understand.'' So, she gaed awa and got twa buckets and put lids on them and took them doon and they makkit fit they caaed a ''shakky-doon'' in the wash-hoose and they stuck his airms intae the boot stockins till the mornin and boy, fen they took them aff and aathing wis washed aff, there wis gapin holes aa alang his airms. So ma granny, she washed him and bound him up and he had scars, but fae that day onwards, he never seemed tae hae a byle worth caain, ye ken.

'Anither thing fen they were at the herrin, one o' the biggest plagues wis herrin scales, believe it or not. Fen they were shakkin the herrin oot o' the herrin gill nets so that they fell doon intil the hull and hingin the nets up, the scales were fleein aa wey, ye know, and if one actually lights on yer eyeball, it adheres immediately like a contact lens and ye cannae get it oot because ye cannae see it. Ye've got the maist affa job gettin it oot and ye've got a soor time tae suffer till ye come ashore and get intae the doctor's tae get it taken oot.

'Anither thing at certain times o' the year wis 'scalders'. A scalder is a jellyfish, a big brown jellyfish wi lang goons like rhubarb streamin from it, and fen ye're shakkin the herrin net and ropes are aa greasy, the sting in them is really quite somethin! Some people were driven crazy wi't, ithers were mair used til't, but especially wi the young laddies jist stairtin tae the sea, it put them clean aff.

'The meetins were verra important tae the fisher folk because they were verra religious people. They were by no means aa meetin people, but a lot o' them were and in fact, some o' them were conscientious objectors fen the war broke oot. That didnae go doon verra weel wi a lot o' people, but havin said that, there wis nae vandalism o' their property or onything like that. In fact, I never saw or ever heard o' onything like that being daen.

'Fishin has changed quite a lot and it's still changing in front o' oor eyes richt noo, not always for the better in my mind because as far as the herrin is concerned, the drift net has disappeared aathegither. The drift net, in my opinion, was a reasonable livin for a good mony people. It had its ancillary work as weel which employed people; it employed blacksmiths and aa, that had tae shoe horses. It also employed coalmen, cairters, the usual services and each boat cairried echt o' a crew. On the ither hand, the purse net can be imagined as a thing that can encompass St Paul's Cathedral and Nelson's Column standing on top o' it; it's like a huge colander and it's drawn up and up and up and everythin swimmin within it is a prisoner. Noo, these purse netters can afford tae lay tied up at the pier for six months, and there's nae sae mony o' them as there wis drifters, but they mak a goodly livin for verra few folk. So in my opinion, it's nae such a viable proposition conservation-wise as the herrin drift nets.'

INDEX TO SONGS

Other titles by Polygon

Elegies for the Dead in Cyrenaica	Hamish Henderson
Radical Renfrew: Poetry from the French Revolution to the First World War	Tom Leonard (ed.)
An Aghaidh na Siorraidheachd (In the Face of Eternity): Eight Gaelic Poets	Christopher Whyte (ed.)
Salutations: Collected Poems 1960–89	Alan Jackson
St Nynia	John MacQueen
Scotland Before History	Stuart Piggott
Kings, Queens and People's Palaces: An oral history of the Scottish Music Hall 1920–1970	Vivien Devlin (ed.)
Voices from the Spanish Civil War	Ian MacDougall
Voices from the Hunger Marches	Ian MacDougall
Odyssey: The Second Collection	Billy Kay (ed.)
The Eclipse of Scottish Culture	Craig Beveridge and Ronald Turnbull
Towards Independence: Essays on Scotland	Paul Scott
A Claim of Right for Scotland	Owen Dudley Edwards et al.
Archaic Cosmos	Emily Lyle